Dinah Maria Mulock Craik

A Hero

Bread upon the Waters, Alice Learmont

Dinah Maria Mulock Craik

A Hero
Bread upon the Waters, Alice Learmont

ISBN/EAN: 9783337141516

Printed in Europe, USA, Canada, Australia, Japan

Cover: Foto ©ninafisch / pixelio.de

More available books at **www.hansebooks.com**

A HERO,

BREAD UPON the WATERS.

ALICE LEARMONT.

BY THE AUTHOR OF

"JOHN HALIFAX, GENTLEMAN," "A NOBLE LIFE,"
"CHRISTIAN'S MISTAKE," "TWO MARRIAGES,"
"A LIFE FOR A LIFE," "OLIVE,"
"FAIRY BOOK," &c., &c.

New Edition.

NEW YORK:

HARPER & BROTHERS, PUBLISHERS,

FRANKLIN SQUARE.

MISS MULOCK'S WORKS.

BOOKS FOR CHILDREN.

A HERO.
BREAD UPON THE WATERS.
ALICE LEARMONT.

INTRODUCTION.

"A HERO, my nephews?" echoed Uncle Philip, stealing in upon a conclave that was being held to decide the merits of a "fellow," who was universally considered the head of the school—in fighting at least. "Pray, my good lads, what do you mean by 'a Hero?'"

His nephews were silent. Probably they thought Captain Philip Carew was the person best fitted to answer his own question. For though not yet forty years of age, he had been bronzed in the Tropics, frozen in the Arctic Seas, had led forlorn-hopes in China, and commanded Pacific expeditions to the South Seas, and finally had returned, invalided by a shot on the field of Moultan in India. He had gone through many tribulations of divers kinds, yet he was still a handsome-looking fellow, with more brains and more heart than nine-tenths of mankind, even though he was a soldier.

He repeated his question, "Pray, what is a Hero?" Still no answer.

"Get the dictionary!" said Uncle Philip. He looked out the word. "*Hero, a great man!* Short and
terse, truly. Now boys, define that: 'A Hero, viz.,
A Great Man.'"

A few tried to do it; but nobody gave a clear reply.

"You are all puzzled? No wonder. That same
definition has puzzled the world ever since it was a
world. I myself racked my poor brains on the subject
for three whole months. But I think I solved the
question at last."

"How, uncle?" some one ventured to ask.

"Oh, it would be a long story. It happened many
years ago, when I was a boy."

It was a magic beginning, "When I was a boy."
Young people do so delight in a bit of autobiography.
There was a general entreaty for that portion of Uncle
Philip's history which taught him the true definition
of a Hero.

He hesitated a little, for many reasons; but then he
was such an unselfish kind-hearted soul, the very per
fection of a bachelor uncle.

Soon, he hit upon a plan.

"Boys, there are twelve days between now and the
New Year; and every day we have an idle hour or
two between the lights, or just before bed-time. Now,
in that hour I'll tell you, if you like, my adventures
in search of a Hero. If by New Year's Eve, I have

not found him, nor you either, why—" here a sudden and rather mysterious smile danced in Uncle Philip's brown eyes—" we must look for him in some other way."

_____

The tale thus told, or rather the sketch of boyish life, too simple to be called a tale, has been preserved by the present Author.

She has done so, for the amusement of all boys, a race whom she heartily loves, from the petticoated urchin to the big hobbledehoy. But especially this book is written for another Philip—

PHILIP BOURKE MARSTON;

now a little year-old child, but who, his god-mother hopes and prays, may one day mingle with the world of men, and there prove himself—in the noblest sense of the word—a Hero!

A HERO.

CHAPTER I.

" I HEAR they are all very nice children, your Scotch cousins and one of them in particular is quite a little hero."

These were a few of the many parting words my mother said to me, when I, a lad of twelve years old, was trusted to pay my first visit from home. It was to my uncle, my father's half brother, who lived in the north, and whom neither I nor my English mother had ever seen.

A little Hero! I remember the word stuck fast to my memory—for I had been deeply studying Plutarch's Lives, until my mind was full of Epaminondas, Alcibiades, Aristides the Just, and "all those sort of chaps," as you school boys would have said. Also—with my Scottish visit in prospect —I had read up tolerably in the history of Wallace and Bruce, though I still thought the Greek warriors much the finer fellows. With some dim notion that my cousin might be one who wore a kilt and wielded a broadsword, and was ready to fight every body in the fashion of Sir Walter Scott's Roderick Dhu, I asked my mother which of the boys he was and what did she mean by calling him a "hero."

She perhaps thought she had said too much, so gave me unsatisfactory answers. But I persisted.

" What sort of a hero is he? Does he fight with a shield

A*

and a spear, like the Thebans; or in armor, like William Wallace? or with guns and pistols like—"

Here I glanced up to where, over the mantle-piece of our little cottage parlor, hung my father's rifle, sword, and belt. Suddenly I remembered a letter my mother once showed me, in which it said that "Lieutenant Henry Carew died the death of a hero."

I stopped—for my mother's eyes following the direction of mine, had fallen on the sword and belt. She never looked at them without crying. So I did not like to put any more questions about heroes.

Nevertheless I thought a great deal of my cousin, and speculated very much, and not without considerable fear, as to what sort of a person he would turn out to be. This curiosity was so strong that it actually helped to make me less sorrowful at parting with my mother and sisters—don't laugh, boys, for I was rather tender hearted then, and much petted, being the youngest, and the only son. But I'm not ashamed of it—no, upon my word I'm not. It is only a coward who is ashamed of being fond of his mother and sisters.

Well—I said good-by to them all at home. I remember pretending to have a bad cold as a sort of apology for taking out my pocket-handkerchief—a very foolish cheat on my part; but I did not like to be thought a baby. It was only when we had long left our quiet village, rattled over London streets, and my poor mother and I sat on the deck of the ferocious looking steamer that was to carry me away far north—where neither she nor I had ever been before—it was only then, I say, when she, half crying herself, kept telling me to "cheer up," and "be a man"—that I proved myself to be still a mere baby, by bursting out blubbering on her shoulder.

("I'm not ashamed of it now, not in the least," said Uncle Philip, speaking very thick and blusteringly, but growing rather red about the eyes—"She was a good woman always

·—your grandmother—God bless her! and, as they say in the
East, may she live a thousand years!"

Which sentiment being universally echoed, Uncle Philip
went on.)

I don't remember much about the voyage, except the pre-
liminary incident of my mother's wanting to put me in the
ladies' cabin under the care of the stewardess, and of my indignant protestation against the same. It seemed a positive
insult to a boy of my mature age—thirteen; though my poor
mother would persist in considering me a baby, and unable to
take care of myself. The matter ended in my being assigned, with the dignity due to my sex, to the gentleman's
half of the vessel, where I was tossed about and scolded incessantly during three interminable days, during which I lay
in all the helpless misery of a first sea voyage, heartily wish-
ing I could be quietly dropped overboard, and so come to an
end at once, without any body's being the wiser.

At length somehow or other I began to feel better, and
took courage to crawl up the ·companion-ladder, in order to
find out whereabouts in the wide world I was ; for I had an
uncomfortable fear that the boat must have tumbled through
an entire ocean since I last went on deck, and that we should
find ourselves somewhere in the middle of the Atlantic. An
idea not very pleasant to a small individual, who however
he might admire heroes in theory, was by nature a rather
timid boy.

("Oh, Uncle Philip," broke in one or two astonished voices
But Uncle Philip repeated that it was quite true. He seemed to take pride in the fact, as if to show how much force of
will could effect in the formation of character.)

It was late one evening when I crept on deck, and crouched down in a woeful half-frightened condition behind the man
at the wheel. I could see nothing but him, for the night
was very misty. The boat appeared to be going through a

dense white fog, dashing on nobody knew where. We might
be off the shore of America for all I could tell—it seemed
such an awful length of time that we had been at sea. I
was very cold too, though it was summer time—so I begun
to think that we must have come within the line of the floating icebergs, which, as I had somewhere read, are often met
with in the Atlantic on the voyage to North America. My
geographical notions—indeed all my ideas, were rather confused ; but then it must be remembered that I was at best a
queer-like old fashioned little fellow, brought up at home,
entirely among women, with no brothers or school-fellows.
Moreover I had been sea-sick for four days, which does not
materially improve one's faculties.

I could not get the notion of icebergs out of my head, and
as the mist cleared a little, I looked anxiously over the ship's
side Lo ! there was a confirmation of all my fears ! A
great, gray, mist-enveloped thing, rising right out of the
water—seeming to be floating down upon us, or we upon it ;
for my still dizzy head could not distinguish which. I looked
in terror on the man at the wheel, but he appeared quite
comfortable, standing there, the light from the compass lamp
just showing his hard, ugly, weather-beaten face, and his
big shoulders, all the bigger for an enormous pea-coat. That
man was my nightmare, afterward, for many a year ; whenever I ate overmuch supper (as boys will do, more shame to
them), I always dreamt I was turned into a steamboat, and
he sitting on my deck, *i. e.* my lungs—was steering me right
against an eternal succession of ice-bergs.

I looked at this man, then at the misty object standing
upright in the sea, then down the solitary deck of the vessel,
and lastly at the man again. I got positively frightened,
every thing was so silent and strange. At length I plucked
up spirit to go nearer him, and say in a small voice—" If
you please—"

But the man at the **wheel** might have been cut out **of rock.** He took no notice. Most likely, he neither heard nor **saw me,** so engrossed was he in his duty, honest fellow ! **It** never struck me, as he stood there, his eyes keenly fixed for-**ward,** doing nothing but turn his **wheel a** little way round and back again, that with every slight motion of the hand he was guiding this large vessel's course.

Curiosity, or dogged perseverance, or obstinacy—I had all three—impelled me not to give in, but to address my man again, for I was beginning to think him something **super-**natural ; especially as, in my universal search after knowl-edge, I had read a queer sort of poem, which I greatly **ad-mired, but** did not altogether understand—the " Ancient **Mar-iner."** So I just took courage to touch the sleeve of the **pea-**coat, and finding that it was quite real, as well **as the arm** within it, I gave both a good pull.

" **Hollo !"** shouted the sailor, **rather startled,** until he per-ceived my small self. He merely shook me off, as if I had been a puppy dog pawing him, and turned to the wheel again.

Now, as I said, I *am* rather obstinate by nature ; and moreover my dignity was hurt. I pulled his arm again, ad-dressing him boldly, as—" You, sailor !"

" Ahoy !"

" Where are we, sailor, **if** you please ?" I asked **meekly** " And what is that great thing there ?"

" Yon's Ailsa Craig, and ye're aff the **coast o' Scotland."**

This information, given in a very grumpy **voice, was** all I could get out of him. I thought him **a most unpleasant** surly fellow, little knowing that on his **strict** minding of his duty depended all our lives. Afterward, **as I** grew older and wiser, **this** little adventure taught me that it is best not to " bother' unnecessarily **those** who have **our** guidance in their hands. I found this **plan to tell** through life, especially with **regard** to those who, speaking metaphorical.y, have **the** steering of the family ship. So, boys, whenever you are disposed to plague your father about trifles, or make complaints to your tutor, or any thing of that sort, just remember one little maxim that you may find written up in all steamboats— "*Don't speak to the man at the wheel.*"

I went down below, and slept—my first real sleep since I left home. It could not have lasted long, however, when I was awakened by a great trampling overhead, and by the engines letting off steam. The steward, putting his head in, bawled something about "Greenock," which, as I suddenly remembered, my mother had strongly impressed on me as being the place where my uncle was to meet me. In a great fright, I huddled on my jacket, collected my properties together as well as I could, and went on deck.

("It is a curious thing," added Uncle Philip in a parenthesis—"how well I remember every little circumstance of this journey, the first important epoch of my life. All seems as clear as yesterday—and clearer as I go on. I must certainly have a capital memory. But so much the better for you, my young audience.")

Now, as I said before, I had never seen my uncle, nor indeed, from some family differences, had I ever heard much about him, except his name, which being rather un-English, I had in the bewilderment of the moment quite forgotten. No unlucky boy could feel more thoroughly desolate than I did on that momentous day, when, at four in the morning, I found myself on the steamer's deck off Greenock quay, jostled hither and thither amid the confusion of hurried passengers and shouting porters; feeling queer and half asleep, for it was not yet broad daylight ; and bewildered by the clatter of strange tongues, some Scotch, some Gaelic, though both were alike unintelligible to me. I do not think that at any after portion of my life did I ever feel more dolefully miserable. I sat down on a coil of ropes, with my little trunk beside me and in **truth was** very near crying, had **I** not remembered that *that* **would** disgrace a boy of thirteen years old.

Soon I heard, through the din of cross passengers' voices, one—not cross certainly, though it had a peculiar tone—very **Scotch I** thought   Nevertheless, nothing ever impressed my childish mind more than the first tone of that voice—strong, deep, steady, and kind, giving one at once a feeling of respect, slight fear, and instinctive trust. It sounded distinctly through all the confusion of the vessel, as its owner walked down the deck, looking round him.

" Is there any boy here named Philip Carew ?"

I jumped up, with a sudden instinct of joy, jumped almost into the arms of my Scottish uncle.

He gave me a quick hearty welcome—there was no **time** for more : caught up my luggage with one hand, **and myself** with the other, and in **a minute we were** standing on the **quay.**

Then it was I managed to steal an inquiring look at my uncle. He was a tall, big man—with rather harsh features, **tanned as** brown as a **berry ; and a** quantity of gray hair flying about in all directions, in a fashion that irresistibly re-minded me of a hay-stack in a high wind. At first sight **he** seemed a very formidable person—especially to a shy English boy—but as soon **as** he began to speak **there was something** in his smile so very good-natured, warm-hearted, and **cheery,** **that** I took courage.

" Lift up your head, boy : let me look at **you !**"

He did so for a long time, and then turned his head away I afterward guessed why. **He and his half-**brother had been boys together, but, **when** young men, had suddenly parted in **anger, and never met more**   I was considered very like my father, and perhaps he noticed it.

" Norman !" shouted my uncle abruptly, as **we stood or** the now deserted **quays ;** a boy **of about my own size came**

forward, I did not notice from whence. "Here, lads, shake
hands. Philip Carew, this is your eldest cousin, Norman
MacIlroy. (That then was the queer name I had forgotten.)
Be friends with one another, as your fathers were before you
—and mind, never quarrel, never quarrel!"

Saying this he walked off hastily to another end of the
quay, leaving us two boys together. I eyed my cousin very
curiously. To this day I remember the look of him.

A slender, tight-made little fellow, any thing but a beauty
—(now I myself was "a very pretty boy" I believe). He
had a thorough Scotch face—high cheek-bones—a freckled
skin—and hair which, in many an English school, would have
assuredly gained for him the pleasant nick-name of "Carrots."
Not that it was really carroty, being a rather pretty color,
I thought, but nevertheless decidedly red. He was dressed
in a jacket and trowsers (which I should certainly have
scorned as being apparently made out of my mother's black
and white plaid shawl), and he had on a queer sort of cap
without a brim—a "Glengarry" bonnet, as I afterward
found out.

We stood and eyed one another rather suspiciously—Scotch
boy and English boy—just as if we had been the two opposing armies on Flodden Field, of which I had lately read. At
last, the idea seemed to strike us that it was very funny, our
staring at one another in this stupid way; for, with one impulse, we both burst out laughing.

"That's right, old fellow," said my cousin, patting me on
the shoulder—"we shall be capital friends directly."

We made no more fraternization than this, for boys are
very shy of an outward expression of liking; but somehow
we got into friendly talk. When Uncle MacIlroy came back,
he found us sitting together on the steps of the custom-house,
quite sociable; Norman having learned from me the whole
history of my voyage, while he, in return, was communicating

various pieces of information **as to** where 1 **now was, and** whither **I was** going.

I observed that he had, like his father, an **odd sing-song way** of speaking which I could not at first catch, and which sometimes made me laugh. I concluded **it was only the** Scotch accent, **and** exulted **in** the vast superiority **of** my own cockney tongue.

" Well, lads, how are you getting on ?" said my uncle, taking out his watch—" 'Tis now just five, and the first Dunoon boat does not start till seven—What will you **do ?** Would you like something to eat, Philip, or wait till you join your aunt's breakfast table at eight ?**"**

Being in a state of excitement and bewilderment that en**tirely took** away my appetite, I said I would wait—though where **I** was **to be** taken to eat this problematical breakfast **I had not** the least **idea.**

" **Come** then, here's enough to keep you from famishing for **an hour or** two."

He pulled out of his pocket a three-cornered thing which he called a *scone;* a queer looking cake I thought, but really very nice. I **ate** one, and Norman another, with considerable gusto ; then we **walked up** and down the quay, looking at the shipping close by, the broad river, and the **hills** beyond.

I don't think, nephews, that I ever shall forget that **morn**ing. **It** was the first morning I had seen the sun **rise, being, like** most other spoiled children, a very lazy little fellow, and a disgraceful lie-a-bed. Until **now** I had no **notion how** the world looked at four or five in the morning, especially in **Scotland.** That picture still remains, so firmly riveted was it **on** my childish memory—the silent, solitary quay—the ships **lying** motionless alongside, as if they were half asleep—the **broad** bars of amber and rosy clouds streaking the east—the distant hills painted **of a** deep lilac—and the **river** between taking all sorts of colors according as the sky changed I never saw such a scene as that—never! It made me an early riser for the rest of my life.

Norman tried hard to amuse me, and put my geographical powers to their utmost stretch, by pointing out, with a very natural pride, the beauties of his country.

Ben Lomond was over there—he said, I had surely heard of the great Ben. Perhaps I might see him now, unless, as was probable, he had his nightcap on.

"His nightcap!" I repeated, rather puzzled.

"I mean the mist that is almost always seen covering the top of very high mountains," explained my cousin.

Upon which there luckily flashed across my mind a sentence out of my geography book—"*Highest mountains in Scotland are Ben Lomond and Ben Nevis.*" So I merely observed—"Oh, of course!" and hid my ignorance beneath a very wise shake of the head.

"There's Dumbarton Rock, so celebrated in history," continued Norman, but talking in a very quiet way, not in a show-off style at all. "You may see it clearly, far down the reach of the river, toward Glasgow. It's a curious place; I once climbed to the top of it, to Wallace's watch-tower."

"Oh, William Wallace," said I, anxious to exhibit my acquaintance with Scottish history. "I know all about him. He was a great hero, don't you think so?"

"Yes," said Norman, rather indifferently, for he was watching his father, who happened to be looking grave just then.

The word hero set me off on my old hobby, and reminded me of my mother's still unexplained words, concerning the one of my cousins who was "quite a hero." It could not be Norman. Such a quiet looking, plain little fellow, in a plaid jacket and trowsers! not at all the sort of hero I had expected. Perhaps there might be another of the family.

" How many brothers have you ?" said I abruptly.

" There are five of us—I am the eldest."

" You !" I exclaimed with some surprise and a little dis
dain, for my hopes of finding the "hero" became less and less.
" All younger than you.   What babies !"

" Not quite," said Norman laughing.   " I'm not over tall
myself, though I'm older than I seem ; but if you like a great
big fellow, there's my next brother, Hector."

" Ah, that was it ! Hector must be the hero—called after
his great namesake, the defender of Troy.   I was thoroughly
" up" in that history, having been lately put into Virgil (for
I was rather a clever boy), and having got safely through the
second book of the Æneid.   Here was the secret out ; Hector
was certainly the hero my mother meant.   I prepared myself
with no little expectation, and with some alarm, for the expected meeting.

So full was my mind of this, that I don't clearly recollect
any thing more that happened, until the steamboat landed at
a pier, very quiet and desolate compared with the London
quays , and I, quite out of breath with climbing a terribly
hilly street which Norman called " a brae," found myself at
my uncle's door.

In the little parlor, at the head of the breakfast table, sat
my aunt.   I did not notice her much then, except that she
looked kind, and kissed me.   But I was dying with curiosity
to see my hero-cousin.   There were in the room three small
boys, the youngest quite a baby.   I was quite relieved to hear
my uncle call out " Where's Hector ?"

" In his bed—Hector's always lazy," said some of the
younger lads.

" Hector rowed us half-way to Greenock and back last
night," observed Norman, in his quiet way.

" So he did," cried my uncle, smoothing a rather angry
brow.   " But surely he has had rest enough.   Go, Philip,

help to pull your cousin out of bed ; we can have no lazy loons here."

Alas, for my expected hero !

Hector was a great boy, much bigger than Norman. He looked very handsome too, though he lay fast asleep with his mouth open : which was not becoming, nor, indeed, at all like a hero. Nevertheless, when we had fairly roused him—a difficult matter—and he was up and dressed, I regarded my cousin with much respect. He was a very fine fellow, tall and strong, with sunburnt cheeks and curly brown hair, and oh ! such a loud, merry, hearty voice. I greatly admired him, and thought that I must be right at last in my hero, even though he had neither kilt, pistols, nor broadsword, but came down to breakfast in the ugly plaid jacket and trowsers like his brothers.

The rest of my cousins I remember I scarcely looked at, but set them all down together as " the children." There was among them but one little girl.

(Here Uncle Philip paused, but continued after a few moments—" Some of you elder ones may remember ' Cousin Gracie,' as you called her, who spent some months with grandmamma, and died ten years ago, before I went to India."

The children looked grave, for most of them had heard something about a Scottish lady who was to have been Uncle Philip's wife, and for whose sake it was thought he would always remain an old bachelor. After a brief silence, the story was continued.)

Norman came in, carrying his sister in his arms, for she was lame in her ankles, just then, and could not walk. Gracie had always been delicate, they said ; but she smiled sweetly, and thanked Norman so cheerfully when he set her down, that no one would have thought she was ill. She was one of those patient creatures who make sickness so beautiful that afterward we remember them as if they had been angels.

(Uncle Philip's voice altered ; and after a sentence or two more, in which he tried to continue the story by a description of his first breakfast in Scotland, he came to a dead stop, observed that it was bed time, and finished the history for that evening.)

OF course, children (said Uncle Philip), you don't expect me to go on telling you categorically what I and my cousins did every morning, noon, and night. That were impossible to the best memory in the world, while still a childish memory. When we think of our young days we can but remember circumstances here and there ; particular days, hours, or events, which stand out clear from the rest, like bits of a distant landscape viewed through a telescope, which appear wonderfully distinct and accurate so far as they extend, but which only comprise a small portion of the view.

Thus I shall tell you at hap-hazard fragments of autobiography—certain days or certain adventures ;—the rest of our life at Dunoon you must imagine for yourselves.

The first thing I remember was that same evening, after I had been sent to bed by my sensible aunt, and had slept throughout the day as sound as a top. I woke up to tea, and then stood looking out of the window on the beautifu' river. Now I had never seen any river or large sheet of water, except that day when I sailed down the Thames and over the sea. O miserable voyage ! enough to give me, in a moral sense, a perpetual hydrophobia. ("You understand, boys, I don't mean mere dog-madness. Look to your Greek derivations—*hydro-phobia*," said Uncle Philip parenthetically.)

I had thought and said to Norman that the very sight of water would be enough to make me ill, henceforth ; but I changed my mind when I looked on the magnificent Clyde.

"That's the Clough point opposite," said Norman, good naturedly telling me the various places down the shore. "Farther down are two islands, the Greater and Lesser Cumbraes, we call them. About there the Firth divides and goes round either side of the Island of Bute. A long way beyond, you may see something like a two headed cloud lying on the horizon."

I did, with some difficulty, for my eyes were not accustomed to such distances.

"That's Goatfell, the topmost peak of the Island of Arran. A curious island it is, all formed of hills, or rather granite rocks. It's awful fatiguing work to climb Goatfell, but my father says we lads shall try to do it some day. Did you ever climb a mountain, Philip?"

I confessed somewhat with shame, that until to-day I had never even seen one. And I further confessed, that in the sight I had been a good deal disappointed. "A mountain isn't half what I thought," said I, "I expected they would be a great deal higher, and would rise right upright like the side of a house, very awful and grand. Now those hills there are nothing; I could run up them easily."

"Could you, my boy?" said Uncle MacIlroy, coming behind us. "But that is what we all do on entering the world; we imagine to ourselves mountains, and find them mere molehills—we try to climb molehills and find they are very considerable mountains, after all. Hout, tout! (a queer expression he had) bide your time till ye are wiser, Philip Carew."

I did not then understand my uncle's quaint saying, but I have since.

We were interrupted by Hector's shouting from the garden below, "Norman! Cousin Phil! will you come and have a pull?"

"What does he mean?" said I, "what sort of a pull?"

"A pull at the oar," answered Norman, laughing. "Did you never row?"

I certainly never did, in fact I had never been in any boat but a canal-boat drawn by a horse. I tried to explain this, my sole experiment in navigation, as I was going down to the beach with the boys; but Hector burst into such fits of laughter that I found the story too humiliating. In fact when I saw these two sturdy, active, fearless Scottish lads haul up their boat, drag me into it, and dash off amidst threatening rocks, and waves so high that the little boat went up and down on them like a cockle-shell, making me inclined to scream with fright—I began to feel that as regarded all manly exercises my education had been very much neglected.

I had seemed to myself a very fine fellow strutting about among my mother and sisters at home; I shrunk into a mere baby, sitting in the stern, with those two lads, little older than myself, so brave and independent, sweeping among the waves and under the shadow of the hills, which, I began to think were really grand, after all.

"It's growing misty over the river," said Norman, stopping in his laughter and jokes with his brother, which, I must say, they tried to make intelligible and amusing to me, but hardly succeeded; I still felt so strange to all about me.

"Never mind mist, it will be moon-rise directly," Hector cried, giving a long, sinewy stroke with his oar, and then laughing to see that with his greater strength he could pull his brother round—that is, he could make the boat turn till her bow was where her stern should be. She spun round and round till I was quite frightened.

"Hector, you're too daring," said Norman.

"And you're too—" Perhaps in the excitement of the moment he was going to say "too cowardly;" but he stopped.

"Hector," said Norman again, in a very low tone I was

a good deal surprised to see that Hector gave up his too ven-
turous fun and rowed steadily for full ten minutes. But when
I had got over my fright, I am not sure that I did not admire
the daring reckless younger brother a great deal the most, and
became quite convinced in **my own mind that** he, and none
but he, was the Hero.

We pulled on merrily, at least they did ; while I sat watch
ing them in **longing** admiration ; for nothing impresses a boy
with so much respect as the exercise of physical power. I
remember I carried my enthusiasm on this point to such an
extent, that afterward I actually reverenced the first fellow
who ever gave me a sound thrashing, more than I did any
other boy in the school.

"Phil **! would you like to take** an oar ?" shouted **Hector**,
more in bravado than kindness, I fancy.

Now I, having got somewhat accustomed to my novel position, **was longing for** an opportunity of **doing** that which the
two lads seemed to do with so much ease. Nevertheless my
boldness and self-confidence were not over great, and I was
half deterred by Hector's unpleasant manner of making the
offer.

"I should like very much **to row,**" said I, hesitating,
" but—"

" But, you're afraid ! **Well, I** dare say you're right, **my**
little fellow," answered my cousin, in the rather contemptuous and superior tone which big boys delight in using toward
smaller ones. **I was a good** deal nettled, but had sense enough
to hold my tongue. Hector went on laughing and talking,
quite indifferent to, or oblivious of me. I thought this scarcely
polite ; but he was such a good-natured hearty fellow that
nobody could be angry with him long.

We got into smooth water in the curve of the bay.

" **Now,**" **said** Norman, calling to me from the bow—he
always gave his brother the stroke-oar, which dignity Hector

would not easily have relinquished, I suspect ;—" Now, Phil.
come over here and I'll give you your first lessons in pulling ;
we must make you as good an oarsman as any of us, before
you go south again.—Hola, there ! take care !"

His cheery voice and good-natured way of helping me, as
I " crawled" down the length of the boat, in the midst of
Hector's suppressed grumbling, made me feel wondrously
grateful to my cousin Norman.

I clutched the oar eagerly, and of course did what every
body does the first time of attempting such a feat, easy though
it is afterward, when one gets into the knack of it. I made
an awkward dolt of myself ; got red in the face, struck myself
breathless by a blow on the chest with the oar, " caught crabs"
innumerable, and all that sort of thing ! The boys burst into
shouts of laughter ; even Norman could not help doing so, until
he saw tears of vexation in my eyes—for I was a very touchy
little fellow, and very self-conceited too.

" Come, never mind ; you've plenty of pluck, I see ; you'd
row capitally in time," said he, " only do not splutter and dash
the water about, and make such an awful fuss and exertion
over it. Take things coolly, my lad. Look here."

He took the oar from my hand, and showed me how in
this, as in many other things throughout life, quiet work makes
quick work ; for a simple and adroit turn of the wrist effected
all that was necessary. He pulled a few strokes, which seemed
to me wonderfully clever ; doing so readily what I had done
with such desperate effort. Now I understood the mystery ;
it was quite a treat to watch him, dipping his oar noiselessly
and quietly without producing one ripple in the water, and
bending forward his body with ease and grace at every stroke.
My admiration rose immediately, and with it my desire of
emulation.

" Let me try again," I entreated. Hector looked rather
cross, and said something about " keeping back the boat,"

and "spoiling fun ;" but the elder brother took no notice, and I had my will.

I have known many a pleasurable excitement in my life ; many a thrill of triumphant pride ; but I do not think I ever felt so proud, as in the moment when, my awkwardness overcome, I first found myself really " rowing ;"—sweeping the boat along with the force of my own single strength. It was a sense of victory, of power, of independence—feelings, the most delicious to either man or boy ; Alexander the Great (always my pet hero), when he had conquered his millions, could not have felt prouder than I, when I conquered the waves of Clyde, and looked over the whole river, conscious that with a little boat and an oar, I could at any time be free master of it all.

("I have owed my cousin Norman a great many things in my life," continued Uncle Philip, smiling, "but one of the greatest debts I owe him, was teaching me to row. From that night I date a pleasure, which I shall never cease to delight in while I live. Children, I don't think Uncle Philip is ever so thoroughly happy as when he is pulling away over a broad river, the boat dancing on like a feather, with the waves lapping at the keel—nothing but water around, and the blue sky overhead—Ugh !"

Captain Carew here gave an unearthly grunt, probably expressive of intense satisfaction, and after a minute's pause went on.)

Henceforth, I took such a liking to the water, that Uncle MacIlroy declared I must certainly have been born amphibious. My first letter home contained such glowing accounts of my daring aquatic exploits, that I am sure my poor mother must have been terrified out of her senses, and never expected to see her only son return alive. But this was before the time of penny postage, so I had no opportunity of frightening her often.

We began to lead a very happy life—my cousins and I ; it was a life of entire holiday, for my uncle lived in Glasgow He was one of the masters in the High School there, and a very learned man too, having been educated for a minister. The family had only come to spend a few weeks at the coast before the classes recommenced.

Uncle MacIlroy was one of those wise people who think that work should be work, and play, play ; so he gave his boys full liberty, and even made himself quite a boy likewise among them all. This however was only at times ; and amidst all the freedom he used, and allowed them to use, one could see that it was merely the pleasant condescension of a supreme ruler—so certain of his authority that he could afford to let the reins loose at times. I did not quite understand him then, and was somewhat frightened of him besides ; but I have since thought that there could never have been a better father of a family than Uncle MacIlroy. Firm he was, never allowing the slightest breach of discipline ; his will was in all things supreme, his "yea" was *yea* and his "nay," *nay ;* no body ever dreamed of opposing either. Yet he was so right n all he did, so just, above all so thoroughly *true*—exact in speech, punctual alike in commands and in promises—that every body loved, and in the best sense of the word, honored him.

When I came to live with Uncle MacIlroy I first learned to regret, what I have often regretted since, that I had never known what it was to have a father.

Of my aunt it is hardly necessary to speak, except that she was a worthy wife to such a worthy man. She is living still, and I think if she heard it, this my simple description of her would be the very one of which she would most approve.

Nephews, I hope you don't find these facts very uninterest-ing. I state them, not as being what I observed then, but as the results of after reflection concerning those boyish days If you object to my dilating so much upon " elderly" people, I can only say that in telling this story I prefer rather to raise your minds above their level than to depress them, remember ing that you can't ever be younger, and that you are fast advancing toward the time when you will yourselves be grown men and heads of families.

(There arose a little laugh at this, but it was soon stilled by Uncle Philip's extreme gravity for he was on his hobby, one not rare to old bachelors, the proper mode of ruling a family. No one could get him off it, so there was little more autobi ography that night.)

CHAPTER III.

("**AN** adventure, an adventure to-night, Uncle Philip! Surely you must have had something of the kind during the time you were at Dunoon."

Uncle Philip, who was just about to begin his relation, looked puzzled. "Do you mean the sort of adventures that used to happen to me in the Punjaub, such as attacks from the natives, or tiger fights in jungles, or being half drowned in crossing rivers, or those sorts of little tribulations?"

His nephews laughed, and said they only wanted boyish adventures; something queer, and interesting, and true, and dangerous, but in a small way, of course.

"Land or water adventures?"

There were dissentient voices, but "water" carried the day.

"I have it!" said Uncle Philip "Fetch me the map of Scotland.")

Now, boys, I daresay it seems to you but a small distance from Dunoon, round that point of land and across to Greenock; yet I assure you it is nine or ten English miles. This was the longest pull we boys had ever had.

We planned it, I scarce remember why, one day when Uncle McIlroy was away at Glasgow. Otherwise probably we might not have been allowed to do it. But it was such a delicious exploit, that even the long-headed, prudent Norman gave in to the excitement of the plan.

Another reason we had, was that little Gracie, who, in spite of her weakness, was a fearless child, and very fond of the water, longed to see more of the river than in her helpless state she was ever likely to see, except in our nice boat, where she was carried every day, and sat in the stern on cushions, looking, as one day Norman said—"just like Queen Cleopatra sailing down the Cydnus.'

She begged to go, and as she was a great pet with us all, why—she went.

I well remember that day. It was about eight in the morning, for of course we had to start very early. There was a soft mist over the river, but not so as to make our boating dangerous, and the sun was very bright and warm. We had picked out our crew with great care and pride; choosing only those who could be useful and row; so the number dwindled down into Norman, Hector, James the third brother, a funny, clever little fellow, who we thought would keep us alive with his jokes, save that though he could handle an oar pretty well, he was apt to get excited and terrified—and lastly, myself. Little Gracie was our only passenger.

She asserted that we ought to have, in true nautical fashion, a distinguishing mark for our boat's crew; so, determined that we should do every thing grand, she fastened sprays of ivy in all our hats, just where the sailors wear the name of their vessels. A pretty fancy of the child's; and we were all ready to please her.

At last we started from the West Bay, greatly to the admiration of a group of boatmen, who, when we told them the port we were bound to, opened their eyes wide, and wished us safe back again. But we were bold, and had no fears.

After some discussion, we settled that the wisest way to steer our voyage, so as to keep clear of our great terror—the steamers, that were then beginning to ply up and down the Clyde pretty frequently, though in nothing like such numbers as at present—was to go right across to the Clough Point, and then follow the windings of the shore up to Greenock.

This being decided, off we flew like an arrow; Gracie

striking up one of her merry songs. She had the sweetest
voice I ever heard in a child.

(Uncle Philip here spoke hesitatingly, as he always did
whenever he alluded to little Gracie ; but he seemed to think
she was necessary to the history, so always mentioned her
name with the rest. The children heard it silently and with
awe, as young people always listen to the mention of one that
is dead.)   .

We had not started long when there arose one of those dif-
ficulties which prove the unerring truth, that in every collect-
ive body, there must be one to rule. There lie, a little way
in the river, opposite Dunoon, a small cluster of rocks, called
the Gauntlets. Now, Hector wanted to row outside the
Gauntlets, and little Jamie, who was terribly afraid of steamers, and ready to scream if he saw the smoke of one winding
up the river two or three miles off, insisted on going inside the
rocks. And, he being steersman, while Hector and I had the
oars, he guided the helm and turned the boat in one direction
while we were laboring hard to pull her in another ; the consequence was, our making no way at all. In fact, after rather
a vehement altercation, we ended in lying upon the water,
quite stationary.

Gracie ceased her singing, as well she might amidst such
loud voices. She looked appealingly to Norman, who was
stretched his length in the bow of the boat very cosy indeed.
He waited for a lull in the storm of contention, and then spoke.

"Pray, boys, do you ever intend to get to Greenock to-day?"

"Of course," said Jamie.

"Then you'll reach it somewhere about six P. M., if you go
on at this rate. Do you not think it would be better to use
your oars than your tongues?"

This reproof, given so cheerfully and merrily, made us all
laugh, and then James and Hector began to explain their
several wrongs to their elder brother. I fancy I see him yet;

the old fashioned little fellow, sitting listening as **grave as a** judge, but **with** a queer twinkle in his bright eye, that made us laugh amid all our quarrelings. For I was as bad as **the** others, thinking it very shameful that our pleasure should be spoiled by Jamie's foolish fears.

"I'll tell you what it is," said he at last. "Father's saying is quite **true, 'that there's no** doing any thing without a **head.'** Every kingdom must have a king, or-even if it's a republic—a president; every expedition must have a leader, and every ship a captain. Now ours has no captain **at all;** that's why we have all gone wrong."

Every body assented to this fact; but, as was to be expected, in trying to remedy it, the matter became more puzzling than before. Every body wanted to be captain.

However, James seceding from the contest, the choice lay between Hector and me. Hector seemed to expect the honor of right, as being the biggest and boldest of the crew, until Gracie gently suggested that in a ruler and guide prudence **was** as essential as courage, and I was much the more prudent of the two. Strangely enough, but naturally, in the heat of our contest, nobody seemed to think that the best captain, and the one who had chief right to the honor, **was** the only one who sat quiet and held his tongue.

When the war of words grew hottest, Norman's voice was at last raised, and so seriously, that we heard it **above all ours.**

"Hollo, you foolish fellows! Look ahead!"

We had good need; for there was a steamer, **which** in the **height** of our uproar we had not **noticed,** bearing down upon us as fast as ever she could **come.**

James uttered a shrill scream and let go the helm, which little Gracie, terrified as she was, had yet the sense to hold.

"Pull away, Hector," I shouted.—"Pull for your life."

But Hector's bold cheek had turned quite white, **and his**

B*

hands seemed trembling and paralyzed, so that instead of long strokes, his oar only made ineffectual splashes in the water.

"Hold still, James," said Norman, in the loudest and most commanding tone I had ever heard from him. "Hector, give me the oar! Steady with the helm, Gracie dear! Now, Phil, pull away, right into the middle of the stream, outside the Gauntlets."

James gave another scream at this order.

"*Outside* the Gauntlets, I say. Do you not see she's keeping close in shore? We'll be out of her track in two minutes, and then we're all right."

Frightened as I was, and I own to the fact, there was something in my eldest cousin's steady, resolute, and perfectly composed manner, which gave me strength. The two other lads sat quite still and subdued. Gracie, pale as death, but perfectly quiet, kept her eyes firmly fixed on Norman's face, and implicitly obeyed his orders about the helm. He and I pulled together with all our might, and in about three minutes we were clear of the steamer's course, and far into the middle of the river. But it was the longest three minutes I had ever known in my life.

"Now, lads," said Norman, when we all paused to breathe and consider the danger we had escaped, "you see what you would have gained. You were so busy squabbling, and I watching you, that we never saw that boat at the pier. Another minute and she would heve run us down."

"I do not believe she would," said Hector, brightening up. "Steamers always keep a good look-out for small boats. I think you made a great fuss about nothing, Norman."

"Look there!" cried Jamie. "She has passed over the very place where we were lying. We should all have gone to the bottom for sure. I'll never go in a boat with Hector again. Oh! how will we ever get to Greenock alive!"

Here poor little Gracie, who had sat quite calm during the

danger, now that it was over began to feel the effects of her
terror. We had to dip our hands in the salt water, and dash
a little on her face, and pour down her throat some of the
ale that Norman had wisely brought with us, before she came
quite to herself. This little incident subdued us all very
much, and I even proposed rowing back ; but Gracie would
not allow it. Only she hinted a plan, which I believe in our
hearts we were all thankful enough to assent to—that for the
rest of the voyage Norman should be made sole and supreme
captain.

And a very hard business he had of it, poor fellow, with
such an insubordinate crew. The helm was left in Gracie's
care; it pleased her, poor child, and kept the duty of steering
out of Jamie's hands, which was a great blessing. Nevertheless, he or Hector got it sometimes, and as one always
wanted to go close in shore, and the other far out into the
river, the general line of our course became something in
the shape of the letter Z, which did not exactly shorten the
voyage.

Nothing further of any consequence happened, except the
perpetual warfare about steamboats, in which Norman, like
many another ruler, was sometimes forced to yield a little
to the follies of those under his sway. Consequently, once
Jamie's frantic terrors nearly ran us aground in Gourock
Bay ; and again, insisting on being instantaneously put ashore
—a slight impossibility, considering we were about half a mile
toward the centre of the channel—he sprang to the boat's
side and threatened to jump overboard. I don't know whether
the threat were really in earnest, but if Norman had not
stretched out his firm hand and pulled the little fellow in, we
should have been capsized in a moment.

I state this to illustrate the truth of one of Norman's wise
axioms—vainly impresed upon some of us—that there is no
thing so dangerous as cowardice.

Nevertheless, with all its alarms and disasters that day stands out clearly in my memory as one of the most delightful my boyhood ever knew. I could shut my eyes now, and see the broad Clyde spread out on either side, so dazzling, yet so sleepily still; the two lines of shore, the hills misty with sunshine; a big ship coming up now and then, exciting our curiosity and admiration, or the smoke of a steamer seen curling far off and coming nearer, until we, having let her pass at a respectful distance, would take courage, row toward the great waves she left in her wake, and there, shipping our oars, lie rocking up and down with a motion so pleasant that even Jamie was not frightened. It was a delicious day!

("And nothing happened? You got to Greenock safe, after all!" inquired one of the nephews, seeing that Uncle Philip paused and was growing rather prosy over his pleasant reminiscences.)

That we got safe is most true, at which fact I now often wonder, for never was there a more dangerous expedition— dangerous, not from itself, but from the various conflicting wills of the young crew, whom even the sensible captain himself was not able to rule.

I own it *was* a satisfaction when our keel grated on the Greenock shore and we lifted out little Gracie safe and sound. When we had hauled up the boat, which we did with the assistance of a stray passer-by, whom we informed with great pride that we had pulled all the way from Dunoon, Norman and I carried Gracie between us, in the fashion they call "ladies' cushion." Hector went before, poising the oars, one on each shoulder, and Jamie followed with the rudder. In this triumphal procession we reached the house of the good folk with whom we intended to spend the day, and, I must say, slightly "astonished the natives" by our sudden appearance and the story of our exploits.

We performed no more feats, however, as we were not

allowed to row home by ourselves. Our small crew was
divided into two boats, and in the early evening merrily we
again set sail. We had no more hair-breadth escapes or
perilous doings; but I remember we had a great deal of fun;
our two boats' crews running races, splashing each other with
oars, and hallooing contemptuous defiance over the quiet
river. I remember too—though faintly, for I was too young
to take much notice of such things, except that I had quiet
fancies beyond my own age—I remember how black and
grand the hills looked after sunset, and how a red ball of fire
rose out of the river behind us, at which I was half frightened
until I found out that it was the full harvest moon.

Also I remember Gracie's singing out of the other boat,
(Hector had made me come and pull with him in our own)
—how very beautiful, and at the same time melancholy, the
voice sounded, especially when they gradually rowed away
and disappeared in the mist that was creeping over the water.
I listened, catching at times a fragment of Gracie's singing,
or of their talking. I did not mind so long as we could hear
them, if ever so faintly; but when all ceased, the river seemed
wide and dark. They reached home first.

("Well boys," said Uncle Philip, abruptly stopping, "I
think this is enough for to-night.")

CHAPTER IV.

Wᴴᴱɴ next day Uncle MacIlroy came back, and heard of our exploit, which even now I can not help thinking *was* an exploit, considering that we were all lads under fourteen, and none of us, not even my cousins, had had much nautical experience—when my uncle learned the fact, he was half angry and half amused. He compared us to Ulysses sailing west in search of the Fortunate Islands, Jason rowing to Colchis after the Golden Fleece, and various other naval heroes of antiquity, with whom his own boys at least were quite familiar.

But he strictly forbade our again voyaging to Greenock, or any where else, without the parental permission.

" There is nothing I admire more than a courageous spirit," said my uncle, " but remember, boys, that fool-hardiness will never make a *hero*."

This observation sent me back to the old notion about my cousins, which I had never got out of my head, though I could not by any means form a decision on the subject. This last adventure on the river, wherein Hector, the object of my great admiration, had proved himself at once so foolishly daring and so dangerously timid, made my mind more uncertain than ever.

" Pray, uncle," I asked, with desperate resolution, " which of my cousins is it who, I understand, is a hero ?"

He seemed at once astonished and amused, and began to laugh so heartily that, in great confusion, I ran out of the room without waiting for an answer.

The same day, we being still considerably tired and stiff

with our long pull, were glad enough to do nothing but take a quiet walk along the shore. The first place that we went to was the Castle-hill, a curious ruin, on which my uncle lectured very learnedly to his boys. I myself found the conversation dull enough, and took far greater pleasure in running up and down the little hill, chasing the sheep that were feeding there, and leaping from side to side of the crumbling gateway, the chief remnant of mason-work left, at the imminent risk of my precious life.

I was alone too—even Hector, usually my associate in all kinds of fun, had for once given up his frolics to listen to his father's learned dissertations. For Hector, in addition to his physical advantages, was a very clever boy, and was being educated for a minister. When he chose he could be as sedate as Norman; and I sometimes thought his intellect was the stronger, certainly the brighter, of the two.

I happened to come behind the father and sons while they were talking; it was about the olden times, when this dilapidated place had been a fine fortress, under the hands of the Campbells of Argyle, and another ruin which Uncle MacIlroy pointed out down the shore, Castle Toward, was in the possession of the head of the Lamont Clan.

("This is possibly uninteresting to you, lads; but stay till you grow older. Information is always valuable;" observed Uncle Philip.)

"They must have been a lot of brave fellows in those days," said Hector, his eyes brightening while his father related some of the incidents of warfare that took place between the Clans of Lamont and Campbell, "I never knew they were such grand heroes."

"Heroes! I am not so sure of that," answered my uncle, thoughtfully (and you may be sure, boys, that I listened attentively as soon as I caught his first word). "It depends upon what consists our notion of a hero. Remind me, Hector that I read you a passage out of an old book I have, when w. get home."

("Now, nephews," **broke off Captain** Philip Carew, "if one of you will bring me **that big volume** there, I can read **you** the very passage which I then heard from my uncle. It **made a** great impression on me at the time, and rather altered **my notions concerning the** 'heroic days' of ancient history.")

The quotation ran thus :

"In 1646, certain **of the clan** of the Marquis of Argyle, having besieged and forced **to surrender** the houses of Toward **and** Escog, then the property of Sir **James** Lamont, did most treacherously fetter the hands of near two hundred persons **of** the said Sir James's friends and followers, detaining them prisoners, with a guard, their hands being bound behind their backs like thieves, within the said Sir James's house and yards of Toward, for the space of several days, in **great torment** and misery. In pursuance of their further villainy, **after** plundering all within and without the house, they barbarously murdered several, young and old, yea, sucking children, some of them not one month old.

"**The said** persons, in 1646, most traitorously and perfidiously did **carry the whole** people who were in the houses of Escog and Toward, **in boats to the** village of Dunoon, and there most cruelly cause to hang **upon one tree, near** the number of thirty-six persons, most of them being **special** gentlemen of the house **of** Lamont, and vassals to the said **Sir James.**"

("A pretty set these 'heroes' must have been," observed Uncle Philip, **looking up** ; "but," he added, with a sigh, remembering **the Punjaub,** "we are not much better now.")

"Others were likewise barbarously and unchristianly murdered with **dirks,** and cut down with swords **and** pistols; John Jamieson, then **provost** of Rothesay, being shot through **the body, they** finding some **life in him, did** thrust several dirks and skeans at **him, and** at last did **cut his throat with a long** dirk. And **to** manifest their further cruelty, **they did cast some of the** aforesaid persons into holes made for them, **who were spurning** and wrestling while they were suffocated with **earth ; having** denied them any time to recommend themselves to God, although **earnestly** begged and desired **to do** so by the said murdered persons. Insomuch, that the Lord from Heaven did declare His wrath against such inhuman cruelty, by striking the tree whereon they were ᵃ

nanged, in the said month. of June, being a lively, fresh-growing tree, at the kirk-yard of Dunoon, among many other trees with leaves; the Lord struck the said tree immediately thereafter, so that the whole leaves fell from it, and the tree withered, never bearing leaves thereafter."

"Not very likely, after having borne the unprecedented fruit of six-and-thirty hanged men," observed Uncle MacIlroy, when he had read the passage which I have just now read to you. "But," continued he, "this is no matter for jest. It is a pretty specimen of what, in those days, was generally considered heroism."

I started; as well I might.

"But, father, surely all the heroes of that time were not as brutal as these Campbells," said Norman gently—he had a faculty for always hinting, or insinuating the best side to every subject.

"No," answered Uncle MacIlroy, turning over the leaves of his big book; "here is a story, about the same part of the country, which to my thinking, quite counteracts the former one. I'll tell it to you, not just now, but when we come home from our evening walk; it will put out of your poor mother's head the horrible story of this massacre at Dunoon, which I see she is still shuddering at; and, moreover, will give you lads some notion of what I consider a hero."

This was a brilliant idea. So we took our twilight walk, talking over the account my uncle had read. Very strange it was to see the hills looking so quiet in the direction of Castle Toward, and to climb the deserted castle-hill of Dunoon, with the moon shining over it. How different, when we thought of those olden days ' in which, nevertheless, we took a marvelous interest; boys do so delight in stories of warfare and battles

We talked the whole subject over thoroughly, and even walked round by the kirk-yard, trying to imagine where stood the marvelous ash-tree, and to picture how it must have

looked, with the six-and-thirty hanged wretches dangling in
the air, amid the beauty of that June night, in the year 1646.

"Norman," said I to my cousin, as we passed on, "do you
think there ever was any body who deserved to be called a
hero?"

He smiled, but made no answer; for just then we were
entering our own door.

After tea, Uncle MacIlroy told us the story he had prom
ised; a true and well-authenticated legend, which I will
here relate—not in his own words, as of course I can not
remember them exactly—but I shall keep close to the facts,
which have not in the least faded from my recollection.

The Lamonts of Castle Toward, for a number of generations, headed the most powerful clan along the northern bank
of the estuary of the Clyde.

("Most of you English boys know what a *clan* is," said
Uncle Philip, interrupting himself; "still, for the benefit of
the younger ones, I may as well say, that it means a numerous tribe of men, all bearing the same surname, and probably
originally sprung from the same stock, united under one chieftain, whom they implicitly obey, continuing their allegiance
from father to son. It is, in truth, the Scottish form of the
feudal system, which you have all read about in your History
of England—except that the Highland retainers all bear their
chieftain's surname, and mostly claim the same descent from
one patriarch of the race. This is the simplest form of government extant, and dates from the earliest times; in fact,
we may consider good Father Adam himself to have been
the first chieftain of the first clan."

All laughed at Uncle Philip's odd conceit, and professed
themselves quite satisfied with his explanation.)

Some centuries ago, though no date is assigned, the chief
of the Lamont Clan happened to be a mere youth. His
father had probably been killed in one of the various squabbles

which were common then, when every body seemed at once
to fight to live, and to live to fight; when nobody thought
of working, but if he wanted a cow, or a drove of sheep, stole
them from his neighbor, and kept them till his neighbor grew
the strongest, and stole them back again.

In truth, the system of public law then was very much
what it is in boys' schools now—might, not right, was the
general rule, and the best fighter was sure to carry all before
him. Thus, the Lamonts, being very numerous and strong,
held the whole west country in subjection; and did so, until,
as you may remember, in that black year 1646, the Campbells of Argyle made such havoc among them. But the
story I now relate happened long before then.

Young Lamont was on friendly terms with another chieftain, Macgregor of Glenstrae—I know nothing of Glenstrae,
having never been there, but I believe it is on the shores
of Loch Fyne. Macgregor had an only child, a young lad,
something near Lamont's own age; and one day, during a
visit that the latter was paying at Glenstrae, the two youths
went out hunting together.

At night-fall, being far away from home, they, with some
of Macgregor's retainers, took up their lodging in a hill-side
cave; as, indeed, was and is the common habit of the hardy
mountaineers.

During the night, from some trivial cause, on which tradition is silent, there happened—what alas! was likewise not
unfrequent in those warlike times—a quarrel between the
two young chieftains, mere lads as they were—lads, who
nowadays would just have had an honest battle with fists,
fought it out, and been friends again. But in this blood-
thirsty age the case was different. Young Lamont, in the
heat of passion, drew out the dirk, which a Highland chieftain always wore, using it indiscriminately to slay a wounded
deer, or to destroy an enemy. In a moment, while the pas-

sion was upon him (and most of you lads know what the fury of passion is) he had stabbed the boy Macgregor to the heart!

It is worth pausing a moment, to think what must have been the feelings of Lamont—a noble and generous fellow in the main, as his after life shows—when, his momentary passion spent, he stood in the cave, looking at his playmate, his merry companion of an hour since, now lying there, a dead body and nothing more. People in those days thought more lightly of human life and of the sin of murder, than we do now; yet the young chieftain's sensations at the moment must have been of a very horrible kind.

Almost by miracle, Lamont got safe out of the cave; which, had the Macgregor clansmen detected him, he certainly never would have done, since the law of " blood for blood" was very strong, indeed almost the only *law* those lawless times could boast.

He escaped, and wandered about the forests for many hours, until he quite lost his way. At last, seeing a light in the distance, he made for it, and entered a house.

It was the very home he had quitted that morning—the home he had now made desolate.

Old Macgregor received him with unaffected cordiality, forcing him to enter. The unhappy murderer must have done so, scarcely aware of what he was about. But very soon Macgregor discerned that something had gone wrong, and knowing well the fierce passions of those times, was at no loss to guess the whole truth; or else, which is not improbable, young Lamont confessed all.

It is hardly possible to imagine a sterner honor, a more rigid justice, or more heroic self-control, than that evinced by the father of the murdered boy toward the slayer of his only son; especially in those times when, as I said before, the law of vengeance was almost the sole law existing.

The old chieftain not only shielded his wretched guest from
the present fury of the Macgregor clansmen, who at day-break
returned with the evil tidings, bearing along with them the
body of the poor slain lad, but he himself concerted a plan to
save young Lamont's life. Whether this was from a strong
sense of the sacredness of hospitality, or whether from a merciful judgment of the deed—the same which in our days would
have led a jury to pronounce it not exactly murder, but un-
premeditated manslaughter—can not now be known. Certain it is, that the bereaved father acted in this heroic fashion
In the middle of the next night, he rose up, ordering Lamont
to follow him. He led the young chieftain over hill and
forest, far away from Glenstrae, down to a place called *Dùn-
na-ràmh*, on the shore of Loch Fyne. There, were lying a
boat and oars.

"Take these," said the Macgregor sternly. "Use them
for your life; on the opposite shore is your own country.
Once there, let the murderer save himself if he can."

Lamont took the boat, with what words of gratitude the
history does not relate; he rowed safe over to the other side
leaving the childless father standing on the shore.

.   .   .   .

Despite the unrelenting pursuit of the Macgregor clan, the
Lamonts were too powerful for any harm to reach their head.
He lived safely entrenched in his own Castle Toward, and
grew up from youth to manhood, from manhood to middle age
He is believed to have made a just and generous chieftain, and
the clan Lamont flourished under his rule. Possibly, the awful
event of his boyhood influenced his after life; but at this distance of time his character can only be judged by what is, in
deed, the sole way of judging any character, in history or tradition—his recorded actions.

While the Lamonts prospered, the smaller and less power-
ul clan, Macgregor of Glenstrae, was fast sinking. Its head,

the childless father, the last of his race, was incompetent to
rule ; the whole clan, impoverished and weak, were oppressed by their stronger neighbors on every side. At last, by
some great but not uncommon wrong-doing, Macgregor was
stripped of his lands, and for no cause whatever, but merely
to make a show of justice, declared a criminal and an out-
law.

.   .   .   .   .

One day, when Lamont was in the height of his power,
there came a poor old man to the gates of Castle Toward. It
was the unfortunate Macgregor of Glenstrae, who could find
no shelter on earth, save with the man who had slain his only
son, and whom he himself and his whole clan, had pursued
with unrelenting but useless vengeance for many years. A
curious instance of the strange mingling of barbaric, ferocious
justice and chivalrous honor, which prevailed in the middle
ages.

Lamont joyfully received his former enemy, and became
as a son to the unfortunate father whom he himself had made
childless. For many years, Macgregor lived at Castle Toward, treated with infinite respect and tenderness. When
he died, it was under Lamont's roof ; and the chieftain's own
hand closed his eyes. He was buried, tradition avouches,
with all the honors due to his rank, as the last Macgregor of
Glenstrae. His place of burial was until very lately pointed
out ; it was in a little chapelry, dedicated to the Virgin, of
which a few relics only now remain, situated on the farm of
Toward-*na-uillt*.

" Now," said my uncle, when he had finished the story
which I have here repeated, though I can not give it with
half the force that he did, with his terse impressive language,
and his strong yet pure accent (for, as I afterward found out,
my Highland uncle, well educated, and learned in many lan-
guages, spoke, and taught his boys to speak, far purer English

than I did myself). "Now," said he, turning upon us his bright blue eyes, "that is what I call a hero."

We assented eagerly ; but the next moment a difference arose as to which chieftain was meant. Some stood up for young Lamont, and others for Macgregor of Glenstrae.

At last, little Gracie, whom, during the story, I had more than once seen with tears in her eyes—she was such a tender hearted little lassie—Gracie solved the difficulty by proposing that they should both be considered as heroes.

The matter ended ; Hector and I resolving to walk next day to the farm of Toward-*na-uillt ;* in order if possible, to find out the grave of Macgregor—which we did.

("I wonder," continued Uncle Philip, musing, "whether the old chieftain's *manes*—you classic students know what *manes* are—were gratified by this homage paid by two school-boys to his memory. Well ! it only shows how long a truly heroic action is remembered in the world. All the Lamonts and Macgregors that ever tore one another to pieces in blood-thirsty conflicts, have passed into comparative oblivion, from which is only rescued the memory of these two— real heroes !"

Captain Carew looked thoughtful for a minute ; then, seeing his small audience were all dropping to sleep, he gave an impressive grunt, and ceased moralizing.)

I THINK, that the brief time we staid at Dunoon, just two or three weeks, renders my memory more vivid concerning all we did. There was one day, that with its termination (which had nearly been likewise the termination of our lives) recurs to me particularly just now.

It was the day before we left. My uncle had already gone to Glasgow and begun his classes; Norman and Hector ought to have likewise commenced theirs, only my aunt fancied that the former was delicate, and begged an extra week or two of holiday.

"How shall we make the most of this last day?" became the general question; some voted for boating—we certainly had grown water-mad. But Norman suggested that we could not possibly row up and down the Dunoon shore all day, and we were forbidden to go any further.

"Besides," as he sensibly remarked, "would it not be better to tire our legs out first, and then resort to our arms? I propose that we should take a good long ramble up the hills all day, and have a nice pull in the evening."

So off we started; Norman, Hector, James, and I. There was a slight squabble previously, as to whether or no we should take any lunch with us; but we all had such an intense aversion to carrying a basket, that my aunt's entreaties were vain. However, I saw her quietly put a slice or two of dry bread into Norman's pockets; every body was thoughtful over Norman, as he, in his turn, was thoughtful over every one.

We started, promising to be back in time to give Gracie a sail—poor Gracie! who set us off so merrily, and yet when we reached the gate, we saw her looking after us with such longing, wistful eyes.

Boy-like, we could not think of going up into the hills by the regular path, but determined to ascend up the bed of a stream, a beautiful *burn*, that came pouring merrily into the Clyde at the West Bay. It was a remarkable place, the water dashing over the slate rocks that formed high braes on either side of its course. I hear that now, when Dunoon is so changed, this stream has been bridged over, its wildness brought into elegant order, and an English chapel of the fashion called Puseyite (though I don't quite like such nick-names in religious matters), built on the top of one of the braes. Nevertheless, no modern innovations can have altogether spoiled that lovely little **burn.**

Nobody, **who has** lived only in a flat country, can have **the least idea** of what a stream really is in the Highlands. Not a quiet, babbling, good-tempered brook, but a perfect torrent, which, be the volume of water great or small, is equally impetuous. It comes leaping from rock to rock, circling the larger stones, dashing over the little ones; divided here and there into half a dozen zig-zag channels, or again joined into one, flow for perhaps a few yards, until the rocky impediments break it once more. Mostly, it is so shallow, that you **can** step through it, but by places it sinks into deep, still **pools** under the hollows of rocks; tempting, transparent, crystal baths, where you can almost see to the bottom. But it must be a very venturesome bather who would put his foot in *there.*

Such a stream was the one I speak of, up the channel of which we four merry boys went.

What fun, what laughing we had! How we took off our shoes and stockings and slung them over our shoulders, that we might the easier cling to the smooth stones. How deli-

C

cious it was to feel the water dashing coldly over our bare
feet, as we tried, by the puny resistance of those said feet
planted across lesser channels, to stop a current that was as
resistless as time, or fate, or any thing else of that sort.

("Upon my soul '" cried Uncle Philip breaking out into
the only asseveration that, soldier though he was, he was
ever known to use. "Upon my soul, when I talk of these
things, I almost wish I were a boy again! But it won't do,
it won't do !"

He continued, making an attempt to laugh :)

No felicity is without its vexations, and I remember we
were desperately tormented by the midges, that would come
about us in myriads, settling on our faces and.stinging, till
they almost drove us crazy. At length we stuck great leaves
of fern, or bunches of heather, in our caps, with which the
little wretches contented themselves in some small degree ;
though still they were all but insatiable. (So, boys, it is worth
while to remember that the greatest merriment and happi
ness in life is sure, more or less, to be accompanied by—
midges !)

I can not call to mind every portion of our walk, or rather
scramble, for we scorned any thing like regular locomotion,
but I know that our next tribulation was something worse
than midges. We got into a bog.

I never can understand why, on mountain sides, which one
might naturally expect to find dry, there should be such a
deal of bog land. To me, an English boy, quite unaccustomed
to such a thing, I own it was not over pleasant. So unexpected, too, for the marsh we crossed looked pretty and green,
had magnificent beds of moss; with, oh! such heather!
And Gracie wanted some of both to take home to Glasgow.

On I plunged, choosing for a footing the greenest looking
mosses, and always finding them the deepest in water. But
I was too proud to confess the fact ; so floundered silently on

seeing the other lads far before me. At last Norman turned and shouted for me to come on.

"Presently," answered I, putting a bold face on the matter; "but it's *rather* bad walking."

It certainly was; I being just then busy hunting for one of my shoes; in the search for which I left the other shoe behind me.

"Come on, Phil!" shouted the boys once more.

"I can't," cried I, piteously, despair at last subduing my courage, "I've lost my shoes, and I can't walk home barefoot. Will nobody come and help me?"

"What, you expect us to go back all through the bog!" Hector replied, from near the top of the hill. "Hurrah! I'm out of the moss now, and it's such a beautiful view. Make haste, boys."

Very easy that—with some dozen yards nearly impassable between me and the enviable hill top, to say nothing of the lost shoes. Except that I was ashamed, I could have sat down and cried. Once I thought of calling for Norman, but then I did not care so very much for him. Hector was my chief friend, and Hector had deserted me.

However, when I was standing sulky and disconsolate, looking at my stockings all tramped in holes, and my trowsers wet up to the knees, I found Norman beside me. He had come all the way without my asking him.

"Well, old fellow, and what's to be done for you? Here has Jamie been in just the same plight." (Oh, what a comfort that was!) "Come, cheer up, never mind!"

"I don't mind," said I proudly, "only if I could but find my shoes, considering I haven't another pair, and am not at home as you are." And I began to think mournfully how my poor mother had charged me to be very careful of my clothes, since she was not rich enough to buy me more for a long time. Horrible visions rose up of my having hencefor

ward to go about barefoot, like the little ragged Scotch boys
I so despised.   It was an accumulation of woes.

Perhaps Norman saw I was sulky, and tried no more con
solation, except in a practical way.   He said nothing, but cut
a long stick from a fallen tree, and poked about in all directions for a dozen yards round, until at last, after infinite patience, he found my shoes.   I shall never forget my joy when
he jokingly exhibited them one stuck upon each prong of the
long stick.

"Thank you, Norman," I cried, energetically.

"Stop, Phil, you can not put them on.   See how soaked
they are ; they'd be the death of you !   Come, off with your
stockings too ; put them in your pocket and sling your shoes
over your shoulder ; then you'll be quite sure not to lose
either."

I own, I somewhat objected to this plan.

"Oh, nonsense, it will only teach you to be hardy.   Feet
were made to walk on ; do you think father Adam wore
shoes ?   Squeeze the wet out of your trowsers and roll them
up to the knee ; then start off ; you need not mind the bog
now.   Bravo ! that's the way to get over a difficulty."

His cheery voice and manner would have encouraged any
body to do any thing.   He made so light of the trouble too,
and bore his part of it—for he had got desperately wet—so
uncomplainingly.   Before I knew what I was about, I found
myself laughing merrily—stepping from heather-tuft to heather-tuft as he told me.   (Which general hint I throw out to
all bog-trotters, that where there's a heather-tuft, there is sure
to be safe footing.)   Very soon, we had nearly passed the
region of my woes, out of which I had moreover contrived to
bring a magnificent nosegay for Gracie.   At last we stood on
the hill-top, and looked back on the bog we had safely got
through.

("And that bog," added Philip Carew, meditatively, "was

not the last from which, during our troubled journey through life, my cousin Norman has brought me safely out.")

This hill-top, which I have never climbed since, nor am ever likely to climb, afforded a scene which, boy as I was, I have never forgotten. It was a very narrow peak, quite bare, composed of a few rocks or stones thrown together like seats, with bits of heather, moss, or lichen growing upon them. The peak was high enough to afford a view of the Firth of Clyde, from Rothesay up to Greenock, or possibly further, only that the afternoon haze was stealing on. The river was perfectly calm, with very few boats on it—there was not a sound among the hills—not a cloud stirring in the sky—every thing was as still as death; although it was such bright sunshine. There were a few sheep feeding far below us, but they only looked like white stones scattered on the hill-side: we never saw them move.

Somehow, wild boys as we were, the scene quieted us. We sat on the hill-top for half-an-hour, without talking at all—or only in whispers. Then I put on my shoes which Norman had managed to dry on the hot sunny rocks, and we started off down the slope.

Now another disaster arose. We found as we penetrated further down the woody side of the hill, that on it were feeding not merely the harmless sheep, but some Highland cattle, and little Jamie was dreadfully afraid of cows. His terrors were this time not quite so unfounded as usual, for I remembered that Uncle MacIlroy had himself warned us to be careful where we went, since there were sometimes very ferocious bulls found in unfrequented parts of the hills.

And when unluckily a black cow, rather wild and shaggy-looking, as all Highland cattle are, being possessed of an inquiring disposition, walked foward a dozen yards to take a mild survey of James, the poor wee fellow ran off screaming. The noise disturbed the animals still more. They began to

look at one another, and at us, and really even I grew rather
uncomfortable.

" Pooh !" said Hector disdainfully, " who's afraid, even if
there is a buil ? We must pass this way, and those that do
not choose to go may stay on the hill-side all night."

With that, he went daringly forward to meet our foes, and
so outraged the feelings of the aforesaid black cow that I really
think she would have run at him, but happily there was a
broad ditch between them.

" Hector, do not be fool-hardy ! Come back !" shouted
Norman, in the imperative elder-brother tone he so rarely
used ; and Hector came, probably not very reluctantly, leaving the indignant little Highland beast to watch him with
ferocious eyes.

" We can not go through that pasture, it's quite evident,"
said Norman.

" But we will ! Nobody is afraid but Jamie ; let him stay
behind."

" Now, Hector, that's not talking common sense. How *can*
we leave the little fellow behind ? Whether he's foolish or
not is another matter ; anyhow there's no conquering his fears."

" He should have staid at home then."

" So I think, Philip ; but since he *is* here, we must jast
make the best of him. The question is, are we to leave him
on the hills all night, or are we to get back another way ?
Try it, lads ; there's great fun in finding out a new road.
Here goes !"

He plunged into a small copse of nut trees and brambles
whence Jamie's frightened voice was heard in different directions, frantically calling on us all in turns. Hector and I
looked at one another rather discontentedly : Hector muttering something about " little cowards that always spoil every
thing,"—then we followed. Somehow or other, whether we
liked it or not, Norman generally had his way

It was a great consolation to find lots of nuts in the nut-wood, and in the enthusiasm of hunting for them, we quite forgot to abuse poor Jamie. We compelled him to cram his pockets with our surplus nuts, until we found that he ate them so fast as to be any thing but a trusty guardian of the spoil. So we quarreled and made it up again, grumbled and laughed, shouted and sang—Norman being as wild as any of us; until suddenly we discovered that the sun was getting low, and the nut-wood dark; and besides, we had not the dimmest notion where we were. We were very hungry too, in spite of all our nut-eating, and were beginning to feel tired and cross, especially Jamie. He had just proposed our going home, when the unpleasant idea presented itself, that we really did not know how to get there.

We three elders had a serious consultation, while Jamie sat and cried.

" Look," said Norman, " there's a white line running along the foot of the hills. Now that must be a high road, and a high road must lead somewhere. Suppose we strike to it, in a straight cut, through bushes, bogs, and every thing. It will be an adventure; and as to mud, why, we can't be much worse than we are now."

We looked dejectedly upon our torn and dirty habiliments, soaked to the knees, and acknowledged that fact at once.

" Come then, before it grows late ; let's start boldly."

" I canna," sobbed Jamie, "I'm so hungry, and nuts are not like one's dinner. I'm so thirsty, and we have not seen a stream."

" You goose," cried Hector, " do you think we are not all hungry and thirsty too, only we would be ashamed to make such a fuss about it. Get up, James, and let's be off."

"Stay, lad," interposed Norman, catching his little brother by the shoulder, and arresting a most pitiful and disconsolate outcry Then, out of that blessed pocket of his, he drew a

great lump of dry bread—very dry indeed, and warmer
through ; but, nevertheless, eatable bread. Did'nt we eat it !
with most hearty gusto too, though I'm afraid we were too
hungry to say " thank you." Except that Hector, having
finished his piece, and wanting some more, which was of
course not to be had, slapped his brother energetically on the
back, saying—

" Never mind ! you are a trump, old fellow."

" Now for water ; there must be some hereabouts," observed Norman, and we went a little way and listened. Sure
enough, there was the faint tinkle of a spring, falling a drop
at a time. We followed the sound, so indistinct, that except
in that region of perfect quietness we could not have heard it
t all.

" Bravo ! here it is," shouted Hector. " Now, Phil, do
you wish to see a Highland spring ?"

It certainly was the slenderest rivulet imaginable, oozing
drop by drop out of a moss bed, and running under the roots
of the heather, a mere thread of water. But it *was* water ;
and it grew and grew, we tracking it a few yards by the sound
of its trickle, though we could not see it, until at last, coming
to a rock a few feet high, it had to make a great leap, and in
that leap suddenly discovered itself to be a stream.

Oh, the delight of drinking it up ! which we did literally,
for it was such a tiny runnel that our mouths laid across the
current stopped it up entirely. Moreover, the water had in
a slight degree the peculiar iron taste given by running through
bog land. Nevertheless, we thought it delicious ; and I looked
upon Norman with as much respect as if he had discovered
the source of an important river, which, for all I know, he
really had, since every river must have been, once upon a
time, a little trickling mountain spring.

All being refreshed, Norman gave the word to start. What
a scramble it was, down a sloping thicket of nut-wood and

brambles, a descent always at an angle of forty-five degrees (you boys know thus much of geometry). A descent, likewise, which **was** marshy ground the **whole** way. Nothing was heard **but** plunges, tumbles, and outcries; **yet** the thing was **so funny,** we could none of us help laughing. Except Jamie, **who** in despair gave **himself up to his fate and was quite sure** he never should reach **home alive.**

" **Well,**" said Hector, " if the worst comes to **the worst, we can** but stop on the hills all night, as people do when **they go** deer-stalking. I should like it very much; it would **be just** like Robinson Crusoe."

But, seeing that this alternative frightened the **tired Jamie** more than ever, Hector, really a kind and generous boy, **took** his little brother **on his back, and they two went floundering** on together.

" Good **news !**" cried **Norman, who was in advance,** " we **have** come at last **to the foot** of the hill **and** the end of the **bog. Here is a stream, which must** run somewhere, and I think from the direction it takes, must run toward the high road which leads toward Dunoon. Jamie, you're clever at the points of the compass, tell us what you think ?"

Jamie, thus ingeniously appealed to, stopped crying at once, **and looked about** him. He declared he knew the **place, and** that the little **loch we** saw close by **was near the high road** from Loch Eck to Dunoon.

" He's quite right ; **Jamie's a sensible wee fellow,**" said the elder brother kindly. " If we track the **course of** this burnie, we'll come out all right, and to save trouble in getting through the brambles, I propose that we take off our shoes and stockings and wade."

This plan **of** aquatic transit **was** greatly admired, and certainly the **bed** of the stream made a most admirable pathway, quite easy compared with the bogs we had gone through. We performed the exploit capitally, with much laughing and

c*

fun, and without any disaster ; only as we neared the high
road, we heard the voices of some Dunoon ladies passing, and
at my earnest entreaty, we four torn, muddied, bare-legged
laddies crept under a bush until they had gone by. For
which act of timid propriety on my part, my cousins tormented me the whole way home ; telling me I had always lived
among girls, and was just a girl myself ; until I furiously
proposed they should all fight me, and try.

Somehow or other, we got home. Little Gracie was sitting in the bow window, watching for us very anxiously. My
aunt had been too busy to vex herself much ; besides it was
not much later than we usually came home. Returning, we
had mutually agreed to keep our own counsel, and tell none
of our dangers and disasters, that night at least. So when
after tea Gracie innocently asked if we had enjoyed ourselves,
and if, supposing we were not too tired, we would take her
one last sail in the dear little boat ? it became necessary to
answer yes.

Looking out, we found the twilight had gradually melted
into the most lovely moonlight. Gracie crept to the hall
door, holding by Norman's shoulder, and came back singing
one of our English nursery rhymes which I had taught her,
and which took her fancy very much—

> "The moon doth shine as bright as day,
> Boys and girls come out to play,
> Come with a rattle and come with a call,
> Come with a good will, or come not at all."

She sang it so prettily ; she could put a tune to any thing she
liked—she was such a clever little girl.

Well, I don't remember how we coaxed my aunt to let
us go, seeing it was eight o'clock at night ; but we certainly
did get leave, promising to remain out but a little while, at
which promise we were ready enough, being much tired.

But somehow the brilliant moon making every thing as

clear as day, the river being very calm, and our boat lightly laden (there were in it just Norman, Hector, Gracie, and I) —we staid out longer than we intended. Gracie was so merry; singing at the very top of her clear voice, clear as that of a little golden wren; it made one wonder how such a volume of rich sound could come out of so slender a throat.

We were pulling up and down the West Bay, listening to Gracie's singing, or at intervals making a tremendous noise ourselves, by shouting to an echo that we had found out at a particular spot in the bay, and which answered us from shore in most unearthly mimicry of our words, and especially our laughter; the latter became a " ha, ha !" perfectly demoniacal.

Gracie suddenly stopped us with " Look ! is not that a steamboat at the pier ?"

" I don't think it," Norman answered, " it's too late an hour for steamers. Yet that certainly must be one; I wonder which way her head is. I did not see her pass up, so she must be coming in our direction. Pull away, Hector; Phil, take the other oar !"

" No, no !" cried Hector, who was showing off his skill with both oars " we are quite far enough in shore ; besides, I would like to catch her waves."

" Ah do ! and let us have a nice rock on them; 'tis for the last time this summer," begged Gracie.

Norman assented, knowing that there was no danger in the harmless see-saw of the waves, which his sister was so fond of. In fact, there was no time for refusal, since when he was yet speaking the steamer, which in the uncertain light proved nearer and larger than we thought, had passed us by. For a minute all was still, and then I saw her waves—great long rollers, hills of water, with deep clefts between—advancing slowly in the light of the moon.

" Ship your oars !" cried Norman, who was looking fixedly at the rollers, which Hector, sitting backward, could not see.

"Oh how nice and large they are!" said Gracie, quite fearless.

They were indeed large, larger than I had ever seen ; they came on huge, steady, resistless. I remembered having heard Norman say there was no danger to any boat in a mere swell, but only when the waves rose into breakers, curled over, crested, and broke. And looking at these, I saw slowly gather at one end a white crest of foam.

"Steady! Keep her head to the waves! Now ship your oars," said Norman, in a quick whisper. Our eyes met, and *we* both understood—we two only—that the next minute would decide whether the boat, already sinking aslant in the watery hollow, should again rise up on the wave, or go down to the bottom like a shot.

Boys! it was an awful minute. I remember seeing Norman steal his arm firmly round Gracie ; I knew what he did that for. She, poor child, sat smiling, and Hector too. It was, I say again, an awful minute!

The boat plunged down head foremost—and rose up again! We were saved.

Other waves came, but less than the first ; the little boat rocked harmlessly on the swell.

"It's grand!" cried Hector. "But, Norman! Philip! what's the matter with you?"

"Only that we have all been within an inch of our lives, and are safe. Thank God!"

I had not thought of that thanksgiving. It made me feel that Norman was a better boy than I.

"Now, pull ashore, quick!" added he, taking the trembling Gracie in his arms. Hector, horrified at the past danger, obeyed. We rowed home and landed without speaking a word.

•

CHAPTER VI.

(" WELL, boys, are you not getting tired of my story? It is becoming as long as those of Dinarzade, in the Arabian Nights. Do any of you, contrary to the Sultan, want to cut off my head, in order to put an end to my tale?"

Uncle Philip's question, with its very mild amount of humor produced great merriment, and hearty " Noes," on the part of his young audience, who settled themselves at once for an· other " night's entertainment.")

You will hear no more Highland adventures, nephews, since after the last unlucky boating we left Dunoon ; which, I now think, was very fortunate ; Hector and I were growing so wondrously daring, or rather fool-hardy (for there is a mighty difference between fool-hardiness and courage), that otherwise I don't believe we should ever have quitted the place alive.

Very loth we were to quit it, nevertheless, and grumbled extremely all the way up the Clyde ; especially Hector and I, for Norman was too busy looking after the luggage, and making jokes for the purpose of keeping the younger children quiet. We used to call him " the nursery girl," from his care over his little brothers, and his great popularity among them ; which popularity Hector and I rather disdained than emulated. But Norman only laughed at our quizzing.

The steamer went lazily between the narrowing banks of the river, very much like an overgrown goose trying to swim along a small, dirty and ugly stream—I never saw any water so muddily black as the beautiful blue Clyde becomes near

Glasgow; only it was some fun to watch the boiling eddies that the steamer produced on either bank as she passed, so extremely narrow was the channel.

"Really," said I, "how stupid the people were to build Glasgow here. I wonder any ships can ever manage to get up this poor dirty bit of a river. We should never think of it in England."

"Very likely not," answered Hector with wondrous dignity, "but we Scotch can do any thing any where, and make any thing out of any thing."

Of course I indignantly scouted this fact: but I half begin to think there was some truth in it. And, viewing Glasgow, not as I did then, with prejudiced and limited boyish vision, but as I should now, it seems to me a wonderful place. Ugly as it is, or was in those days, it keenly strikes a thoughtful mind, as every commercial city must. One may liken it to the roots of a great tree, tangled, dirty, unsightly fibres, but which nevertheless stretch out far and wide, often wider than the branches, and upon whose strength the whole stability, health, and beauty of the tree depends. Therefore I have a marvelous respect for the western metropolis of Scotland, and say with all my heart, as says the motto on those atrocious'y ugly city arms, " *Let Glasgow flourish!*"

Little did we boys then care about these things; we only thought, as we landed at the Broomielaw (which I remember I had unaccountably supposed to be a bank of flowering broom and discovered to my confusion, that it was a thicket of masts just like St. Katharine's Docks) we only thought that we were coming back to a disagreeable town life—to dullness and school.

"Ah," sighed Hector, as we passed the ferry, where the ferryman sat in his clumsy barge, handling his still clumsier oars: "Ah, that is all the boating we'll have for months to come! just crossing the dirty Clyde and back."

We both pulled melancholy faces and thought it very hard.

It was on a Saturday that we came home—I now called my uncle's house *home* quite naturally—on the Monday the boys were to begin their "classes," for here I found every body said "going to classes," instead of "going to school." On Sunday night, Hector, Norman, and I lay awake for hours—we all slept in the same room, they in their bed, and I on the floor, which I thought great fun. There I heard a deal of talk, to me quite mysterious, about "third year," "fourth year;" "dux," "Doctor Cowe," "prize," "examination," etc., etc. In the midst of which I gradually fell asleep.

I was awakened, at what I thought an unearthly early hour, by the ringing of a most unearthly bell. Norman jumped up, shook Hector into wakefulness, at the which he growled furiously, and then performed the same kind office for me.

"No use grumbling, Phil!—up at seven—prayers at half-past—breakfast at eight—off to classes at nine! It's father's way, and *must* be done. Tumble up, lad!"

I did "tumble up" very sulkily, with strong intentions of rebellion against Uncle MacIlroy. But as soon as ever I saw him, I began to fear my bold resolutions were all thrown away.

He came down stairs, his hair flying abroad more than ever, with a most resolute, business-like, head-of-a-family look, quite different from that he wore in our holiday-time. As I have before said, Uncle MacIlroy was a very good man, and a very kind man; but I never saw any body look more stern than he could, when he chose. And when he, in his quiet way, issued a command—"boys, do so and so!"—you would as soon attempt to jump over the moon, as not do it.

So when, after prayers and breakfast were over, the latter being almost as gravely gone through as the former, while

Norman and Hector, both very quiet now, were busy looking over their books—my uncle called me into his study, I did not dare to refuse.

An awful place was that study, all lined with books, and thickly scattered with papers; he was such a learned man, though fate had ordained that he should never be any thing more than a schoolmaster.

"Philip, come here ; nay, do not be frightened." (I dare say I looked so.)   "Have you ever been to school?"

"N-no, uncle, not exactly!"   In fact, I had gained all my little learning from my poor dear mother (a very clever woman grandmamma was in her youth, boys.)   I timidly stated this to Uncle MacIlroy.

"Um—yes—I see.   Has she taught you Latin?"

"A little."

"Delectus?—Cæsar?—Ovid?"—my uncle never wasted words.

"I'm in Virgil ; my mother likes Virgil best."

"Oh ! let us see what you can do," and he took down a great musty looking Æneid, all mouldy and dogs'-eared inside, though most carefully bound ; no doubt a very valuable edition, but it only frightened me the more.   "Now, Philip, begin."

"*Arma virumque cano*," tremblingly I commenced, pronouncing my *a*'s short, English fashion.

"*Arma(y) vyrumquee ca(y)no*," mimicked my uncle, shaking his head—"boy ! that will never do here, you would be the laughing-stock of your class.   There is not a country in the world where they pronounce Latin so, except in England. Try it this way."

And in his sonorous, musical voice—broadening out the *a*'s and *e*'s, Italian fashion—he read the lines :

> "Arma virumque cano, Trojæ qui primus ab oris
> Italiam, fato profugus, Lavinia venit
> Littora."

"Now, Philip, go on."

I was obliged to do so, my Saxon pride rebelling at every word. Though now I think my Uncle MacIlroy and "every country in the world," are quite as likely to be correct in their notion of pronouncing Latin as the solitary opinion of John Bull

("Oh, oh, oh!" groaned some of Uncle Philip's audience, staunch Westminster boys

"Well, nephews, the thing's not worth fighting about," smiled he, and continued.)

Whether or no I passed my examination with credit, I can not tell; certain it was, that my uncle, putting away the terrible Virgil, desired me to get ready and join his class in the High School.

Here was an encroachment on the liberty of a boy and a Briton! I absolutely stood aghast.

"And," continued my uncle, not taking the slightest notice, "since, as you will not be here all the session, it is useless your taking other classes, I shall give you evening lessons my-self in whatever I may think you require. Now away with you; the boys will show you my class-rooms. Remember, half-past nine, *invariably*. I never excuse want of punctu-ality."

He patted my head ("The old hypocrite!" I thought) and sent me away.

There was no help for it. All the nice long lounging mornings I had planned, to be spent in drawing Gracie's little carriage, or playing jack-straws and cat's cradle with Willie and Wattie, for at heart I dearly loved laziness, all—all were put an end to! I regarded my uncle as a terrible tyrant, and thought if any of my cousins had been the "Hero" my mother alluded to, they would not have stood it for a single week. I had some notions of setting up for "a hero" myself, and running away home. I had even got the map

to calculate how far it was from Glasgow to Surrey, when I
heard Norman's voice calling me, and found that I must
make up my mind to be a slave—for one day more.

"But to-morrow, to-morrow"—I said to myself; and kept
my counsel safe, even from my cousins.

They, honest lads, trudged merrily through the muddy
streets, for it was what malicious strangers call "a regular
Glasgow day," which sort of day is the most abominable
specimen of weather I ever met with any where.

"Never mind it, lad!" laughed Norman. "Mud never
killed a body yet ; and smoke, Glasgow smoke, is considered
very good for the lungs. 'Tis the healthiest town in Scotland, father says."

"Probably," said I, maliciously , and stumbled on, trying
hard to feel cross, and not being able to manage it.

"You'll not be in the same room with us, Phil," observed
Hector, as we entered a quadrangle, where stood a building
looking very scholastic and college-like. "Father has the
third year this session, and we are in the fourth year."

"What do you mean by such nonsense as third year and
fourth year? Surely I am not going to be set to learn with
little brats three years old ?"

"That's a good joke—go it again, Sulky !" cried Hector,
in great glee. But Norman explained to me that the classes
were arranged in this fashion, according to the number of
years the boys had learnt Latin.

"As Hector said, we are in the fourth year, under Doctor
Cowe. Isn't it a droll name? And he is such a funny old
fellow. But—hush! here he comes."

We drew back on the dirty—yes, the very dirty stone staircase, which looked as if it had been muddied and dirtied by
the boys' boots for ten years—and let the master pass by. I
could draw his picture now.

He was a tall man, in a rusty black doctor's gown He

stooped in the shoulders, and his face must have been decidedly
ugly, for I remember he had little eyes, and a large, clumsy,
under-hanging lower jaw, which he had a habit of twitching
nervously from side to side, until the effect was not unlike
that of a cow chewing the cud. He was rather fat, and had
an awkward, ungainly, cow-ish walk. Or else, which was
not improbable, his queer name set me off at finding these
resemblances, as it had the other boys. Altogether, the
effect was irresistibly droll.

When he had passed, Hector—no, I think it was Norman,
for Norman had an immensity of quiet fun in him—slyly
pulled me aside to show me a cane that the doctor had stuck
in his right hand coat pocket underneath his gown, which it
hitched up most comically.

" He always carries the cane so; we call it the Cowe's
tail. And doesn't it give us some pretty hard switches sometimes! But for all that, he's an excellent fellow, the old
doctor. And we must not keep him waiting, or he'll get
cross."

" Here's your door opposite, so go in, and good luck to you !"
said Hector, as he followed his brother into the class-room ;
and I was left outside, my good-humor quite restored by
laughing at the Cowe's tail. I wondered if my uncle kept
one too !

But soon these speculations ceased in the trepidation of
making my first entry into a boy's school—a crisis formidable
to any lad—and most especially formidable in such a public
place as the High School of Glasgow.

I just poked my head in, following two or three boys who
then entered, and who stared at me as if I had been a strange
cat, which indeed I much resembled, prowling about in this
forlorn way. The class was evidently not begun, so I popped
out again, and again prowled about the staircase. I might
have done so till night-time, without gaining courage for a

second appearance, had not Uncle MacIlroy suddenly come
up the staircase, and seen me.

Now, if there was one thing in the world my uncle liked
to see in young folk, it was punctuality. His rugged face
dilated into a good-natured smile.

"Hallo, Phil! here already? Capital beginning this, and
good beginnings make good endings. Come in."

"I—never went to school—and—I never had any body to
teach me but my mother," whimpered I.

"Poor lad!" and as my uncle looked at me I knew he was
thinking of my father that was dead—he now and then did
look at me thus, with a remorseful kindness quite incomprehensible to me. "Poor little fellow! Come in with me."

He took me by the hand, and led me into his class, setting
me in a quiet place by myself. Then he gave his gown one
shake, and his hair another—bent his brows, and set his lips
sternly together—altogether putting on an appearance quite
worthy of a pedagogue.

I think Uncle MacIlroy must have been the best teacher
of boys imaginable. He never thrashed—he rarely scolded
at least not in the passionate manner that many schoolmasters
do; but there was something in his rigid inflexible will that
did the work both of tongue and cane. It seems to me now
perfectly marvelous, the way in which he reduced such conflicting elements to discipline and order. He could doubtless
have ruled a kingdom as he ruled that little sovereignty, his
class. He governed it thus well, because, like all good rulers,
he governed that very difficult subject—himself. His temper,
truth, conscientiousness, never failed.

Since even in my boyish imagination one of the chief qualities of a hero was to know how to rule, I seeing, as a quick
child would at once see, how well he ruled his scholars, began
to consider whether my uncle himself was not something of
my grand object of search—a Hero. So by noon I had

determined to put off my running away to England for an
indefinite time, in order to wait and judge. Especially as
having very easy tasks this day, merely to stand up and construe a few lines of Latin in my turn, I got through the class-
hours more comfortably than I had expected.

At mid-day I was set free, and reached home somehow,
having spent an hour or two rather amusingly than otherwise, in losing my way and finding it again. Then I drew
little Gracie about in her chaise, and played baby-play with
Willie and Wattie till they quarreled with one another, and
afterward both took to quarreling with me.

By evening I was so thoroughly tired of doing nothing, that
when the two elder boys set to their books, and Jamie, the
cleverest and busiest little bee imaginable, set to his, I felt not
so much ill-used as I had expected by being called into the
study, and taught there for an hour or two. Of course I still
considered myself rather a victim, and if I did go willingly
and pay some slight attention to the teaching, it was with the
firm conviction that the obliged party was, not myself, but
Uncle MacIlroy.

(" I don't exactly think so now," said Captain Philip, closing
his tale for the night.)

CHAPTER VII.

Thus the first day of my experience at the High School passed off pleasantly enough. But things could not go on so smoothly forever. It was out of the bounds of possibility, and out of the nature of boys.

My first trouble came upon me on the third day. Tired of going home to spend a lazy afternoon, I had sauntered about the quadrangle that formed the playground, in the hope of getting some sort of a game with somebody.

I got a much more unpleasant game than I thought—a sort of practical "Hunt the Hare"—in which I myself performed the part of the unlucky animal.

It happened thus. I had on, as was the custom of boys then to wear, at least in the south, a beaver hat like a man's. I well remember the extreme pride with which my mother bought it, taking me into a hat-shop and choosing it with great care; sighing the while, for she said it made her feel what a man I was growing, and that wearing it I looked more than ever like my poor father. She little thought that the unlucky hat would prove so fatal a *casus belli*, and come to such an ill end.

My cousins had jestingly warned me that the wearing of it was dangerous, since the High School boys had a mortal objection to any thing but Glengarrys. But it was quite impossible that I could constrain my Saxon liberty to wearing a Scotch bonnet, so my beaver stood its ground. Once or twice I noticed it eyed with a cruel smile, as it hung on its peg of dignity, the only hat in the class; but that was all.

However, on this Wednesday, when for the first time I joined my comrades in the playground, the hat's misfortunes began.

First, there was thrown from behind a wall a handful of mud, which lodged on the **brim. Next,** somebody shot a **sharp** pebble, which **made a dent in the crown.** Thirdly, some person or persons **unknown,** quietly stole behind and knocked it over my eyes.

At this, I grew into a furious passion, in the midst of which a little lad snatched my hat away altogether, "to **keep my** head cool," as he waggishly hinted. The next minute I **saw** it stuck on the handle of a whip, and in this manner **passed** from hand **to hand through a crowd of** jeering boys. The fifth indignity was to batter in the crown, the sixth to turn **it** inside out, the seventh **and** last was to stick **it up on the top** of a wall and shoot it with pins from **a cross-bow.**

By this time my rage was unutterable, but its impression **was harmless enough, as a** great **gaunt lad** held my arms pinioned behind me.

"Hollo, what **are** you doing to the wee fellow?" cried Hector's loud voice, and frantically I writhed myself out **of** the big lad's arms into those of my cousin.

"I will have my hat. They've stolen and spoilt **it. I'll** be revenged. I'll bring you all up before the mayor."

"We hae nae mares here, but ye may ask at the Cowe," answered a lad, which atrocious joke was received with shouts of applause, **in the** which my little burst of indignation was completely drowned. Even Hector began to laugh as loud as **any** of them, and in **so** doing imperceptibly slid from my side. **When a joke goes** against a fellow, it's rather bad for his cause.

I sought refuge with Norman. "Help me, do help me. Get me my hat again—my poor hat, that cost my mother so much money."

It was an unhappy allusion. Every body maliciously

wanted to know the precise amount of cash my mother paid,
and how much she had left? and all that sort of thing. Some
even attacked my two cousins on the subject and made a few
contemptuous allusions to " Auntie."

Then Hector's spirit rose up for the honor of the family.
" I'll tell you what, lads, if you don't let Philip Carew alone,
and give him his hat again, I'll fight the four biggest of you,
turn and turn about."

This, I do believe, was exactly what he wished, for Hectoı
was the stock pugilist of the school, and fought battles for any
body or any thing, quite in amateur fashion. Nevertheless,
I thought it very kind of him to champion me, and loved and
admired him very much.

Norman, after a dissuasive word or two, ceased to interfere
He was either too quiet or too wise to go right against the storm.
He only staid close by to see that his brother had fair play.

It was agreed that the combats should be wres'ing matches,
not battles with fists, lest black eyes or bruised .ıoses should
betray any thing to parents ; and so like a young Aιtæos, or
else like his great Trojan namesake, did Hector begin the fray.
He was a capital wrestler, strong, active, bold ; I never saw
his like.   Now I became quite certain that I had found my
" hero!"   He laid the first combatant prostrate in the mud,
was himself laid prostrate by the second, but rose up fresher
than ever, and returned the compliment.   The third lad
skulked crying from the field, and with the fourth Hector was
so well matched that the battle at length ceased, neither
being victor, but both giving up from the very unwarlike fact
that it was getting near dinner-time.

For this all-important reason, when Hector had received a
round or two of applause, the play-ground became gradually
thinned, the circle which had gathered round the fighters
slowly broke up, and the grand bone of contention, having
been kicked about pretty well, at last lay unnoticed in a corː

ner. In this, as in many a more important war, the original matter of dispute soon came to be altogether forgotten. Even I myself, in my enthusiasm for the fighting, had ceased to remember my unlucky hat, and stood composedly in the drizzling rain, bareheaded, until I began to sneeze.

"What's to be done with the boy ? he is not so hardy as we," said Norman kindly.

"Oh, let him take my bonnet to run home in," answered my "hero," throwing it toward me with an indifferent yet patronizing air. "Well, Phil, are you not very much obliged to me for fighting your battles ?"

I said "yes," though I thought he need not have asked the question. And somehow I let the bonnet lie, and tried to pick up and set to rights my poor battered hat.

It was no use, the thing was a perfect scarecrow.

"Nay, let it be, and put on Hector's, since he offers it. You can't go through the streets bareheaded, the folk would 'augh at you."

Hector turned suddenly round. "By-the-by, I never thought of that. Hey there ! I can not spare my bonnet, old fellow." He picked it up again and set it firmly—not on my head, but his own.

"Nay," said Norman, as I began to sneeze worse than ever, for the rain had thoroughly soaked my hair, " Phil needs it worse than you ; and you being a bigger boy, would get through the streets better, even if you were tormented a little. They wouldn't dare to do it long. Think again, Hector."

But Hector, the bold fighter, could not face the humiliation of walking home without his hat. He grew angry, and told his brother "to practice what he preached." I protested against having either's cap, for I did not like to see Hector cross with me, after having defended my cause so bravely.

"Here, take this, and we'll see what is to be done," cried Norman, throwing me his bonnet and running away.

D

" He's only showing off, he'll be back directly," muttered Hector.

But he did not come back. We waited a little while, and then, hunger being strong upon us, we started home both rather silent. Just turning the corner of the street where Uncle MacIlroy lived, we met Norman.

He was walking along, the heavy rain pouring on his head, and running down his neck in little streams. His cheeks were very hot, and his manner hurried, for there was a tribe of ragged urchins at his heels, jeering and pointing after him, calling him " bareheid," " gowk," and " daft laddie." And poor Norman was naturally such a shy, timid boy, painfully sensitive to observation. What he must have suffered in that hour's walk !

Hector and I ran to him, I full of tenderness and contrition, Hector muttering something about " thrashing all the little vagabonds within an inch of their lives." But that proceeding was stopped by an unlucky, or lucky conjuncture.

Close behind us, wearing his most serious look, appeared Uncle MacIlroy.

" What's all this. Tell the truth."

We obeyed, Hector being the foremost to tell it, and to his own disadvantage likewise ; for when his feelings were touched he was a generous fellow.

Uncle MacIlroy heard in silence. He did not even take exception to the matter of the fighting, which Hector had modestly dwelt upon very lightly. All he said was said to Norman, in a tone so gentle that we were quite startled.

" My boy, I am glad to see that you have the best courage of all, *moral courage.*"

Stooping a little, he put his arm through that of his eldest son, who stood by, blushing and agitated as a girl—and so walked with him up to their own door.

I don't think I ever saw Norman look so happy or so proud

("Bois," said Captain Philip Carew, in answer to general request, "do you expect me to tell you circumstantially what happened day by day during the time I was at Glasgow? Because, if you do, I can only say it is an impossibility Remember, all this happened twenty odd years ago, and if I had not the clearest memory imaginable, you would not have the story so respectable as it is. Even now, I have a strong conviction that I am painting things not exactly as I saw them then—for boys have little observation—but as I afterward by comparison found out they were, or must have been. Are you content to receive matters so, or shall I stop?"

"No—no—no—" was the outcry, though there came a very faint deprecatory "yes" from some person or persons unknown.

"The Noes have it, as they say in the House of Commons," cried Uncle Philip. "So here begins.")

Our days at Uncle MacIlroy's well-ordered house passed so exactly alike, that the history of one will do for all.

We rose at seven—then lessons, prayers, breakfast, classes, dinner, play (not much, alas!), tea, lessons, bed. After bedtime came the hour of chatter and forbidden fun, tempered with serious discourse between the brothers, with whom it was a very anxious time.

Now, though of course I had never been in the "fourth year," from constant hearing about it, I knew by heart every member of "our class," his capabilities, and his chance of prizes.

First there came Andrew Caird, the undoubted Dux—

nobody ever dreamed of contesting that point. Next to him
were Norman and Hector MacIlroy, who usually "ran neck
and neck," as sportsmen say ; the elder's diligence still keeping a trifle ahead, in spite of the younger's brighter parts.
But, latterly, the lazy Hector had absolutely suffered his next
class-mate, John Gordon, to get his place sometimes, whence
came sore heart-burnings and fears.

These four were all ministers' sons. I think I said before
that Uncle MacIlroy had been brought up to the ministry
though for some years he had had no church. The four
"ministers' boys" were the pride of the whole "year." They
always kept together at the head of their class, and held
slightly aloof from the lower lads, whose names I don't remember, as they went by the general term of "the other
fellows." Nobody ever thought of them in connection with
prizes. All the excitement, all the doubt, contest, and dread,
lay with the ministers' boys.

Now I, who had never known any thing of life at a public
school, still less at a public school in Scotland, was at first
driven "clean wud," as my northern cousins would observe,
by the constant talk about "our examinations," "our prize
givings," &c. &c.

"Can't you make a little less fuss about it, and let a poor
fellow go to sleep," cried I one night from my shake-down on
the floor. "What does it matter who gets the prize ?"

"What does it matter ?" echoed Hector indignantly
"When all Glasgow comes to look at us, or may come if they
like—when we have to walk up in face of every body, and
the Lord Provost himself gives us the prize !"

I own, the latter fact struck my youthful imagination. I
remembered having once seen the Lord Mayor, and being
greatly awed thereby. The idea of receiving a book from the
hands of a live Lord Provost, only a degree lower than a
Lord Mayor, seemed something very grand indeed.

So I only said "O !"—a great round O of enormous veneration, and sat up in bed leaning on my elbows, and listening
with open mouth to what Hector and Norman were saying.

The former was in what Norman called "a way," "a state
of mind," which may be translated to mean a state of temper.

"I know it's no use," he was saying ; "I know I'll not get
it. There's that confounded fool—"

Here Norman gave a low whistle—he didn't quite like bad
words.

"I say it again, that confounded fool, Johnnie Gordon,
whom I thought I could beat by just lifting my little finger,
has kept my place as often as I have kept it myself, or
oftener. He is sure to get the prize. And if he does, I'll
thrash him within an inch of his life."

Norman whistled again. I began to think that, hero as
my younger cousin was, he had rather queer notions of might
and right. Nevertheless, I earnestly wished he might get the
prize, or if not, that Johnnie Gordon might get the thrashing.
I felt convinced that both were equally deserved—as indeed,
I still think they were.

"Now, Hector," Norman answered, "if you'd only listen to
reason, and take things coolly. You did so a week ago. You
said you did not care a straw about getting any prize at all."

"He did say that, for I heard him," added I, at rather an
unpropitious moment. Hector made an angry lunge out of
bed. (He was rather fond of pommeling even me sometimes,
but it was quite in a friendly way, and I always took it
quietly—I was so fond of him). The lunge missed me, so all
I got was a polite "Hold your tongue ! Bother !"

"Don't practice beforehand on poor Phil, in mistake for
Johnnie Gordon," said Norman, laughing—he knew good-
humor was ten times better than scolding ; "If you want to
keep your hand in, I'm bigger. Hollo !—let's have a round !"

He leaped up in bed, tucked up his white shirt sleeves, and

his bare arms—also very white, for I remember we used to
tease him mercilessly about their lady-like color—shone in the
moonlight.   Altogether he made such a comical show of warfare—poor Norman, who never could fight—that Hector forgot
all his ill-humor, and burst out laughing, until Uncle MacIlroy
coming up stairs, rapped warningly at the door.

So we all slunk into bed again, and were doomed to whispers—under cover of which, I managed to learn the real facts
about the prizes, and about Hector's wrath.

In the High School of Glasgow at that time, and even now
for all I know, prizes were given in this fashion :—the boys
took places in their class ; each day it was set down in writing
where they stood, first, second, third, and so on.   At the
year's end these numbers were counted, and the lowest
number, which consequently ranked highest in the class, received the prize.   In my cousins' class there were three
prizes, the first of which would doubtless fall to Andrew Caird
or Norman—the second was pending between Hector and
Johnnie Gordon.   All the winter and spring these two had
run nearly equal—in their Latin at least, which was the
'hing chief thought of—but after the holidays, Hector's soul
had been left behind with the boats and the Clyde, and he
lost his place continually.   Doubtless the score would turn out
very much against him, poor fellow !

"It's a great shame," cried I warmly, after which loud
exclamation I took the useless precaution of smothering my
mouth in blankets lest they should hear in the next room

"It is a shame, when he could beat Gordon and me too, if
he tried.   If Hector were not such a lazy fellow I should be
shaking in my shoes," said the good-natured elder brother.
"But after all it is not sure for a few more days.   Hold up
to the end, lad !   Never say die !"

And he began counting the other chances Hector had,
supposing the Latin prize failed.   Alas ! all the other chance

were likely enough to fail **too.** In Greek, figures, mathemat
ics, drawing, **there was always** some unlucky impediment
Perhaps the real impediment was what Uncle MacIlroy,
teaching his boys at night, often said, and what I then considered an atrocious libel and **a** cruel **instance** of paternal in-
justice—that Hector **was** one of the laziest **fellows** the sun
ever shone upon !

" **What's to be done ?"** cried the poor **lad, waking** up to his
disastrous situation. " Oh, what will father **say if I** get no
prize at all !"

Here was an awful prospect !—the more so as " **Father**
had of late been so busy teaching me **in the evening, that he**
had not **looked after his own boys** quite so carefully **as he**
ordinarily **did.** Nevertheless, **from little things which he said**
sometimes, **we knew how much he counted on the success of
the cleverest of his sons, in whom, though he tried to** hide it,
he evidently **took great pride.**

I too, **began** to speculate **on what Uncle** MacIlroy would
say, did Hector win no prize this year ; and as the brothers
began to talk in a lower voice, and very earnestly, I was left
to my own meditations. These **I** suppose, gradually melted
into drowsiness, and drowsiness into dreams ; for I remember
fancying that the prizes were to be given away that night, in
our bedroom—that **the Lord Provost,** sitting in **state on the**
chest of drawers, was delivering numberless rewards **to every**
one but Hector, whom he sentenced to be beheaded. **That**
thereupon my uncle came in, dressed like the executioner of
Charles I., carrying instead of a **hatchet, the dogs-eared** Virgil,
with which he solemnly cut off Hector's **head,** the decapitated
body falling across the bottom of **my bed.**

At which I screamed **myself** awake, and found it was only
Gracie's **immense black cat,** who had leaped on my feet, and
was purring **himself** to repose as contentedly as possible

Hector, however, was still **alive, if I** might **judge** by his

vociferous snoring ; in the which I doubtless very soon joined
But before then, I recollect seeing Norman lie, his wide open
eyes and anxious face distinctly visible in the moonlight.   He
might have been thinking of his prize ; I fancied so then, but
now I don't believe he was.   Poor Norman ! I did not always
do him justice, in those days.

CHAPTER IX.

WEEKS and days, nephews, seemed a great deal longer to Philip Carew then, than to Uncle Philip now. The time at last arrived when the public examination was only a fortnight distant, and the boys were daily expecting to be informed how the prizes stood. The examination, I should say, was mere ly complimentary, to show off the boys' acquirements, and had no reference to reward of merit.

Of an evening we were always a very studious set, but during the last few days of suspense we worked like Trojans! I could picture us now, all gathered round the table with our books and exercises before us, Hector conning his, fast, loudly, im-patiently—his cheeks flushed with excitement ; Norman sit-ting very quiet, trying to knock every word of the lesson into his honest head, poking his fingers in and out among his stiff hair—then decidedly and obnoxiously red, but which, as Gracie lovingly foretold, would grow into the prettiest color imagina-ble. And Gracie was right.

James too, the busiest little laddie of ten years old, what an indefatigable student he was ! With all his terror of four-footed beasts, how bravely he could decline *bos, bovis!* and what wonderful long sums he got through, perfect mountains of multiplication ! Only, he never could learn any thing with-out digging his elbows on the table, and squeezing his fists into his chin, and knitting his pretty brows like an old philos-opher. Poor little Jamie ! I wonder if he does the same to this day in his learr ed college at Calcutta !

My aunt always presided at the lesson-learning, the head

D*

of the household being then safely deposited in his study, to
somebody's great relief, I confess ¹ Now and then, however,
we knew by my aunt's looking up and smiling, that he had
re-appeared at the parlor door, to carry off some unfortunate
wight for a lesson ; and again silence fell on every body, except
for the click of Mrs. MacIlroy's scissors as she mended those
eternal pairs of stockings, little and big—grey and white—
socks and long hose. Poor woman ! I dare say she almost
wished, after the formula of the Emperor Nero, that her
numerous household had but one foot; the only hope for a
termination of her labors

Nobody was allowed to talk during the hour of lessons.
This was a positive law, which like many another, was by
some loophole or other slipped through.   Gracie did it chiefly
Nobody could see her lying on her little sofa in the corner,
telling fairy-tales to Willie and Wattie, without listening with
one ear at least.   Most interesting tales these were, always
beginning " once upon a time," and ending with " they lived
very happy all their lives.'   What wonderful people "*they*"
must have been !

But Willie and Wattie was not always satisfied even with
them.   Continually the wee fellows, Willie especially, would
come creeping to the table, pulling Norman's sleeve with the
interminable " Please, tell me a 'tory !"

And continually Norman would lay his book down, rub his
fingers over his forehead, to send the cobwebs away, and
patiently launch into some astonishing adventure, told in an
under-tone, with the gravest face imaginable.   He certainly
was the very perfection of an elder brother, as regarded the
babies of the family.

In fact, whether a Hero or not, in all cases of difficulty he
invariably turned out the best elder brother in the world.

I remember one Saturday night—it must have been Saturday, our weekly holiday—his taking me aside and warning

me to be especially "jolly," and say no word about the all
engrossing subject—the prizes—if I could help it.   From this
I guessed that Norman had good reason for thinking that to
day was the critical day with the masters, and that Monday
would decide every thing

I felt very uncomfortable ; for little as I went among the
High School lads, I had heard enough to know what the
Fourth Year generally thought of Hector's chance ; and that
it was but the turning of a feather between my elder cousin
and the steady-going patient, wooden-headed dolt, Johnnie
Gordon.   Very hard, that !

However, I made myself "jolly," as Norman desired, and
helped him to make the rest so.   Hector did not heed us ; he
was, or seemed to be, in very high spirits ; he had been third
in the class for five days now, and thought that Johnnie Gordon's star was paling.   He was so easily swayed either to
hope or fear, poor fellow !

After tea, Norman put on his comical mood—which, when
he chose, was very comical indeed.   He took little Willie on
his knee, and told him the queerest 'tories, until we all gathered round in curiosity.   As for the child, his pretty face
lengthened with amazement, and his eyes were almost start-
ing out of his head.

" Not quite so wild as that, my boy, you'll frighten the
little ones," said the mother, with a gentle—a very gentle
reproach, for she had been watching Norman all night, and
doubtless guessed his motive, though she said nothing.   " Come,
Willie and Wattie, before you go to bed, shall mamma tell you
a 'tory ?"

Mamma's 'tories were so rare, that at once there was a
delighted assent, and all crowded round.   I could see that little
fireside group now ; my aunt in her arm-chair, with Wattie
on her knee, Gracie lying on the sofa opposite, so smiling and
content, with Norman sitting at her feet, and Willie too, who

never would leave his elder brother on any account. In the
intermediate space sprawled Hector, James, and I, dividing
the hearth-rug with the big black cat, which Norman's wag-
gery had christened Tea-kettle, on account of his color, his
fondness for sitting close by—nay all but on the fire, and his
habit of hissing indignantly at every opportunity.

" Now," began my aunt, " If any body knows what I am
going to tell, they are not to say any thing until it is over."

It was a mysterious commencement, and I paid attention.
Every word almost of the story I remember to this day.

" Once upon a time—now, listen, Willie and Wattie, and,
Jamie, do not be pulling poor Tea-kettle's tail—Once upon a
time, there were a papa and mamma living together at a manse
far up in the Highlands.   Perhaps Philip does not know what
a manse is ?"

Ay, but I did ; having grown familiar with Scottish words
I at once stated that it was the clergyman's house.

" The minister's," said Aunt MacIlroy, correcting me ,
" and this papa was a minister.   He had an immense parish,
all among the mountains ; indeed, he had to ride sixty miles
to get from one end to the other.   In the summer time he was
often absent for whole days together, preaching among the hills,
and leaving his wife at the little manse.   It was a very small
place.   They lived there with only one servant to help the
mistress in the house, and look after the two little boys."

" Two 'ittle boys," repeated Willie with grave interest.
" Mamma, were dey as big as Wattie and me ?"

" I think so."

Den, dey were not 'ittle boys," sturdily persisted Willie,
whose reasoning and intellectual powers far surpassed his
powers of language.

" Very well, they were big boys, then," said Norman,
laughing ; " only do not interrupt mamma."

Aunt MacIlroy tried to go on, but very soon Willie, after a

meditative silence, broke in again. " Please, tell me one ting just one ting."

" Well, out with it !"

" Did de two 'ittle boys wear pinafores ?"

Every body laughed, as indeed we often did at Willie ; he required such very circumstantial descriptions of every thing.

" Yes, I can answer for it ; they did wear pinafores, which they tore just as often as Willie and Wattie do theirs, and often made mamma very sorry." Here Willie, quenched and humiliated, poked his fingers thoughtfully in his rosy mouth, and let the tale go on.

"These two brothers were near of an age, and as there were no more, except a tiny baby, they were left to play to gether a good deal, with no one looking after them except the servant-lassie who was their nurse.

" Dat was Issy, their Issy," observed Willie, with the air of a person asserting a great fact ; arguing, I suppose, that all nurses must bear the same name as his own.

" We'll call her Issy," answered the mamma, smiling. " They were very good little boys, especially the elder, and did not give Issy or mamma any thing like such trouble as some other little boys I knew. So they were allowed to run about the manse-garden and farm-yard ; for the minister had a sort of farm, that is, he kept a horse and two cows, and had a few sheep feeding on the hill-side.

" There were two places about the yard where the children were forbidden to go ; one was to the byre while the cows were in it, and the other was to a stone trough that lay just outside the gate in the manse ; the minister had placed it there for the cattle to drink out of. It was a long and deep trough."

" How long, and how deep ?" inquired the pertinacious Willie, whose great blue eyes were dilating wider and wider.

" About the length of the hearth-rug, and as high as that,"

said my aunt, measuring with her hand about two feet from
the ground. "In summer time, when the little mountain
streams were dried up, it was always carefully kept full, by
the minister's desire, that the poor thirsty cattle and sheep
which happened to pass by might always find something to
drink at his door."

"How kind! Was he not a very good man, these boys'
father?" asked James.

I could see my aunt's eyes silently shining; but she only
nodded her head in reply.

"One summer-day the little boys were sent out into the garden, to play about there, while Issy was busy washing and
drying the clothes, going to look at the children from time to
time to see that they got into no mischief. For though, as I
said before, they were good boys, still they were very young.
Country children brought up as they were have on the whole
more sense than town children, otherwise these would not
have been trusted alone at all. But though the younger was
daring and heedless, the elder was a very wise little fellow for
his age.

"On this especial day they were more left to themselves
than they had ever been before, for the minister was out on the
hills, and the mother was kept indoors, looking after her poor
little baby that was ill.

"She sat nursing it for a long time, an hour or two after
she had sent away the boys. It kept crying incessantly, so
that she could hear nothing, think of nothing but that. At
last it grew quieter, and she walked about the room singing it
to sleep. The window was open, for the day was very warm;
every thing around was quite still, as the Highland mountains always are in summer. But as she stood laying her
baby in bed, she heard a faint sound somewhere outside the
house.

At first she thought it was only the hens calling their

chickens far down the road ; it was very unlikely to be the
voices of people talking, for the manse was in such a solitary place that sometimes not more than one person passed
in a day. And just then the poor baby waking, the mother
turned and sang it to sleep again. When she ceased she
still heard the same faint noise.

What sort of a noise ?" James wished to know.

" Like somebody who was trying to call out and could
not, being half smothered, and the cry sounded like a little
child's."

Here Aunt MacIlroy stopped, looked pale, as if the bare
idea of this critical moment were too much for her motherly
heart.

" The—the minister's wife ran to the window. It looked
on the long garden, at the bottom of which ran the road.

" There she saw the great deep trough, which had been that
morning filled, and above it something which looked like a
little curly hea"

" Nobody can tell how the terrified mother managed to get
down stairs. When she came to the trough-side, there were
her own poor boys—not one, but both ! The younger had
fallen in with his face foremost, nearly touching the water ; the
elder, not strong enough to pull his brother out, had climbed
up and stretched over the side. Baby as he was, he had the
sense to keep his little brother's head above water, holding it
by its curls, while he cried out for "mamma" and "Issy."
He must have remained thus for more than half-an-hour.
Both were nearly exhausted ; another minute—and the little
hands would have given way and the little head have sunk
down, and—O my dear children !"

We all looked in amazement at my aunt, who had leaned
back in her chair, much agitated. The children clustered
round her anxiously, but she soon put them aside with her
quiet smile, and was herself again.

"But the little boys," said Hector, deeply interested "They were saved? They grew up to be men? What a wonderfully brave fellow the elder must have been !"

"And so sensible too," added James.

"Surely," Hector continued energetically, "the younger would never forget what he owed to his brother, even when they were quite babies."

"I hope," the mother answered, "I earnestly hope he never may." And smiling, she looked from one to the other of her two elder boys.

Norman sat uneasily twisting Willie's pinafore. All the while he had not spoken a word; but when he met his mother's eye he blushed crimson.

Gracie half rose; she was the quickest of us all to divine the mystery. "Mamma, it's a true story you have been telling us! And I guess who were the two little boys."

Sobbing, she flung her arms round Norman's neck and kissed him.

Then a light broke upon us all, but Hector was the most confounded. He turned red and pale, and looked more near crying than I had ever seen him.

"Mamma—and I never knew this !"

"Your father desired it should not be told. But it is indeed true. Your brother Norman saved your life."

"Norman saved my life," repeated Hector, still bewildered. But Norman came up and put his hands on his brother's shoulders with a cheerful laugh, "Wake up, old fellow, you see we're both alive now."

Then Hector, quite overcome, did a little bit of sentiment, and the two big brothers kissed one another as if they had been baby playfellows.

My aunt was a wise woman. After her story nobody even so much as thought of prizes.

I went to bed that night looking with rather different eyes

at my cousin Norman   Though I still believed it quite impossible that such a mild easy-going fellow could be in any
way the hero I sought, yet I began to think that during his
boyish life-time Norman MacIlroy had done one or two things
that even a hero need not be ashamed of.

What say you, nephew?

CHAPTER X

On that Monday—the very day of all others that I intended to stay about the school after my uncle's class was over—which I did not usually do, the High School lads teased me so—on that Monday I had to come home at once, for poor little Gracie was ill, and my aunt wanted me to deliver some messages. Of course, I was always glad to do any thing for my kind, good aunt, and little Gracie.

I came direct from school, hearing no word of the prizes. Indeed, I forgot all about them till dinner time.

Then, as I sat at the window, trying to keep the little ones quiet, I saw my two elder cousins coming down the street. One look at Hector was enough to explain the truth—that he had failed, and Johnnie Gordon had won.

Poor Hector; the proud, handsome, merry lad! How I hated that Johnnie Gordon!

I did not like to run and meet the boys, lest it might wound Hector's feelings; so I listened till the hall door opened, and very soon Norman came in alone. His brother had gone away up-stairs.

"Well?" said I in a whisper, for Gracie lay on the sofa asleep.

"Well!" said he; and nothing more. He looked almost as unhappy as Hector himself.

"How many has he got? Any or none?"

"One—second for writing. But that's nothing!"

"And you?"

"Oh, Phil, be quiet! Just three!" His vexed voice

though he spoke of three prizes, might have seemed like affectation or hypocrisy ; but even in my most unjust moods I never could find the like of either in Norman MacIlroy.

We said no more, for Gracie was just waking, and ill as she was, we knew it would grieve her to know how unhappy her brothers were. Very soon I went up-stairs to poor Hector.

Nephews, I have long been a grown man, and seen much of vexation and disappointment in the world, but I own that the recollection of Hector's misery rests upon me still. It was perfect despair.

"Hollo!" shouted he, when I opened the door. "Keep off, will you? Who wants you? If you come in I'll send this book at your head."

I did come in, for I was so sorry for him ; and he did send the book at my head, only luckily I ducked down and it missed me. By that time Hector's passion was cooled ; he lay sullenly on one bed, while I sat on the other, looking at him.

"Hector," said I, "if I were you, I wouldn't care."

"I do not care!—who says I do?—I've thrashed four of the class, and kicked Johnnie Gordon half way down stairs, and now I m satisfied. Doctor Cowe and his prize may go to the devil if he likes."

This certainly was language not quite becoming a minister's son, or indeed any body's son. I was quite astounded. For, though I know the boys in public schools generally get a habit of using ill language, and are even so deluded as think it fine and manly, it was not so with my cousins. Uncle MacIlroy had brought up each of his sons to be, like himself, a Christian and a gentleman.

"Dear Hector," said I meekly, for all the girlishness I had about me from being taught by women, came back when I saw him in such trouble. "Please, don't talk abou' the devil. It isn't right, and it won't get you back your prizes Never mind, try again!"

" I'll not try again. I'll never try any more. I'll drown myself—or go to sea—or— '

" Come and have dinner," said little Willie at the door.

This apropos conclusion of his sentence would at any other time have made Hector laugh his ill-humor away, but it was too deeply seated now.

" I'll have no dinner. Yes,"—he added with a sudden thought—" I'll go down, just to show them how little I care."

It happened fortunately for Hector that his father being out, and his mother busy over Gracie, the dinner that day was a very desultory affair. Nobody took much notice of him.

He made a great show of eating heartily—being always a big, stout, hungry boy ; but, looking at him, I could fancy he swallowed down more tears than mouthfuls. He seemed in a state of perpetual choke, poor lad ! All the rest were very kind to him, and bore his sharp speeches without a reply ; for, though the young MacIlroys often squabbled a little, as all families of boys must, there was always a tender combination over any one of the number that was either sick or in trouble. I have no doubt that if Hector that day had abused us all round we should have taken it quite patiently—so sorry were we for him.

But he did nothing of the kind. He ate his dinner, or pretended to do so, and went up again to his own room as before, save that this time he locked the door. Which proceeding made me very unhappy, for I thought him such a desperate, daring boy, capable of any thing. All the romantic stories I had ever read, of incarcerated or wronged heroes secretly putting an end to themselves, came horribly into my mind as I sat by that bolted door. Every now and then I called to Hector ; he made no answer, though I heard him moving

about. **At last, as the afternoon** darkened he seemed to grow
quieter. **My** terror only increased the more. Every **minute**
I expected to hear the click of a pistol, or the fall of a heavy
hanged body!—A very brilliant imagination of mine, considering there were no sort of fire-arms in the house; **and** certainly Hector, whose hands were not adroit at any thing but
fighting, would never find out the correct way to hang him-
self. My knowledge of his want of manual dexterity also
put to flight another fear—that he had torn the sheets into
strips, made a rope-ladder, after the fashion of De Latude and
other prisoners, escaped out of the window—a very useless
trouble, when he could so easily have gone out **by the front
door**—and so ran off to sea, never to be heard of **more!**

But **it would be idle** to count up my fantastic **and romantic** speculations **during** the two hours that **I kept guard at**
intervals **over** Hector's bedroom. **I had nobody to** speak to,
Norman **having** disappeared mysteriously after dinner. I
thought it very unkind of him so to go and leave his brother
in such a state, and my love and pity for Hector rose tenfold.

After a while the poor lad seemed comforted, for I did not
hear him dashing things about, but still I could get no answer, not even when it grew dark and I begged him to come
to the parlor fire. At last, when a quarter of an hour's silence
had rather frightened me, I bethought me of **sending in a**
potent consoler.

I waylaid Tea-kettle on the stairs and made him **scratch**
with his fore paws at the door, his accustomed token that he
wished **to be** let into the boys' **room.**

The door was half opened. Hector was certainly growing
mollified—toward Tea-kettle at least. But little hope there
was for me, **who** only had the door shut in my face with a
cross " Get along !"

I certainly won " more kicks than halfpence" from my
Hero ; **but then I** was rather a devoted little fellow, and

had always that peculiarity, more suited to a woman than a
man, of loving those I did love entirely for themselves, without
reference to the way they treated me.   Likewise it shows
what a generous, frank-hearted lad Hector must have been,
and how many good qualities he must have had, since he
made me love him so well, though he was such a tyrant.

It was useless meddling with him any more till Norman
came in—Norman who could coax any body to any thing.   I
bethought myself of the rhyme my mother used to say to me
in my sulky moods, a rhyme into which she put a mighty
deal of moral meaning.

> " Little Philippe
>   Has lost his sheep (viz. his *temper*)
>   And doesn't know where to find him;
>   Leave him alone
>   And he'll come home,
>   Dragging his tail behind him."

I never exactly comprehended the force of the last line, nor
do I now, but doubtless it had a significance, so I determined
to follow out the axiom and leave Hector alone.

Only once, unable to keep away, I crept up the dark staircase and listened at the door.   There was a hollow, smothered
sound inside—regular—coming at intervals like groaning.
Had he really killed himself?   I was on the point of running to alarm the household, when I remembered Tea-kettle
—the wise sensible cat, that was so fond of Hector.   And I
fancied that in the midst of the groaning I heard loud purrs.
O lucky Tea-kettle!   There could not be any thing very
wrong.

Nevertheless, it was an infinite relief when, tumbling
down stairs, I felt somebody else tumble up against me, and
found it was Norman.

" Hollo—who's that?"

" Only me.—Oh Norman, come up here and listen!—
What's wrong with Hector?"

Norman leaped up three stairs at a time, tried the handle, and then put his ear to the door.

What a relief it was to hear him burst out in one of his merry laughs! "Bravo! you're a pretty goose, Phil. He's only snoring. Here—Hector lad! wake up. Open the door. I've got some news for you."

That loud cheery voice would have wakened the sulkiest sleeper. We heard Hector roll out of bed and unlock the door.

"Well, I hope you have had sleep enough; here have I been all the way to Doctor Cowe's and back."

Hector threw himself down again, and told Norman to hold his tongue.

"I will not, for I have a notion in my head. I've been to the old Doctor about the Greek verb."

This was decided Greek to me, and I durst not give any sign of my presence by inquiry; but I afterward found out what Norman meant. There were, beside the prizes, a few medals given at the High School, and one of these was for the best writing out of a Greek verb. This was considered one of the chief competitions in the class, and Norman, who was pretty well on in Greek, had done his, but Hector had been too lazy to try.

"Let me alone," muttered he, "what do Greek verbs matter to me?"

"A little, for I've a plan, as I said. Hold up, lad, and listen. Do you think I'd have walked all the way to Patrick and back for nothing? No, though the old Cowe did give me a drink of milk and a big apple. Here it is!"

But Hector, with a return of his old ill-humor, sent the offered apple spinning across the room.

"Well—if you will not listen," said his brother, somewhat hurt.

"I will listen to *you*, only do not tease me about old Cowe and the 'prizes.' I hate and despise them all."

" Would you despise a medal if you got it ?" said Norman
smiling.   You might; there's plenty of time.   The Greek
verb can not be decided till just before the prize-giving, as the
Principal wishes to judge it himself, and he is away from
home.   Though my verb is done, Charles Henderson's is not,
nor John Menteith's.   The old Cowe himself says that if you
were to try hard and work steadily, you might get the
medal."

" Does he ?" cried Hector, leaping up in bed, and nearly
extinguishing poor Tea-kettle, who began hissing at a great
rate.

" Ay, and I think he would be glad too.   He knows what
you *can* do ;—and he would be greatly hurt that father's
cleverest boy should gain nothing."

" But I will—I'll get that medal or I'll die for it," shouted
the impressible Hector.   " I'll brush up all my Greek, I'll
work early and late."

" And I'll help you—that is in the writing, because perhaps
you do not write Greek quite as well as I do, and the verb
must look very neat, mind.   But you'll soon manage it.
We'll get up at six instead of seven, and practice that abominable *al pha, beta,* till you'll write Greek as well as you,
write your copy books.   I think you have a very good chance
of the medal.   What says Philip ?"

I could hardly speak, I was so glad !

" Hey, little Phil, are you there ?" said Hector, patting me
on the back.   " Come, hunt for my other shoe, will you
there's a good lad ; I'm going to get up to tea."

He did get up, and was soon his old merry self—kinder
than usual to us all, especially to Norman.   Gracie grew
better toward night, which added to the cheerfulness, so that
after all our woes we had quite a merry evening, and Norman told such lots of quaint fairy tales and hobgoblin stories,
that little Willie's curls almost stood on end.   But when the

little ones were fairly gone to bed, out came pen and ink, and the two lads were writing Greek verbs until the very last minute before their father came home.

All that week and part of the next we had nothing but Greek verbs. Of course all they did was mere practicing; for the verb itself had to be written at school, on magnificent white parchment. But every bit of it was copied out a dozen times beforehand, by the indefatigable Hector, under his brother's instruction. Our bedroom resembled the cave of Virgil's Sibyl, being strewed with innumerable leaves of waste paper, scraps of tenses and moods; and I'm sure I went to sleep every night to the sound of

$$\text{Τυπτω} \qquad \text{τυπτεις} \qquad \text{τυπτει}$$
$$\text{Τυπτ}—$$

("Lack-a-day!" cried Uncle Philip, laughing—"if I haven't quite forgot my dual number.")

E

HECTOR's verb was done in sufficient time; and, as his brother positively informed me—and Norman never exaggerated any thing—" it looked stunning."

We were all very glad, for the poor lad had worked harder and more steadily than Hector had ever been known to work before ; and counting on his deservings, we began hopefully to anticipate the medal. As for the other competitors, Charles Henderson, and John Menteith, Norman declared there was nothing to be feared from them, their verbs were so much inferior to Hector's.

It was very odd, but—probably from his saying so little about it—we had all of us quite forgotten Norman's own verb —completed some time since, and put away.

The examination day arrived. Though nothing of importance depended on it, still it was a day of great expectation and delight to the High School boys.

" You are allowed to come to our Year, and mamma, and Gracie too," said Hector to me. " Doctor Cowe is glad to see every body. He hopes they will come early, because the Ovid begins at ten, and he wishes father to question us. Any body may put to us any questions they like."

" Even I, Hector," cried Gracie, mischievously, holding up her merry face ; she was quite well again now—at least, well for her.

" Even you, little goosie ! Supposing you choose to do such a very foolish thing, and exhibit your ignorance."

" Thank you," she laughed, putting her arms round his

neck as he carried her down stairs to her little chaise ;—rough boy as he was, Hector never had a hard word for Gracie. Indeed none of us had, she was such a gentle little darling.

Hector and Norman started first, but the rest soon followed in a body; my uncle and aunt, James, little Willie, Gracie and I.

It was a very formidable thing, opening that door of the Fourth Year; almost as formidable as the entrance into Uncle MacIlroy's class-room. For little boys, and girls too, persist in the notion that every body is looking at them, when in fact every body usually happens to have something very much better to do. If each shy person, boy or young man, could once believe of how very small importance he is to society in general, and how rarely any body sees whether he is in the room or out of it—what he wears, or does not wear--what he does, or does not do—and that, provided he does not do any thing very extraordinary—such as standing on his head, for instance, the chances are that nobody is taking the least notice of him ;—if only he could be made to understand this, we should have much less foolish bashfulness in the world.

("There's a lecture for you, boys," observed Uncle Philip. His nephews gave him such a hearty round of laughter and applause, that nobody could for a moment accuse them of bashfulness.)

I have no doubt I blushed as deeply as if the whole three-score pair of boys' eyes were concentrated on me alone, when probably every body looked at my aunt and Gracie, and nobody at me. And I remember feeling quite nervous as to whether I ought or ought not to smile in answer to the applause, or "roughing," as my cousins called it, which greeted our entrance, quite forgetting that this tremendous racket of boys' feet on the boards was meant in compliment to the favorite among all the High School masters, my uncle Mac-Ilroy.

"They always 'rough' father very much," whispered Gracie to me. "And he looks so pleased!—Ah, mamma sees our boys. Look, Philip, there they are."

Among the long line of boys' faces, I could not at first find out the two familiar ones. At last I saw them. Norman looked gravely quiet. Hector all gayety and happiness. What a handsome, bright, clever face it was!

"There are the rest of the class. I was sure we would know them," said Gracie. "That must be Andrew Caird at the top. What a little fellow he is to be so clever. How pale and delicate he looks! I wonder will he live to be a man?"

(Gracie had a curious habit of speculating as to whether children she knew would live to be men and women. But she had so many strange ways, and looks, and thoughts.)

"And there's that hateful Johnnie Gordon," added I "Look, Hector is talking and laughing with him. How generous!"

Gracie assented, with affectionate eyes. Nevertheless, she gave me a sign to be quiet;—for Doctor Cowe was just saying, in a pompous nasal tone, which nearly made me laugh,

"The Reverend William MacIlroy will commence with prayer."

But the inclination to laughter ceased the moment my uncle began. He uttered a few solemn, simple words of extempore prayer, Scottish fashion, suited for the occasion, and such as boys could understand. He was evidently in earnest, a father looking at his own and other fathers' sons, all growing up, either for good or evil. He made even thoughtless lads in earnest, too, for the moment, and there was not a careless gesture or a smile, until he had ceased.

"Now for Latin class. What shall it be, sir?" asked Doctor Cowe, who was very reverential to my uncle, as the best classic present. There had gradually dropped in a good many Glasgow gentlemen—stout fathers of families, and stupid bailies—who looked very wise, but whom, as I told Gracie, I should just like to have seen stand up and construe a page of Ovid. We schoolboys could have beaten them hollow, I know.

My uncle turned over his Virgil. Doctor Cowe handed another, with a very solemn bow, to my aunt, and a third to Gracie and me. Very kind of the old Cowe—and Gracie had fine fun in making believe she understood Latin.

" We will take the Æneid, second Book,

'At regina gravi jamdudum saucia cura.' "

began Uncle MacIlroy, as mildly as if he had not the whole poem at his fingers' ends—as we boys all knew he had, together with almost every other Latin and Greek author. But he bore his learning quite meekly—a great deal more so than Doctor Cowe.

" Very well, Sir. Now boys. Duncan Brown first," pompously cried the latter individual.

Duncan Brown rose up. I had heard a great deal of him. He was the cleverest lad in the whole year; Dux in every thing. His power of work was prodigious. He was reported to have sat up whole nights at his books—the ragged old books that Doctor Cowe lent him, when he came, three years ago, as a big ignorant boy, of whom nobody knew any thing except that his name was Duncan Brown. Few knew any thing more now, except that he had outstripped every lad beyond him, had become the Doctor's favorite pupil, the glory of the whole class, and was going next term from Glasgow High School to Glasgow College.

Gracie and I looked with some curiosity at Duncan Brown. I remember his face quite well, even at this distance of time It was very handsome, something like the portraits of Byron as a lad of seventeen, save that the mouth was less full and

more sweet.   It was the sort of head we call aristocratic.   I
don't know why, since there is but one true aristocracy, that
of genius and talent, and this boy had it, most surely, even
though no one knew where he came from, and his name was
Duncan Brown.

But I am getting tedious.   ("No—no—" said the obliging
nephews.)   Well—well, I am not going to construe *Æneidos,
Liber IV.*, with all Doctor Cowe's corrections, and all Uncle
MacIlroy's clear explanations, and all the ludicrous hints of
a certain pompous bailie, who thought himself very learned,
and to whom Doctor Cowe listened in polite silence, though
he, and all the boys, even I, saw quite plainly that the old
fellow had mistaken the sense of the passage, and was as
arrant a dunce at Latin as his own youngest son.

I shall pass lightly all this—how Duncan Brown construed
magnificently, and answered every thing that every body else
could not answer, coming off with wonderful eclat.   Also how
Norman went through his part very creditably, and how Hector, twice as quick as his brother, was in great glory, answer-
ing his own questions and a dozen others, some of which were
wrong, but generally right.   And how, altogether, though
Uncle MacIlroy pretended not to notice his own boys, and
to be absorbed in the general examination, it was easy to see
how gratified he was, when at the end he stealthily looked at
my aunt and smiled.

I could not then understand why amidst all his pleasure
the tears stood in my good aunt's eyes.   But it is a weakness
natural to all mothers, I suppose.

After the Virgil class, there were other examinations, which
I forget, only I remember my two cousins got though them
honorably, and were regarded with great pride and veneration
by Gracie and me, as well as by Jamie, who was next year
to be promoted to the High School.

I also remember that, in conclusion, the old Cowe (whose

'Tail" for this day only **had** become invisible) stood and read with much importance **a** written speech, in which he **mentioned** the general behavior of the boys—while at the end and **often in the** middle of every sentence, arose a great amount **of** " roughing," in response to any thing or nothing, **just** because **the** boy's feet wanted a little exercise. But when at the last occurred the **name of** Duncan **Brown, and the** worthy old Doctor, with a voice rather tremulous, spoke earnestly of the Dux's industry, attention, **and** perseverance, saying that he **had** never had a fault to find with him since he came to the **school,** and how, in leaving for college, the best wishes of every master—and he was sure he might say every class-mate— went with Duncan Brown—there arose a perfect storm of " roughing," of the sincerity of which there could be no doubt.

The Dux rose, looking very pale—bowed hurriedly—and then sat down, leaning his elbow **on the** opposite form, the massive forehead, and wonderfully intelligent eyes just visible above his thread-bare coat sleeve.

" **Good-by to** Duncan Brown!" whispered Gracie, with tears in her eyes. " I hope he will be a great man yet!"

" The other day," said Uncle Philip, pausing in his narrative, **" I sa.w** advertised a scientific lecture by a Professor Duncan Brown, **F.R.S.,** and **D.C.L., of Glasgow.** I think, though it is more than twenty years since I saw him, I should **almost** recognize the lecturer).

CHAPTER XII

("I am now coming," said Uncle Philip, "to the last portion of my history about a Hero. You must give me time to
think it over carefully, and I will try and remember it as
closely as I can."

Every body congratulated him on having hitherto done
wonders in the matter of memory. Captain Carew smiled.

"Perhaps I have, even to a degree that may seem unnat-
ural. But the coloring of childish recollection is often mar-
velously vivid and minute;—and those three months in the
north exercised such an influence on my after life-time, that
every trifle connected with the time, stands out as clear as a
picture."

His beautiful brown eyes grew thoughtful; he took his
youngest niece on his lap, played with her baby curls for a
little, and then began.)

The examination lasted several days, for there were a
great many classes in the High School. We boys, with most
sedulous pertinacity, insisted on going to all, and we tried hard
to persuade my aunt to do the same. However, her interest
did not extend beyond her own sons, so she staid at home
until the last morning, when Norman coaxed her out to see
the performances of the writing-class.

It was early in a clear autumn day; and no one who had
seen the City of the West under foul aspects can imagine
how cheery and pleasant Glasgow looks on a fine day. Very
merrily did we go down Buchanan Street, my uncle and aunt
first, and we three lads following Either Hector had got

over his disappointment about the prizes, or ese his facile and sanguine **nature was content** with looking forward **to the** medal—which he continually talked about—and seemed **to** expect with certainty. But by Norman's advice, or by tacit consent, we lads kept this little mystery to ourselves and did **not** enlighten the family **in general either as to** what Hector had so energetically accomplished or what he hoped to win.

On the High School staircase a little incident occurred My uncle suddenly turned round and called his eldest son.

" Norman, I quite forgot to ask about your Greek verb, over which you were so anxious. Did you get it finished **all** right?"

" Yes," said Norman briefly, glancing toward his brother, who luckily was not within sight or hearing.

" Do you think you have a good chance of the medal?"

" I—I don't know."

" Never mind, do not be shy about it," said the father, kindly. **" I am sure you** have tried your very best, my boy. —I do hope he will get the medal," added Uncle MacIlroy, turning to his wife, "for I know how the lad's heart has been set upon it all this year."

I looked at Norman, and Norman at me. This was **a** view of the case which I at least had altogether overlooked. " What," said I, "if Hector—"

" Hold your tongue, stupid !" muttered Norman. **I knew** he must have been **in what we called a " a state of mind,"** or he would not have spoken so rudely. I could not **tell** what **to make** of him. But just then **Hector came** leaping up-**stairs,** and we all went into the writing-room. All, I think, **except** my **uncle, who had** business elsewhere.

The **writing** class made a capital show. We passed down **table after** table all covered with fine specimens of caligraphy. There **were copy-books** numerous enough to have been the work **of all** the young scribblers in Glasgow put together

Hector went merrily down the line, showing off all to his
mother, making jocular remarks on every thing and every
body in the room, which was half full of masters, parents,
and ladies. With these latter Hector MacIlroy was always
quite a little beau, being so handsome, ready-witted, and
gay.

Norman kept rather in the shade. He was generally very
quiet-mannered with strangers. More than once I saw him
stand quite still and thoughtful, making believe to look at the
copy-books ; and then there came across me his father's words.
" *His heart has been set upon it all this year.*" I couldn't
understand my cousin Norman yet !

One of the masters, who was very polite to my aunt, now
guided her to the farther end of the room ; where, he said,
was something that would afford her great pleasure.

There, hung against the wall in all their glory, were the
important Greek verbs. Hector leaped forward with a flush-
ing face—Norman hung back.

" It is not often our writing-class is so adorned," said the
master, evidently looking with great pride on the fair white
card-board sheets, on which the beautifully written Greek
meandered in rivers of moods and tenses, a network of confu
sion, yet when one came to examine, proportioned in mos
perfect order. You can have no idea, nephews, what a pretty
thing was that same Greek verb. " I was sure you would
admire it, madam," continued the teacher smiling, " yet these
two are much inferior to the one just beyond. Will you
look ?"

My aunt did so, and hardly suppressed an exclamation of
delight when she read, at the corner of the card-board, " Hector MacIlroy."

" My dear boy, how beautiful—how exquisite ! When
did you do it ? Why did you never tell me ?" But Hector
was too pleased and proud to answer any of these ques

tions. He could not take his eyes from his own handiwork, which was so much more successful than he had dared to hope.

"Indeed I must congratulate you, Mrs. MacIlroy," said the polite writing-master—all masters are so wondrously polite on examination-days. "There could be no doubt of Hector's winning the medal, except for one possible rival, your other son."

He pointed to the last of the four verbs, which was Norman's. Hector started, and rushed to examine it. So did I. We were both struck with a cold fear, a fear so ungenerous, that meeting each other's eyes we both blushed for the same.

"It is—very—beautiful," at last said Hector boldly, though I saw how his face had changed.

"Very beautiful indeed," repeated the mother, looking uneasily at each of her boys ; I never knew any parent so guarded in showing preference "Both seem so good, I could hardly tell which was best."

"That is what all we masters say. The decision will be tough I think ; and, upon, my word I am glad that judgment rests with the Principal, for I should be fairly puzzled.— There can be no doubt, if Master Norman's were not there, Master Hector's verb would be successful—still—as it is.— However, madam, I must congratulate you once more on both your sons."

My aunt bowed—the master bowed—and we passed on.— All but Hector, who still leaned on the table, looking from his brother's work to his own, and then back again. His rosy face had turned all colors—his mouth had sunk in ; he was evidently in extreme agitation. I don't know how Norman felt, or looked, or did. I only saw Hector.

At length the latter touched my shoulder. "Come out with me, Phil. I feel so stupid—so dizzy." He looked up

and saw his brother lagging behind anxiously. " Get along,
Norman ! Do not be staring at me."

These were the first and last words of anger the poor lad
said.

We were invited that day to lunch with some old ladies,
who lived beyond Glasgow Green ; and there being no reason
to the contrary, we went. Norman walked with his mother
—Hector with me. We did not speak a word ˙the whole
way. This was such a new thing with Hector, always so
loud and passionate in his troubles, that I began to feel quite
frightened.- He had evidently taken the matter very deeply
to heart. I feared that in his silence he might be harbor-
ing the bitterer wrath against his brother; but it was not so.

The old ladies gave us all sorts of good things, and wondered very much that we three hearty lads did not consume
all before us. But for once in a way we were not inclined
to eat. For myself, I felt as if the rosiest apple in the dish
would have choked me like sawdust. But then I was a very
soft-hearted and sentimental little fellow.

It was a great relief when we turned out into the garden
to gather apples for ourselves.

I don't know whether it was the apples that put it into my
mind, but when I saw the two brothers left alone together,
I had an uncomfortable recollection of Cain and Abel. I
wondered very much what my cousin would do.

At first, they diverged apart, each taking an opposite path,
Hector pulling the leaves of gooseberry bushes, and Norman
walking quietly on, his hands in his pockets, until by some
sudden turn the two paths met, and the brothers likewise.
The elder put his hands on the younger's shoulders, and looked
him in the face—so kindly—so sorrowfully !

" Hector !"

" Well, Norman !"

" You are not vexed ?"

Hector paused, and at length said, sturdily, though it must have cost him much. " No, I'm not. It's a fair fight—quite fair. If I lose, I lose."

" That is not sure yet."

Hector brightened up, but only for a minute. " No, no ! However, if I must be beaten, it is better to be beaten by you ; mind, I acknowledge that. Now, we'll talk no more about it—it makes me sick."

He did indeed look very wretched and ill, and soon his mother saw it would be advisable to take him home, and let his feelings grow calm of themselves. I thought I had better keep out of the way, so I walked back alone, Norman having already started. Nobody knew wherefore—but he was such a strange boy.

Passing by the High School I thought I would just go in once more—to judge for myself, quietly and alone, which of the two Greek verbs had the best chance. It was getting almost dark, and many of the masters were leaving. In the writing-room were a few figures moving about with lights putting by the copy-books, and taking down the ornamental writing that was fastened to the walls. One of the junior masters was in the act of rolling up the Greek verbs.

" Stop a minute, please, Mr. Renton, let me take one more look."

" And me too," cried another lad, rushing up the room quite breathless. It was Norman.

Seeing me, he started back surprised, and, as I thought, a good deal confused, but soon recovered himself. We looked together at the two sheets—we and the master. There was no doubt which verb was done the best—even if Mr. Renton had not said so.

" Yes, you will surely get the medal, MacIlroy ; still, I'm rather sorry for your brother Hector. Hey there !"—as some body happened to call him—"Lads, stay here a minute, only mind the candle and the ink-bottle—Norman, that is your own verb you're holding—take care !"

I looked at my cousin for a minute—he was extremely pale, and his eyes were fixed with an inexplicable expression on his work—done with such patience, hope, and pains. He regarded it so lovingly, that, remembering Hector, I felt quite vexed and walked away.

A minute after, there was a great splash—crash—ink-bottle and card-board rolling together on the floor. The master came up in a passion, but it was too late. The fair white sheet was covered with a deluge of ink. One of the verbs was irretrievably spoiled.

"It's my own—only my own," stammered Norman. "I did it myself, acci—"

He might have been going to say *accidentally*, but stopped for it would have been the first lie the boy ever told. The moment I looked in his face, I felt convinced he had turned over the ink-bottle *on purpose*.

I will not now stop to discuss whether this act was right wrong. I only know he did it.

Having done it, he stood shaking all over, as nervous and agitated as a lad could be ; but Mr. Renton and the other masters were too busy and angry to notice this. They merely called him a "careless gouk"—and thought it a just punishment that he should have only ruined himself.

"Your brother Hector is sure of the medal now, and I'm glad, for he deserves it"—said one.

"Now, if you had had *his* verb in your hands, the case would have looked suspicious against you," said another. "But nobody would be such a fool as to go and destroy his own work, except by accident."

"A pretty figure you'll cut at the prize-giving," observed Mr. Renton. "And what will your father say ?"

The poor fellow winced. I ran up to him—"Oh, Norman,
Norman!" He saw from my looks that I guessed all.

"Hush, Phil!" and he clutched my wrist as tight as a
vice. "If you ever tell, I'll—"

What savage purpose he meant—declaring it with that
broken, tremulous voice—I never knew. I only know that
he somehow dragged me after him into the open air, and
that there, quite overcome, we both sat down on the stone
steps—and, I do believe, big lads as we were, we both cried.

Norman made me promise that I would never "let on," as
he expressed it. I never did—until this day.

("Well," said Captain Carew, coming to an anchor, "does
any body want to know any more?"

Every body did want to know a deal more—indeed sufficient questions were asked to keep Uncle Philip's tongue
going till midnight.

"Hout tout!" as my Uncle MacIlroy would say, this will
never do. I can't engage to give a biography of all that has
happened to all my cousins for the last twenty years. I only
bargained to tell you the story of my discovering a Hero.
Who was he?"

Some made divers guesses, others begged to hear a little
more before they finally decided.)

I have little more to tell. I don't recollect much about
the prize-giving; I suppose my heart was too full. I only
remember sitting in a crowded church (they usually give
away the prizes in the Kirk, in Scotland), seeing boys' faces
filling every pew, and amidst them all discerning clearly but
one face—my cousin Norman's: hearing a long droning speech,
interrupted with much "roughing," which sounded rather
strange in a church; watching a long line of boys winding up
one aisle and down another, past the precentor's desk, where
they each bowed, got something, and vanished; listening for
the name "Hector MacIlroy," and seeing him go up rather

gravely, and come back looking so handsome and pleased,
wearing the red ribbon and shining medal. As he did so, I
mind above all, catching the eye of my cousin Norman, that
gray eye—so soft—so good, though the mouth was a little
quivering, until at last it settled into a quiet smile. Then
I felt very proud to think that in the whole assembly, nay
in the whole world, he and I alone knew—what we knew
And looking at him, as he sat there so quiet and unnoticed,
I felt prouder still to think that I had learnt one thing more
—I had at last discovered—

"A Hero!" shouted all the nephews together. "Norman
was the Hero!"

(Uncle Philip nodded; but somehow his voice was husky,
and he leaned his forehead on his little niece's curls for a good
while before he spoke. However, when he did speak, it was
in his usual loud, cheerful voice.)

"Boys, you are quite right! Since that time the young
MacIlroys have been scattered far and wide. At this moment
probably, Hector is sailing in his vessel round Cape Horn;
James jabbering Hindostanee on the banks of the Ganges:
Willie devoting his inquiring mind to the parallax of the fixed
stars; and wee Wattie speculating whether or not he shall
marry and settle like a Christian in Scotland, or go out like a
heathen to the 'diggings' in California."

"And one,"—added he, with a sudden pause and lowering
of tone—"one of my dear cousins is with God."

"But," and shortly afterward Uncle Philip spoke on bravely, as a good man should speak, who has learned life's hardest
lesson, to bear and conquer sorrow. "But if among all these
you should ask me to point out the one most honored, and most
worthy of honor, I would send you to a certain town in Scotland, where, in a certain house, sits a certain honest man—
husband of a wife, and father of a family—"

—"No,' shouted Uncle Philip, suddenly darting to the

window, clearing the room at a bound, "he doesn't sit there at all. He is now standing at our gate. I knew he would, for he promised. And, having promised, he was as sure to come as—as the New Year! Wait till he shakes the snow off his plaid, and then you'll see him, my boyish playfellow, the friend of my manhood, my cousin Norman MacIlroy! But, oh lads! for any sake, don't let him suspect I have just been showing him up in a character which he has sustained, and will sustain, all his life, without ever knowing it—that of

A HERO."

BREAD UPON THE WATERS.

A

GOVERNESS'S LIFE.

A WOMAN,

THE DAILY RECORD OF WHOSE LIFE RESEMBLES THAT OF HIM, ON. WE DIVINE STEPS SHE FOLLOWS, " WHO WENT ABOUT DOING GOOD."

BREAD UPON THE WATERS.

PART I.

It is to-day ten months since my mother died, and my father has told me that he is about to bring home another wife!—Another mistress of the household, another Mrs. Lyne, usurping *her* place, *her* name! How shall I ever bear it!

I do not think I share the usual prejudice against step-mothers. I know perfectly well, no daughter, even if grown up, can be to her father the comfort that a wife is; and many men, loving their first wives ever so dearly, have in time married again. My dear mother during her long illness several times hinted this to me, accidentally as it were, yet with meaning. But, in one sense, the parallel did not hold; for she was *not* "loved dearly;"—never, alas! since the first sunny year of her marriage, wherein I was born, and she, out of her deep happiness, called me *Felicia*.

I knew, I felt, that my father would marry again. These two months I have been trying to reason myself, ay, and my little brothers too, into some preparation for what must come in time. I even thought that we might learn to love his wife—I and the two poor little fellows to whom the name of "father" has always been a name of fear—that is, if she were a good woman. But—*that* woman!

That woman, with the paint scarce wiped off her face, to come and lay her head on the sacred pillow where my mother died !—That woman, whose name has been for years the town's talk, to bear the name which, sorrowful as her life was, my pure mother bore unsullied to her grave ! It is hard, very hard !—nay, it is horrible !

Yet there is no alternative ; they are already married—my father told me so. He has given me the choice, to prepare to welcome her here, or to go out myself into the wide cruel world—I think I would, except for those little ones, my brothers, to whom, since our mother died, I have tried to be mother and sister both. For their sakes I must have patience.

All day I have tried to exercise what, young and inexperienced as I am, my mother always said I had—a clear judgment, a power of subduing weak womanly emotions and prejudices, and seeing only *the right*. I think I see it now.

My father is perfectly free to marry, and to marry whom he pleases ; no daughter can or ought to stand in the way of that. But oh !—if his wife had only been a good woman nay, even an honest, respectable woman ! His very house keeper would have been preferable to ——.

No ; I will be just and merciful, as my poor mother was ever, to all sinners. This woman may not be so bad as the world paints her ; for the world is very cruel, and a beautiful public singer must often be maligned. Even granting those things which can not be contradicted, I have heard that kindness and generosity have ere now lingered even in the heart of a Magdalen.

I will not leave my home and my brothers, nor—

. . . .

I was obliged to break off, and go down to our friend Mr. Redwood. I wonder if he saw that any thing was wrong with me, that I could not sing when he asked me. I wonder

too, does he **know** of what will happen in our family ? **and**
what will **he** think of it ? Will he come here as usual, **and**
will his mother ?—To think of the Honorable Mrs. Redwood
visiting the woman my father has chosen for his second wife '
Impossible !

Oh ! I wish, I wish I could have told him—Mr. Redwood,
I mean. But how could I, a mere girl, and he so young a
man ? Besides, **I had** no right ; for he is still but a friend, or
rather acquaintance. Only—sometimes—He said he was
coming again next Wednesday ; and I until this minute have
forgotten that that is the very day my father told **me they**
would come home,—he and—Mrs. Lyne ; **for I must teach**
myself that dreaded word.

Ah **me** ! **ah, my** poor little brothers ! ah, **my dear mother,**
my *own* mother, who knows not **what we suffer, and to whom**
no suffering **can ever come more !—For that,** amidst all my
weepings, I look up, and thank God !

They have come home, and I have seen my step-mother for
the first time. She was very sweet and gracious, both to me
and to the boys ; and she is, oh ! such a handsome woman !
Dressed for the evening, she did not look above thirty. What
a contrast to my poor **sick** mother, **worn** out before **her time** !
But **I must** not suffer myself to **dwell on these** things.

Mrs. Lyne entered the house with **an easy** grace, **all smiles.**
She said it was **a** pretty house. I had **taken** pains to have
all in order for her ; for **I** wished **to** please my **father, if I**
could. After the house, she took notice of **us,** shook hands
with me and Henry, and **would have** kissed dear little Aleck,
but he pouted and refused. **She only** laughed, and said " he
was a pretty fellow nevertheless."

My heart was ready to burst, knowing how like the child
is to his mother.

Nevertheless, **both Henry and** Aleck got sociable with her

toward the end of the evening ; for she was so bewitching in
her manners, and children of seven and ten are so easily impressible.   My father showed at first a little embarrassment ;
but she soon talked all that away.   I never knew a woman
with such irresistible powers of conversation.

For myself, I think I behaved, as I had hoped and prayed
I might behave—with quiet self-control, rendering courtesy
where courtesy was due.   In this I was helped, and many of
the discomforts of the evening smoothed down, by Mr. Redwood, who, not having received my message through his mother, appeared as he had at first promised.   I can not tell if he
had known or guessed the change in our family ; but whether
or not, he sustained his difficult position admirably well.   For
even at his age, he is at once a gentleman and a man of the
world ; though the world has not spoiled him.

I wonder if he thought my step-mother handsome !   She
talked to him a good deal, and he always answered with courtesy ; but it was evident he liked better to stay with the little
boys and me.   He played a game at draughts with Henry,
and told Aleck a wonderful story about a hobgoblin ; then he
went away.   As he shook my hand, I felt his eye upon me
with such a kind, pitying look that I could hardly keep down
my tears.   Oh ! he knows what I must suffer—he has such
a gentle heart !

Surely men can not be all tyrants, all selfish !   Surely—
though my mother's sore experience at times taught me almost to doubt the fact—there must be in the world such a
thing as a good husband and a happy marriage !

> " All things are less dreadful than they seem."

How truthfully that line of Wordsworth's rings in my ear
to-night, when, having looked at my brothers asleep in their
little beds, and seen that the house is all quiet and safe—for
it is not till to-morrow morning that I relinquish the keys to

my step-mother—I have come up to **my own** room, to think over the events of the day before it closes.

Nevertheless, I am very glad that this dreaded evening **is** over.

Oh! mother, my mother, **of whom is my last** thought at night, whose example I desire and strive in all things to fol-low—**you see, O mother!** how I try to do my duty, let what **will be** the end—even as you did, until God took you from my love unto His own!

———

It was Henry's birth-day to-day.

(Mem. inserted, as are several others, evidently **of a** much later **date** than the original diary.

Henry was ten years old, I remember, and the finest little fellow imaginable, the pride of the whole Square. He was very tall **and** large made for his **age;** indeed, he used to torment me by stealing my slippers **and gloves, pretending that** they fitted him exactly, which indeed **was a blessing, otherwise, he** would have gone short enough, **poor fellow! After the first three** months of our father's marriage, **Mrs. Lyne used to say that** children were always wanting some-**thing.**

Yet I dressed them very simply, my two boys—for I began to call them mine, seeing there was no one else to claim them. I could see them now, in their dark green blouses and leather belts, each with his books under his arm, just as they used to look turning the corner of our Square when coming home daily from school. They were such handsome boys!)

Henry's birth-day!—We always, in the worst **of times,** made birth-days pleasant days—but this has been very sad.

It began ill. At breakfast I reminded my father of the day, and hinted what he **had** long promised Henry as a **birth-day present—a box of** tools at Holtzapffel's in Charing **Cross.**

Mrs. Lyne lifted her eyebrows, and reasoned mildly about the **" evil of** extravagance."

Now, since she has brought into the house many luxuries --expensive even to my father's large income—I thought this

F

not quite right; still I argued and entreated a little more, I knew how the boy longed for his birth-day present.

"Felicia," said my father, after his wife had talked with him apart, in her smooth low voice; "you spoil those boys too much. They should, as Mrs. Lyne says, be taught self-denial, not extravagance. I will have no more presents given them on any pretext whatever."

So Henry lost his delight. Heaven forgive me if my heart burned against my father; but I thought it very hard, especially as the case was only one out of many, in which that bland moralizing voice had interfered between the children and their little pleasures.

Henry was indignant too, for he was of a high spirit, and had forced me to tell him the truth;—indeed I never can tell any thing else—all comes out of me sooner or later. And when, in honor of the day, he dined with us, he was not quite so pleasant as he ought to have been and was expected to be. At last, seeing a storm rising, for there had been from the first a curious antipathy between our smiling, soft-spoken step-mother and Henry, who, I must confess, is passionate and rather rough mannered—I rose early from table, that I might get him out of harm's way.

We happened to go into the outer hall, just to cool our selves, when we were quite startled by a man sitting there, who caught hold of me, and addressed me rudely, as Mrs. Lyne?" I said, "No; I was Miss Lyne; did he want Mrs. Lyne. He answered, "Yes; but he could wait, since he knew she was in the house:" and his manner was so uncivil that I was glad to get away.

About tea-time, the footman whispered Mrs. Lyne that some person had been waiting all the evening in the hall, to see her. She went out hastily, and returned after a good while, her cheeks flushed even beyond their usual steady color

" Who was it wanted you?" asked my father, carelessly

"Only my dress-maker."

Henry, who had just crept up-stairs, pulled my sleeve, with a look of great astonishment, and whispered, "That's not true, sister—it was the man."

"Mrs. Lyne's eye—she has such a glaring black eye at times—was upon us in a minute, and my father's too.

"What are you whispering, sir?" said he sharply to Henry.

Now the little fellow has one quality that would atone for a hundred faults; he always tells the direct truth. He answered at once, "I said, it was a man who wanted Mrs. Lyne—a great, dirty man, with black whiskers and a hooked nose;—it was! for I saw them talking."

My father looked furious. "What did they say?"

"He asked her to pay his bill, I thought; but I did not stay listening: I never do," said Harry proudly.

Each moment I expected Mrs. Lyne would burst out in a passion, but she did not: she only smiled, and twirled her handkerchief. "Mr. Lyne, my business was certainly with my dress-maker. I thought you knew already that your son has a habit of—of deviating from truth, and is certainly a *leetle* revengeful. I fear I stayed your too lavish hand toward him this morning. Poor fellow!—but I can forgive."

She threw herself back in her chair, smiling her sweetest smile, first at Henry, and then at my father; at which, completely reassured, he would hear no words from my brother or from me. The scene ended in Harry's receiving the cruelest indignity a spirited lad can suffer—stripes; he crying out all the while "that he had spoken only the truth, and sister knew it was so."

His sister did know it, and frantically declared the same, and the result was—But I have no business to think of my own wrongs.

I have kissed and wept over my poor boy. I have prayed

for him and for myself. What shall we do?—I can not tell . . . . .

After writing this, mechanically, with I scarce know what intent, I went to count over what money I had; my allowance having been paid me that day. I had left it open in my dressing-case, carelessly enough, as rich men's daughters do. I found it gone! and never, though it is three weeks since Henry's fatal birth-day, have I seen or heard of it.

The poor lads can have no pleasures for a whole six months, now; but then I shall be of age, and have twenty pounds a year of my own—my very own! Oh, how welcome it will be! I never knew money's worth till now.

I have had to give up my pretty little bedchamber. It happens to be next my stepmother's, and she wants it for her maid: so I am sent to a room at the top of the house. For some things I do not mind the change—it is so pleasant to catch even a dim glimpse of Hampstead over the forest of chimney-pots

Then my little brothers like it, for it is near theirs, and is such a refuge from the racketing and turmoil going on below. We sit there whole evenings, and plan what we would do if we all three lived together, far out in the quiet country; and I tell them of all the country pleasures I used to have, years ago, with the three little sisters who came between me and Henry, and died when they were young, I only being left.

—I am glad I lived, if only for the poor boys' sake.

Yesterday, at one of our parties, I overheard Mrs. Lyne saying—what from her sharp glance and smile I do believe she intended me to overhear—"that it would be an excellent thing if Felicia were married."

She likewise added, apropos of something her neighbor

said, which something I do not care to write down, " Oh, **no** poor Felicia would never please a young man of taste and intellect—how could she, with her little doll-like face, **and** no manners whatsoever ?"

I had been dull enough that night, as **I often** was ; no one, at least no one I cared to talk with, ever appearing at Mrs. Lyne's soirées. **Her** words kept haunting me—foolishly enough ; but when one is young **one has such a** longing to **be** thought pleasing—such a bashful **terror** of one's self !

It is true I have blue eyes, and long, light curls ; but am I really so doll-like and insipid-looking ? I asked Aleck **the** question to-day, in jest, of course ; and the wicked little fellow laughed in my face, and said, *somebody* once told him he ought **to be proud of** such a sweet sister and especially **of her** " pretty, pretty curls." **But** who it **was he would not** tell, and nothing could make him.

What **a precocious, pert** little creature Aleck is growing ! **And** when I confessed about Mrs. Lyne's unkind speech **how both** the boys did torment me, calling me " Miss Doll" But **I** deserved it all for my ridiculous vanity.

To-day has been a day which, in our quiet life, solitary amidst a whirl of gayety, seems full of adventure.

It was the first Monday of the boys' Midsummer holidays, and we went out for a long walk ; nobody forbidding, **which** was rare. The **lads** dragged me on and on, even **as far as** Hampstead ; where, with a sudden thought of strawberries and cream this time **last** year, they wanted me to call on Mrs. Redwood. **But I could not.** Since my father's marriage **I** have scarcely seen her, or any of the family, except **that Mr.** Godfrey Redwood sometimes has called ; and once **or twice** has met my brothers on their way from school, and brought them **home. He is** so kind to them always, **and** they are wildly fond of him. I could hardly make them understand why we must stay on the Heath, and not intrude ourselves at the Honorable Mrs. Redwood's.

It is a pleasant place—that Heath! All day, Harry Aleck, and I, wandered up and down, hiding among furze and fern, lying on beds of thyme. More than once the boys made me sing at the very top of my voice, which I actually did—I felt so cheerful—though doubtless the act was rather improper, and would have justified my step-mother in her declaration, that I had " no manners whatsoever."

I took great care to keep at the opposite end of the Heath to where the Redwoods lived. Yet it happened somehow, that as, rather tired out, we were thinking of coming home, we were overtaken by Mr. Godfrey Redwood. He joined us, saying he was himself going to town.

He walked with us across the Heath, first holding the two boys on either hand. Then bidding Aleck see how weary Sister looked, he slipped the child off, and quietly gave me his arm. We had never before walked together thus, out of doors, in the open day.

It was a pleasant evening, and we talked of many things, chiefly about the boys, and about his going abroad the following week for two months or so. He went very unwillingly, he told me. However, he promised Henry to write him word of all the wonders of the Alps, and even to bring him home something from the very spot where William Tell shot at the apple, which greatly delighted the boy. So talking, he went with us the whole way, and said good-by at our door. We had all enjoyed our walk so much, and were so happy, that I never uttered a less sad good-by. I hardly remembered he was going away at all, until the children obstinately refused to enter the house without seeing " the last of him."

So we all stood at the door and watched him round the Square. At the corner he turned round, perceived us, lifted his hat and bowed. Then we saw him no more.

(No more! The youth Godfrey Redwood—so gracefu., manly gentle, ay and beautiful—for he was beautiful, in heart as in face—I never saw any more!)

Every week, every day, our life at home grows darker and darker. I am my father's daughter in nothing but the name, and in an existence of forced blank idleness, which makes me envy the very housemaid at her toil.

For my two poor boys, they are being slowly ruined. Constant punishment is changing Harry's frank temper into the ferocity of a young tiger; and yesterday, I heard my innocent Aleck—his mother's darling, and her very image—I heard Aleck with frightened lips stammer out—*a lie!*

If *she* had heard him—she who with dying breath left him to my charge!

I sometimes think, when wandering through our beautiful house, or dining at our luxurious table—If people did but know! And then all sorts of frantic ideas swim through my mind, slowly forming themselves into unutterable longings.

To-day I read in the Proverbs of Solomon :—

Better is a dinner of herbs where love is, than a stalled ox and hatred therewith.

Better is a dry morsel and quietness therewith, than an *housefull of sacrifices with strife.*

I wonder, is it very hard to earn one's bread?

My twenty-first birthday has come and gone, without any celebration except that of tears. Only, one consciousness forced itself upon my mind: I am of age, and my own mistress now.

It is nearly Christmas. Mr. Redwood wrote Harry word that he should be at home by the New Year, to keep his own coming of age, which I knew was just one month after mine Yet how much older he always seemed than I!

I am terrified lest he too should see the visible change creeping over my two boys, from which I can not, can not save them, in a home like this. What will be the end of all ?

I wrote that question last night; to-night I answer it. For the last time I lay me down to sleep under my father's roof.

This is how it happened.—I wish to write all the particulars clearly, that I may at no future period have to meet an accusing conscience, or the reproaches of my brothers.—

There was to-day one of the usual domestic storms, in which, by Mrs. Lyne's contrivance, Harry and Aleck were punished sorely ; and this time—though I know they are not such good boys as they once were—punished unjustly. Then, with her usual smile—she is always smiling—my step-mother informed me that after Christmas they were both to be sent from home, to a twenty-pound Yorkshire school, with holidays, as she delightedly remarked, only once in two years. I went at once to my father, and asked if it were so ? He acknowledged it. I reasoned with him, quietly, earnestly, that in such a school the delicate Aleck would not live a year ; and Henry, with his fierce temper, would turn out a perfect demon. He laughed at me. Then I told him, with tears, that I had promised my mother never to part with the lads He answered, what I shall not write.

At last, half-maddened, I cried out, " that they should not go."

" Miss Lyne," said he to me, glancing at his wife, who sat compassionately smiling at my wickedness, " I give you one alternative—either let your brothers go peaceably to the school I choose, or else maintain them yourself."

" What do you mean ?"

" What I say ; you are quite old enough to earn your own

bread and theirs; and I really think, with the prospect of a new family rising up, you would be much better out of the way."

I was in that excited state of mind when nothing appears strange, startling, or impossible. So, after a momentary pause, I said resolutely, "Very well, father; we will go."

He made no opposition; did not even seem surprised. I left the study almost immediately; but before I went, I walked up to him, and shook hands, which I am now glad of. There were no more words or disputes, but the thing was done.

To-morrow I shall remove with my brothers to a lodging, try to get daily pupils, and begin the world, with a good education, youth, health, courage, and twenty pounds a year Not so bad!—the very thought of toil gives me strength. It is like plunging into a cold bath, after being suffocated with foul vapory steams.

A strange thought smote me just now. What will all my friends say?—what will *one friend* say, when he comes back and finds me—a daily governess?

Still, no matter—it must be.

* * *

(The day after writing this I arranged all my plans, telling them likewise to my father; for I wished to deal openly and have no quarrel, which, indeed, I always conscientiously had avoided. He listened hurriedly—for there was a dinner party awaiting him downstairs—wished me success, gave me five pounds (which I quietly left on his table), and bade me not tell my humble address to the servants. Thus we parted, without anger, and, God forgive me! without love.

So, when the guests had sat down to table, I sent off our small luggage, took my brothers in each hand, and went out of my father's doors through the bleak streets, *home*.

F*

PART II.

WHAT a strange, new life is this on which I have entered to boldly! To-day, after paying my weekly rent in advance, making some slight needful purchases, and providing, much too largely I fear, for household expenses and food, I find we have exactly one sovereign to begin the world with. Well as my clever Harry remarked, "Benjamin Franklin began with one shilling;" so we are fully nineteen shillings the richer than that great philosopher. Nevertheless, I am glad that my teaching duties commence to-morrow, and that my first week's salary will soon be due.

(Looking back on these days, it seems to me almost a miracle that I had got this situation, the very first I applied for It must have been some charitable soul who gave me through pity what I took as an ordinary right, not knowing how many a poor unknown, uncredentialed governess waits, hopes, doubts, gradually sinks down lower and lower, despairs, and starves.)

I have taken our lodgings where would be cheapest, and furthest away from our old neighborhood; therefore I shall have a rather long walk into town to my pupil; but exercise is good for me. The boys will be quiet at home; our old servant, who keeps these lodgings, will have an eye upon them; and I shall teach them of an evening. I began to do it to-night, but rather unsuccessfully; they have been too much excited by the change. So I took Aleck on my knee, while Henry placed himself on the other side the fire, quite man-like; and we had a serious talk about "our establishment."

I told them they must not expect many things they had

at the Square, fine dinners, and servants to wait ; that they must learn to wait upon themselves, and would only get a pudding once a week.

"Twice, sister, please—twice !" begged Aleck ; and I yielded.

Also, I tried to make Harry feel how much depended upon him when I was away, and how he could not be a foolish, headstrong, passionate boy any more, but must strive to grow a man as fast as possible. He promised, and to prove it insisted on putting himself and Aleck to bed without my help. Accordingly, passing their door, I found the window slightly open, the candle flaring in its socket in the middle of the floor, and a great round hole burnt in Aleck's socks. But my two darlings were soundly sleeping, as content in that shabby bedroom as if they were still surrounded by the luxuries due to a rich man's sons. My tears fell as I looked at them ; and I prayed God's help that I might bring them up rightly and virtuously, as their mother would have wished. She, who knew what misery often lay hid under riches, would not have minded their being poor.

I have gone through the first week of my life as a daily governess. It has been rather harder than I had thought.

I found my one pupil a very big girl, indeed almost a young woman, taller than myself, and with twice as much spirit. She really frightened me, with her fierce black eyes, and her foreign manner, for she is half French. I felt myself shrinking into nothing beside her. Yet though she chattered French and German to an extent that at first alarmed me, on the score of my own acquirements, I find her lamentably ignorant in the real classic knowledge of either language ; and as regards English she requires the teaching I would give to little Aleck. Nevertheless, she has such perfect self-assurance, such a strong will, such a thorough ease and inde

pendence of manner, that one requires the utmost moral cour
age to attempt to teach her any thing. I try to assume all
my dignity, and the decision of superior years and knowledge,
but yet I am only one-and-twenty, while she is near fifteen.
And oh! if she did but know how dreadfully her poor little
governess is at heart afraid of her!

I believed myself tolerably well-educated; surely I am, as
regards classical literature. How I always reveled in Dante,
and loved the only true French poet, Lamartine, and dived
thirstingly into the mysteries of Goethe and Schiller : yet in
common conversation I find myself nonplussed continually.
It is such a different matter to know a thing oneself, and to
impart it to another. I ought now to go to school again, if
only to learn how to teach.

There it is again in music. Friends call me a good musi
cian (at least *some* friends did), and I know my love for it is
a perfect passion : but there is a vast difference between
singing for oneself, or for those whom one cares to please far
better than one's self—and knocking a poor song note by
note into the ear and head of a girl who has no more heart
for it than, alas! her poor governess has for the teaching. I
had to-day to play and sing before Thérèse's mother in proof
of my acquirements. I chose a song—sang many a time to
such pleasant praises! but in the singing my eyes filled with
tears, and my heart sank down like lead. I failed deplorably;
and I knew it. I had no business to think of such things
now I am a daily governess.

Occasionally, too, I have stings of foolish pride; I had to-
day, when Madame Giraud asked me abruptly, "if I wanted
my salary?" My cheeks burned, as I said, "Yes, if she
pleased," and took the gold, so much needed. I thought—
if any old friends could see me then, would they scorn me?
But I soon got over this wrong feeling, and walking home,
enjoyed the sweetness of first earnings.

Yet at the **week's end I** am very tired, probably with the long daily walk and the perpetual talking. I am so glad to morrow **is** Sunday!

I see clearly, we **must live** somewhat plainer than we do It costs more to feed three mouths weekly than I had expected : **and** as **for my taking** the omnibus to town on wet days **as** Harry insists—wise, thoughtful little man!—*that* is quite impossible ; but I need not vex him by saying so.

How changed we all are in a few weeks! how **it seems** like an age since we "began the world!" The children have become quite used to our new ways, only, poor things! sometimes they can not understand why **they are restricted in** what were once ordinary things, but **have now become** impracticable luxuries. Harry wants to go out **always** in his **best jacket and French kid gloves; and** Aleck still looks and **longs** daily for **the** pudding. **Poor lads!** it goes to my very heart sometimes.

I have not leisure to write my journal often, being every night so glad to go to bed. It is a great blessing that I have such sound, wholesome sleep, which not only refreshes me, but drowns all care for a season.

If I could only send those boys to school, even to the common school they used to attend, I would be so thankful! It is not right for them to be left alone the long, **long day ;** and at night I am so tired, that I fear **I** do not teach them half carefully enough. I must try some plan **or** other for them.

—Certainly, **it** is a kind world, with many good people in it, as I have proved this day.

I "put my pride in my pocket," and went to Mr. Rawlinson, **my** brothers' old schoolmaster. I told him frankly my position, at least so far as I could without blaming my father

I asked him if he would take back one boy, say Henry, and let me in requital give French lessons to his daughters, or in his school.

He not only agreed, but said at my going away—that two lads gave no more trouble than one, and he must have back *both* his scholars : but he will only permit me to give three lessons a week, nevertheless.

My mind is now at rest, and the children are greatly pleased ; they did so weary after their old playfellows, as I plainly saw.

Still, every pleasure has its pain ; and mine came at last. Seeing a cloud gathering over Harry's mirth, at last I got from him the secret—he did not like going back to school in his old half-worn blouse. He said the boys would tease him.

Oh ! how bitter these things are ! But I must bear them : it is not the children's fault.

After little Aleck was asleep, I sat and talked with Henry alone, reasoning with him, as his good sense and manliness deserved, more like a companion than a child.   I told him how poor we were, and must necessarily be, for a long time ; that the only way in which poor people can remain independent and honest, is by resolving firmly that what they can not pay for they must do without—which resolution I had made, and we would all follow.   I always say " we," that the boys may feel we are all as one, to sink or swim together.

" Now, Harry," I said, " I might go to some shop we used to frequent, and get credit, knowing all the time I could not pay.   But would that be honest ? would you feel happy in your new clothes ?"

" No, no !" he cried, sitting up in bed, and hiding his face on my shoulder ; " however poor we are, I will be thus much of a gentleman—' One that does not owe any body any thing.' —You remember who once told me that."

I did not--which was strange.

"It was Mr. Redwood : and he knows what it is to be a gentleman, doesn't he, sister ?"

" Yes," said I quietly, and said no more.

Mr. Rawlinson mentioned incidentally, that some little time after school began, a gentleman had called to inquire if he knew any thing about the two Master Lynes ? and being answered " No," had gone away, leaving no name.

But I know who it was ;—whom alone it could be. He has then come home from Italy. The children will be so glad!

The spring is advancing fast ; day by day, as I cross the Green Park, I see the change. It has been either sunny weather, or soft, warm, "growing"- weather, ever since the boys went to school. I enjoy my daily walk so much ; especially the three days a week that I return from Mr. Rawlinson's with the boys.

Then it seems so strange to walk in our old neighborhood, and see the same shops, and signs, and turnings. But we never go near the Square.

The days are now so light and long, that coming back through Pall Mall and Regent-street I always meet the afternoon loungers. How gay the spring bonnets begin to look ! I could be half ashamed of mine, poor old thing ! It is astonishing how soon dresses and bonnets will wear out, put on daily, and in all weathers. I could be almost foolish enough to sigh with Harry—" I want new clothes."

However, it signifies little, rushing through the streets as I do, not meeting a soul I know. But, if I did meet any one —I in my unneat winter wrappings, and a bundle of books under my arm ! If any one saw me, spoke to me;—*would* they speak ? I—that was a young lady in her father's house, and am—only a daily governess !

One friend I know—proud, refined, over-delicate in all that

regards women—might start, to think how through this win
ter I have run through London streets alone, unprotected, in
fair weather and foul, in dark or light, often long after dusk—
I, that was never allowed to cross the Square by myself!
He might think too that it was "strange" or "improper," my
living alone in lodgings, with only my young brothers.

O, wide gulf of worldly distance—opening wider and wider
before my eyes! I now begin to see into what I have
plunged. Had I thought, when I was quitting my father's
house!—But no; I am glad I did not : I am glad I thought
of nothing but my poor little brothers, who now live in peace,
so happy and so good.

For me, God will work out my destiny as seemeth Him
best !

I have determined to cease going down the pleasant streets
where I might meet friends I once knew. I walk along back
streets now. Perhaps it is nearest, and I ought to save time
if possible.

My brothers asked me to-day, if now that the long summer
evenings are coming, I would take them up to Hampstead
Heath? · But I told them they would like Blackheath better, and they are quite satisfied, nay, delighted.

How slender is a child's memory ! They never now speak
of the Square, of old times, or any of our old friends, of whom
—as I begin slowly to understand—we may possibly never
hear any more.

Thérèse is a very good girl on the whole ; affectionate too.
She takes care I have lunch daily ; and this morning, seeing
I looked pale and tired with the heat, she brought me a glass
of wine ; saying, her mother desires I should have the same
every day—a great blessing to me ! and how kind of her !
I must try and do my duty by my pupil, even more than I

have hitherto done : though Madame Giraud declares she is quite satisfied.

Waiting for Thérèse to-day, I took up a newspaper, as I do occasionally, just to see the births, marriages, and deaths.   In the latter, one struck me :

"On the 19th ult., Sir Egerton Redwood, of Redwood Hall ; and, same day, drowned near Vevay, Egerton Redwood, Esq., his eldest and only surviving son.   The baronetcy and influential family property fall, therefore, to the next heir, Godfrey Egerton Redwood, Esq., son of the late Colonel and the Honorable Anne Redwood, and grandson of the lately deceased Baronet."

" Sir Godfrey Redwood !"   How strange it sounds !   But he will make a noble use of fortune : God grant him happiness long to possess it !

—I must still look a little longer in the list of " Marriages."

To-day, I have walked more slowly home, nor minded passing through the sunny streets and gay throngs of people in my sombre and dust-spoiled clothing.   It is quite good enough for one who will probably all her life have to earn her bread as a daily governess.

PART III.

Henry and I measured heights to-day ; and he is actually taller than I am. So, coming home from Mr. Rawlinson's he would insist upon giving me his arm, considering that he was yesterday fifteen years old.

(This is the next entry added to my foolish, girlish journal, preserved till now, from the still more foolish tenderness one has over girlish things. I had always a love of hoarding relics, memories, every thing but coin. The long pause in my writing was occasioned doubtless by want of leisure, during four years of a toilsome and yet monotonous life ;—the recommencement of my journal was owing to want of occupation, during that trying period " waiting for a situation "

Remembering his birth-day, puts me in mind that my own is about this time. Twenty-six, or seven, is it ? I have almost lost count. However, I must have been Thérèse's governess five years. This is why I shall miss her so much. Yet it is quite time for her to give up study, and practice housekeeping for a few months before she is married. I wish —as she laughing said—I could teach her *that*, meaning the management of a house. But in the domestic department my own abilities are small ; indeed they have completely died out for want of practice. Which signifies little ; since, as I told Thérèse this morning—I shall probably never have a house to manage.

She looked very sly, said, laughing, how did I know ? and appealed to her father ; who since her mother's death, two years since, has made her his constant companion. M. Giraud took no notice of Thérèse's nonsense ; he is a perfectly well-bred man, just, generous, and kind, so much so, that in these years I have all but forgotten he is by birth the great object of my girlish antipathy—a Frenchman.

He has been very kind to the boys too—my dear boys! of whom I am so proud. Ah, if their mother could but see them now!

Yet I have thanked God that she could not see, that no one could see, all we have passed through; the struggles, the humiliations, the narrow, grinding penury; and, had my health once failed, the awful spectre Want standing ever at the door. But I did not sink: a supernatural strength has borne me up through every thing; and He who gave it knows that strength was not my own

Now, though I am still full of anxieties—terrified when I see Aleck look delicate and weary; or Harry's cheek sharpening out of boyhood into youth; I yet live in present peace, and trust in Providence for the time to come.

Only, if I could hear of another situation before Thérèse's marriage! for I do not like taking my full salary when I teach her nothing, and am only as it were a friend and companion. But she and her father agree in compelling me to this, and I dare not refuse.

Oh, Need—imperious Need—what a tyrant thou art!

————

Strange things have befallen me to-day.

Leaving Thérèse early, I thought I would walk round, as I have done once or twice, by a print-shop in Pall Mall, to see something I should surely see there. There is no need to make any secret about it; it was a likeness of some one whom I knew—before the world knew him, as it does now.

Three years ago, I found in the "Times" newspaper Sir Godfrey Redwood's maiden speech: he had entered Parliament. We were then rich enough to afford a newspaper, so I often saw his name in the Debates. Afterward, when Henry wanted to take in "Chambers' Journal" instead, I managed to read the "Times" at Thérèse's house.

Sir Godfrey Redwood is a celebrated man now; so cele

brated, that besides the print in the shop-window, round
which I daily see a small crowd of curious gazers, I often
catch, in the common talk of strangers, the old familiar name.
Nobody knows, what perhaps I have no right to tell—that
he was once a friend of mine. Nevertheless, it is quite natural
that I should feel proud of this ; and it does not harm him,
or any one, that I have pleasure in seeing his name in the
newspaper, or in coming round now and then by that print-
shop, to look at his portrait—like, and yet unlike. He must
have changed much since we knew him.

To-day, as I stood at the shop-window—an unlady-like act,
it may be, but I feel I am now too old-looking and plainly
dressed to mind much what I do, provided it is not wrong—
there came up a groom and a led horse. Its owner quickly
passed out of the shop, and mounted ; then, just looking round
with a half-smile, that swept indifferently over the shop-window, the little crowd there—and me, off he rode.

It was the glimpse of a moment, but I could not be mis
taken ; I have to-day seen Godfrey—I mean, Sir Godfrey
Redwood.

And he did not know me ! But how could he ? The
years which have made of him a man, have made me—yes,
I am quite right in calling myself "an old woman."

I turned my face again to the shop-window, and gazed in
upon a dazzle of black and white engravings, till a hand
touched me, and some one said—"Miss Lyne ?" I need not
have started so, as it was only Thérèse's father.

He said "he had been watching me a long time . was I
then so very fond of prints ?—he would procure me as many
rare ones as I liked." I thanked him, and was passing on,
when I grew quite sick and weak—it was such a burning
summer day.

M. Giraud took my arm in his, very kindly ; and before I
well knew how it was, I found myself crossing the Park with

inn, in the direction of my home. He said, I believe, that he wanted to consult with me about Thérèse, or the future, or something—I forget what exact reason he gave. But ere long we had reached a quiet, retired walk, and Thérèse's father was talking, not about her, but about himself and me.

I do not know much of love-making; nor did he, this honest, generous-hearted, grave man of middle age, try to "make love." All I know is, that then and there, in that quiet shady walk, M. Giraud asked me to be his wife.

If he had been a foolish boy mocking me with silly, flatter- ing speeches, or a young man whose passionate devotion might torture me with the memory of my own lost youth, I should have felt it less: but this man—asking no love, only the right of showing tenderness; ready to be father, brother, friend, husband—every thing—to poor forlorn me—it went to my heart's core !

I believe I wept much ; but I am quite sure that I gave no answer of acceptance or encouragement, which might afterward smite my conscience. I rather think I said nothing at all ; for, hurrying me home, he left me ; telling me he would wait for my decision until next day.

So this night I have to choose whether I will at once lay aside all my burden of worldly cares, and become a good man's cherished wife. It would be so, I feel ; I know what he was to poor Madame Giraud, what he is to Thérèse and the younger three. That he is somewhat advanced in years, I would not mind ; nor even that he is a Frenchman—when a Frenchman is a true man and a gentleman.

Then, my two brothers, fast growing up, needing soon to be established in the world. And he told me, among other things, that, from the day he married me, he should look upon Henry and Aleck in the light of his own children. That day, he wishes—and Thérèse too, he brought me her own written desire—should be the same which removes his

eldest daughter from his home. Only six weeks hence ;—
one brief six weeks !—and I might be no longer a poor governess, but an honored wife !

I feel almost bewildered. Such a change! not for me
only, but for my dear boys. Surely I ought to forget every
thing except them—to crush out the old life, to tread old feelings into dust, and so walk on that silent pathway—it is *only*
dust, now—quite calm and smiling, up to the very church-
door. But *there*—in the presence of God, before whom, as
well as before my husband, I must take the marriage-vow—
Dare I ?

I have lifted down a Prayer Book—my mother's—and
read the whole marriage-service through.

" *I require and charge you both (as ye will answer at the*
dreadful day of judgment, when the secrets of all hearts shall
be disclosed) that if either of you know any impediment—"

" **Wilt thou** . . . *forsaking all other, keep thee only unto*
him—"

I closed the book.

It is impossible ! Poor I have been, very poor—ay, and
very miserable ; but I have ever borne a clear conscience
before God and man. So it shall still be. I will not per-
jure myself in the sight of Heaven ; nor enter the married
state with a lie upon my soul.

I have written to-night to M. Giraud, telling him that circumstances have made me fixedly resolve not to marry, but
to devote myself entirely to the care of my two brothers. He
is of too generous a nature, and knows too well my firmness
of purpose in all things, to attempt to change my resolution.

One sentence I have on mature consideration added to my
letter—that, should sickness or premature death prevent my
fulfilling my duty toward my boys, I trust to him—the only
man who ever really loved me—to take care of Henry and
Aleck until they grow to be men.

Now, as it is long past midnight, I shall lay me down, and try to sleep. Ah! how quietly those sleep, who, as said the poor dying poet, whose poetry we used to read when I was young, "feel the daisies growing over them!" God forgive me!—me, that have two young souls of His giving to rear up for His eternity!—I must not yet think of the "daisies."

It has all ended as I hoped ; and even my dear Thérèse has forgiven me. I trust, ere long, her excellent father may find a worthy companion for himself and a good mother for his little children : then my mind will be quite at rest.

Though I have seen him no more, he has managed, through Thérèse's husband, to find me some most acceptable pupils ; and he has never ceased his kindness to my boys.

My dear mother used to say, when sometimes we talked, half jesting, of the wooers that were to come to me, "that it was usually a woman's own fault, if in rejecting a lover she also lost a friend." I have proved deeply and thankfully the truth of that saying.

(Two years intervened here—two long, slow, silent years. Of these no records remain, because—I burnt them. It was a great deal the best. Every one who can weed his life, or his life's outward evidences, of all gloomy, erring, or hurtful memorials, is as much bound to do it, as he is bound to root out from his garden all things that might prove painful or injurious to those that come after him.

We should always remember, that in the saddest human life all sad-ness necessarily ends when the tomb closes ; often, with God's bless-ing, long before them. And none of us, quitting the world, should leave behind us the thorns that have mercifully dropped off from our own brows, to cumber and fester young feet.

I am now, in my old age, a firm advocate for that blessed sunshine of existence—a cheerful spirit—which I believe to be, no less than a meek and quiet one, "*in the sight of God of great price.*")

Harry is, I do believe, and every body says so, the hand-somest lad imaginable. I did so wish him to grow six feet

high ; which desire seems very likely to be accomplished
He is strong, too ; especially since last summer, when we
were rich enough to go down to the sea. What a merry
time we had ! and how Aleck, quiet and gentle as he is, became quite boisterous, and wanted to turn sailor. But the
salt-water mania has died away in these two months ; for
which somebody I know is very thankful. Any thing but
red-coats and blue-jackets—as I tell the boys when they talk
of what they will be.

What, alas ! Heaven only knows, for I do not. I can only
find them bread from year to year. As to putting them to
any profession, that is utterly impossible ; and somehow with
a feeling that may be wrong but yet is natural, I shrink
from seeing Henry or Alexander Lyne, sprung from the old
Lynes and Trevethlans of Cornwall, standing behind a coun-
ter, or running about as a lawyer's clerk.

Still, the trial is not quite at hand. Harry's education is
not finished yet ; and I will trust to that good Providence,
which has hitherto enabled me to earn for them not merely
necessaries but many comforts, still to make my way plain
before me.

I think Harry will turn out a wonderfully clever youth,
and that I did right, when good Mr. Rawlinson died, in straining every nerve that the lad should go to King's College
School for a year. He will be seventeen next October, and
then—Well, until then I will wait calmly : " Sufficient unto
the day is" not only "the evil," but the anxious burden
"thereof." We never know what lightening the morrow
may bring.

————

—I wrote yesterday this last line. There must have been
a good angel standing by, and smiling while I wrote. Ah,
no ! our "good angel" wore a human likeness—a likeness
we all knew ! I write this with tears of joy, not so much for

having found **again an old friend,** but for having also **found,** what amidst all doubt I never wholly lost, my faith **in the** ideal **of my youth.**

If from this moment I were never **to set eyes on** the "good angel" I spoke of; or if, harder still, eyes whose kindness I value were henceforth to rest on me in utter strangeness, forgetfulness, or dislike ;—I still should feel the happiness which I feel **now.** A happiness which being wholly without reference to myself, is as pure as that of some forced iconoclast, who, wakening from a miserable dream, sees the broken idol sitting unshattered and godlike fair, nay, sees the imaged marble changed into the visible Divinity. What matters it **into** what dim corner of the great world-temple one creeps, **so** that one knows the glorious presence is still abiding **there** !

—This is certainly a little **piece of insanity,** worthy of the Felicia Lyne **of old : but it is only** temporary ; I shall be " Miss Lyne the governess," **to-morrow.**

After a day or two, I have leisure and quietness to write **down** the circumstance which has made such a change in the boys' future, and consequently in mine.

It was the day **of** the prize distribution at King's College , and Henry had taken his younger brother with him " to see the fun," as he boldly called it—poor **Harry** ! **though** I noticed how pale he was all breakfast time—aware that **his** own fate hung upon the balance. **Since,** till their names are called out, none of the boys know who **are** the winners of prizes.

I could not go, for pleasure must always yield to duty, in my profession ; and I had two music lessons to give that afternoon. Returning home I found to my surprise that the **lads were not come in ; I should have been** foolishly restless, only I knew Aleck's good sense, and how, had any disappointment befallen his brother, no one could calm him better than

Aleck could   So I employed myself in seeing that dinner was
all ready, and in making the room neat—a weary business
where there are two growing boys.   And I am getting such
a fidgety, particular old maid—as **Harry** often tells me;
though he always kisses me afterward, lest I should be vexed.

—How long I am in coming to my story!

It was six in the evening, and I was growing thoroughly
wretched and frightened, when I heard a knock, and a foot
that could be none but Harry's, leaping up-stairs (we live on
the drawing-room floor now).   In a minute, the lad burst in,
all delight, and Aleck after him.

"Oh! sister, sister, only guess!" they both cried.

"No! don't let her guess," said a third voice; and then I
saw that a gentleman was with my boys.   One—than whom
I would sooner have expected to see an angel of heaven
standing in our room!

"I should have known your face any where, Miss Lyne,
though I fear you have forgotten mine."—He was mistaken
in both these things: but it did not signify.

Very soon we had shaken hands cordially, and partly from
Harry, partly from Aleck, I began to hear how my brothers
had met with Sir Godfrey Redwood.

He, now a man of consideration, had been invited to the
distribution; there in the College Hall, he had heard called
out the name of Henry Trevethlan Lyne; and seeing my boy
walk up to receive his well-earned prize, had made sure it
was his old favorite.   Afterward he had spoken to the lads, and
they had told him our whole story.   It was very different
from the one my step-mother had given him concerning us,
some eight years ago.   No wonder he had suffered us gradually to drop out of his memory, unworthy a good man's
thought.

He dined with us that day, though the proud boys were
rather shocked that he should see our humble board.   And

all that evening, with the June sun slanting in upon his face —in which the former boyish likeness gleamed strangely at times, though he is much changed by the thick mustache and beard he wears, foreign fashion—Sir Godfrey Redwood sat talking, sometimes gayly, sometimes thoughtfully, with " Miss Lyne the governess," and her brothers.

I saw in the first ten minutes, that despite his kind courtesy about knowing my face, he, too, was struck by the change which I so clearly perceive in myself; and that if the old "Felicia" had not been long swept out from what could have been at best a mere boyish memory, the sight of "Miss Lyne" had now made it, and all belonging to it, irrevocably *the past*. It was well for me that I had discernment and strength of mind enough at once to assure myself of this, so that our future intercourse may be, as indeed it is, perfectly free and unembarrassed on either side.

Sir Godfrey told us much of what had happened to himself since the days when he used to visit at the Square. It was the ordinary life of a young man of fortune, filled up with many extravagances and follies, all of which he owned so freely, that one could plainly discern—even if his whole countenance, bearing, and the accidental nothings by which we judge of character, had not confirmed the fact—that there had been in him no vice ; that the son of his proud and virtuous mother was, as I had long learnt from other sources, the stay and glory of the Redwood house.

His " wild oats," he said, had been sown early, abroad and at home, and he was now in the midst of manhood's grave and earnest career—the career of one who deeply felt, that as regarded talents, influence, and the power of doing good, to him much had been given, and of him much would surely be required.

Harry asked him if he had been married ? to which he laughingly answered, " No, nor engaged either, though he had been in love and out of love at least a dozen times, as Master Harry would himself ere long."

Then, turning to me, he changed his tone to seriousness, and spoke of all the cares he had had with his younger brothers and sisters, and what a happy and noble mistress his mother made at Redwood Hall. "It would be long ere I should find a Lady Redwood like her," added he smiling ; and then the conversation died.

But now comes that act of generosity, which I find my brother Henry and he had settled entirely between themselves before ever the matter was confided to me, though of course my nominal consent was to be asked as a seal to the bond.

Sir Godfrey is about to proceed abroad as *chargé d'affaires* at ——. He wishes to take with him Henry, who at seventeen—nay sixteen, for it wants three months to his birthday—is as manly-looking and manly-minded as many a youth of twenty. He said the boy should be his secretary, or *attaché*—some nominal office, through which I see clearly his generous purpose of taking all care for Harry's future entirely upon himself.

And Harry must go. It would break the lad's heart did I refuse. I have no right to let any foolish scruple stand in the light of this, the sole chance that may ever offer of my darling brother's earning his bread and making his way in the world in the sole manner that his proud nature would ever thoroughly bend to—as a gentleman. Besides, as Sir Godfrey reminded me, this change in fortune only replaces Harry in the sphere where he was born ; since —like water, the pure blood of the Trevethlans and the Lynes will always find its own level.

When he said so, I smiled, and in my turn reminded him that I was still " the governess."

" Well !" he answered, " and what is more honorable than

a governess, when she is a lady by birth, or at least by education, as all governesses ought to be ? What more noble than a woman who devotes her whole life to the sowing of good seed, the fruitage of which she may never see ? If I have a wife and children," here his eyes smiled with some dim, dawning thought, " I will teach them, that after father and mother there is no one on earth to whom they owe such reverence as to her on whom depends the formation not only of their intellect, but of their whole mind and character. But, accordingly, I will take care that this model governess is worthy of the trust—a true lady, and more, a true *woman*— in fact, just such a woman as you are yourself, Miss Lyne."

I had no answer to that. I—*his* children's governess !

Still, it gives me comfort to think he should so honor the sisterhood to which I belong—unto which I had joined myself in humiliated despair, until at last I began to wear my heavy chains as the badge of a worthy service, and to discover that every governess has it in her power to make herself, and with herself all her fraternity, reverenced and honorable in the sight of the world.

Henry is gone away—Henry, my noble, handsome boy ' my right hand and stronghold in the bitter days of adversity, which hardly seemed adversity when borne for him ! But, please God ! there is only prosperity in store for him now. Also, for me and little Aleck, still *little*, gentle, and pale. But Aleck shall go to college, if he likes, nevertheless ; for he too must be well educated, as is his brother. My mother's sons shall not be inferior in any way to the children who, I hear, cluster round my father's hearth, and will inherit his property. Well ! we envy them not. May they prove a comfort to his old age !

To-night Aleck and I have sat for the last time in our old lodgings, from which we are now removing nearer town. I can not walk so well as I used to do, and we need better rooms, since the situation I have now obtained through Sir Godfrey Redwood, and which I have promised him to hold until he and Harry return home, is one of a higher class and higher salary than any I have hitherto had. Think of my teaching a little Lady Anne !

She is the youngest daughter of a poor earl—I see he is poor for an earl ; but he lives in honest retirement, keeping within his means ; which is doubtless the reason why Sir Godfrey honors him so much. I honor him too, and his three fair daughters, as cordially as if they had not " a handle" to their pretty Christian names.

A quiet yet somewhat dull tea we had, Aleck and I ; and then we sat in the twilight, talking, and watching the shadows in the room, which now seems mean, yet once appeared to us magnificent, compared to the former back-parlor. The poor old room, which has seen so much ! We almost grew sad to think we should no more watch the street-lamp's glimmer creeping in along the wall, so pleasant and dim—besides often saving us an hour or two of candle-light, in times when every small saving was of pathetic value. Ah ! the poor old room !

Soon we broke off talking of the past to speculate on the dawning future, and to wonder whether it would be two years, three, or four ere Harry came back ! and if so, what a man he would be !—Especially when in the constant society of such a perfect gentleman as Sir Godfrey Redwood. Aleck quite envied him that ; for Aleck, with all his quietness, has an exquisite taste for the refinements of life. Nay, coming one day to fetch me home, he has quite fallen in love with my little Lady Anne, and I hear of nothing else from morning till night. The foolish boy ! Sixteen and five feet four to adore eleven and four feet nothing ! But Aleck is a young poet, and so, as I tell him, must fain begin the usual destiny of poets—to be *always* in love !

Love !—-Have I, even I, begun lightly to use that solemn word ?

Aleck is at last gone to bed, and I have taken away his candle, lest he should set the house on fire through reading novels, which would be a pretty climax to our long abiding here.

I go up to my own room, and in its solitary silence think of many things, chiefly of the steamer which, under this same midnight moon, is floating down the broad Thames, and bearing with it my best treasures in this world—bearing them to a future, in which as regards neither, shall I have in time to come any share or claim. Both will ere long have taken to their hearts much nearer ties. To-night Aleck made me laugh, by prophesying that it would not be very many years before I dandled on my knees Harry's children :—and Sir Godfrey Redwood gayly promised I should be governess to his ! All these jests will one day come true ; and then I—this one solitary I—

No matter !—May'st Thou, O God, receive the life-sacrifice on which, year by year, I have thrown all that was lovely and precious in my eyes, and so make the offering—worthless of itself—sweet and acceptable in Thine !

PART IV.

That boy Aleck ! that foolish, comical, impressible fellow !—

(This must have been written two years or more after the time
when Harry went away, and I began to teach the Ladies Airlie. I
say "the Ladies Airlie," because, in addition to my own pupil, I
used occasionally to give music-lessons to Lady Dorothy and Lady
Maud. In fact, I was very much with them all; more like a friend
than a governess. Those two years were a bright portion of my life ;
I was very happy (for me) ; so happy, that I scarcely ever touched
my journal.)—

That boy Aleck will certainly go crazy after his little goddess ! He has had three other child-sweethearts in eighteen
months, and now he has come back to "my bonnie Ladie
Ann." I can now hear him singing to himself that same ballad of Allan Cunningham's, fragments of which he indulges
me at breakfast and tea, somthing about

> " The cherry lip, the creamy loof,
>   Or the waist o' Lady Ann,"

generally going through the whole poem, until he gets to

> " I am her father's gardener lad ;"

at which he pauses, and looks as proud as if the ghosts of all
the ancient Lynes and Trevethlans were peering out from
the eyes of their young descendant. My patience alive ! (a
harmless expletive that, though it seems ridiculous enough
when written), what is to be done with the boy ?

He wants sadly a little reality—some active, busy, earnest
life, such as is led by his brother. How happy Harry seems!
and how beautiful his letters are ! gradually toning down into
manliness. I think on the whole, that though not so much

of a dreamer, he will turn out a finer character than **Aleck**. But then **Aleck is always with me, and** one's heart clings so closely **to those** that are away. " One's heart clings so closely to those that are away!"—How much truth there is in these **words** !

It was my birthday yesterday ; a fact which little Lady Anne coaxed out of me, seeing I looked rather grave. She **also won** from me another secret, which, indeed, I had no reason or design to keep—that I was thirty-one years old.

Thirty-one years old !—It is time I put up my " pretty, pretty curls," which, through a foolish fancy, I have carefully **kept** all these **years**. Nobody would ever **be so blind as to call** them **" pretty" now ; and** whatsoever I did with them, no-body **would** notice **the** change. So, to-morrow, **I will begin wearing my hair quite** plain, which **is** indeed much more suitable to any one who is **no longer a girl.**

Lady Dorothy and Lady Maud **both** gave me birthday presents—quick, warm-hearted, impulsive gifts. Moreover which was better than the gift, Lady Maud kissed me, bend ing over me with her silent, tall, graceful, white-lily-like air. I greatly admire Lady Maud. But merry, frank-spoken Lady Dorothy thought it a very dreadful thing to be thirty-one years old, especially **when** one was **not married,** and appar-ently did not intend to be ; which, she politely observed, was certainly Miss Lyne's own fault, and a very disgraceful de-termination, too !

I laughed, and Lady Maud, whose words, though rare, are always as fragrant as the perfume that comes out of a white-lily-cup—there my fantastic simile holds good !—Lady Maud **said, " It mattered** little : whether old or young, married or unmarried, a woman like Miss Lyne was sure to be happy."

Happy !—**Alone,** in my own home, I sit and ponder over that word

6*

I go out into the world, and see other homes full of selfishness, misery, and strife :—mine is all peace; there is never in it a shadow of disquiet or contention. Except, to be sure, when Aleck persists in sitting up writing poetry till two in the morning.

I see around me restlessness, ennui, young lives wasted in doing nothing—until out of the dull void of an aimless existence gradually forms a chaos, seething continually with all its elements of passion and of pain, from which nothing but the touch of a Divine hand will ever evolve a perfect orb. Now, *my* life—steadily rolling on, with rarely a moment left for weariness or regret, every day bringing its duties, and every night closing them in rest—would I change ?—No.

Young people come to me with their troubles, especially love-troubles ; poor frenzied strugglers through the seas which all must cross ; dashed from rock to rock, of fate, or folly, or wrong, each one thinking there is in the whole world no other sufferer, at least no greater sufferer, than he. I sit and listen so quietly, am sorry for all, and try to help all ; while my outward smile creeps peacefully into my own inward heart, with a consciousness that there are some portions of the solemn life-journey which no one ever has to pass through *twice*.

Yes, I think Lady Maud's chance saying was true ; I believe I am truly " happy."

Was there not an ancient sage who said, " No man can be pronounced truly happy until he dies ?"

———

—Who would have thought it ? who could have told ? So unexpected, too ! But, as Aleck was saying only that very day, every thing in the fortunes of our family seems to happen suddenly. We two were sitting at tea, on Good Friday, of all days in the year : I thinking what I should do during a week of entire holiday, and Aleck rather glum, because though Lady Dorothy had called him " her poet-laureate"--

Lady Maud had said, in her gracious and gentle way, what good a little country air would do to a delicate boy—and little Lady Anne had openly declared she would ask her godmother, Mrs. Redwood, to invite him with them to Dorsetshire ;— still Easter was come, and they had all gone down, save, alas ! poor Aleck, to Redwood Hall.

I had told the boy it was a foolish dream, and that, despite ' all the blood of all the Howards," *i. e.* the Trevethlans, and all the gentle humility of the impoverished, noble household, there was a great difference between them and us ; that he was still but a college-student, and brother of " the govern-ess." But at eighteen one does build such airy palaces ! " Every man his own Aladdin," as I said merrily. " Youths running about barefoot and contented, each with *the lamp* in his bosom."

Aleck laughed, declaring I was growing quite poetical ; so, just for fun, and to pass time away, we began speculating what we each would do, had we the lamp or the ring.

My foolish boy quickly built in imagination a palace, very Aladdinish, on the banks of Windermere (whither I had man-aged to send him after his illness last autumn) ; and was just creating a princess to put into it, which princess strongly re-sembled a full-grown Lady Anne—when he recollected I had not had my turn.

He said, " Now, sister, what would you wish for ?"

I was silent a moment, remembering the days when I used to wish " at the moon ;" but I am not so simple now. So I be-gan to build my Aladdin-palace of real stones—possibilities.

" Then, Aleck, I think if we were sitting just as we are —I am sure we are very comfortable—and if, instead of Henry's next letter, which ought to come this week, there were to come—"

" Henry ?"

I smiled, and was going on, when- -I can only state, not

explain, the odd coincidence—there was a loud, sudden knock
at the street-door. Following the knock, came the old quick-
bounding footstep—three stairs at a time—and Harry was in
the room !

Ay, my own Harry, my real Harry ! though he was six
feet high, with a deep, firm voice, and an awful mustache and
beard ;—though he lifted his little old sister right up into his
arms, frightening her almost out of her seven senses, and by
his foreign and stylish appearance so awed Aleck that for the
first minute or two, the lad hardly ventured to speak to his
brother—still—he was our own Harry !

I had, I thank God ! such entire joy in seeing him, such
perfect home-delight, that I never once thought whether
Harry had come here alone.

He had done so, as he very soon told us; Sir Godfrey
having gone down at once to Redwood Hall.

We had tea a second time for our Harry—the old pleasant
tea-making, which he seemed to enjoy so much, and remember
so tenderly.   He even reminded me of the winter nights when
I used to stretch over between him and Aleck, lying like lazy
puppies on the hearth, and make the toast by the parlor-fire.
My dear Harry !—

He has grown up a perfect gentleman : how could he else,
under the influence of such a friend ?   Better than all, my boy
has kept his own pure heart, only guided into experience by
one that is not only pure but wise.

In every way Sir Godfrey Redwood has fulfilled his trust,
and Henry's attachment to him knows no bounds.   That my
brother, my darling brother, should owe every thing to the
man whom I always held to be the best man on earth—is not
this happiness ?   A happiness, that perhaps is better, deeper,
truer, than what I might have deemed such, once !

Harry says that Sir Godfrey Redwood is very well in
health, and full of joy at coming home.   He sent likewise a

kind message to Harry's sister, saying I should hear from him
soon.

I have heard we are all to go down on a three days' visit
to Redwood Hall. I would fain have declined, being, as I
told the boys, half-frightened at the Honorable Anne Redwood, whom I have never seen since the days when I visited
her as a "young lady at home." She might be proud toward
Miss Lyne the governess. But my two brothers, who seem
to have fairly taken rule over me, will hear no excuse.

Besides, Henry longs for the Dorsetshire shooting, and, as
he told me privately, desires to hear more of a plan which
Sir Godfrey has all but settled for his future career, in which
he Henry Trevethlan Lyne, is to bring great honor back to
the old family. God bless the hand that makes my boy so
happy !

Also, Aleck is urgent for the visit. He knows he shall
meet there his two great patronesses—Lady Dorothy and
Lady Maud, to say nothing of his child-goddess, his "bonnie
Lady Ann." For me, I shall meet—

But I shall meet likewise, what every where has encom-
passed and sustained me—the strength, counsel and guard of
Him who has never forsaken me, nor will forsake me, even
unto the end.

The first day and night of our visit are over.

We arrived just half an hour before dinner : and I saw no
one till I had descended. I was nervous and trembling ; it
was ten years since I had been on a visit any where, at least
in such a stately house as this. It was a positive terror to
me to descend the stairs, until at the foot I perceived some
one waiting for me. At first I drew back—till I saw it was
only Harry, my own kind Harry.

He laughed at me merrily ; and I went in the drawing-room

quite bold and proud—oh ! so proud ! leaning on my boy's
arm .

I can not tell much about the meeting, except that Mrs.
Redwood was very gracious, even tender, for her ; that she
said I was scarcely at all altered (ah ! but she only saw me
by lamp-light, and with her feeble, aged eyes), and that, what
touched me most, she called me by my girl-name, *Felicia*.

For her son, he could not be otherwise than kind.

When dinner was announced, Sir Godfrey left Lady Maud,
with whom he was conversing, and took me down stairs.   I
did not expect that.   From her smile, I think she must have
told him to do it , showing me by this courtesy that I still held
my old position in society.   If so, it was a gentle and generous
act, like Lady Maud.   Once in the evening, when a cluster
of the family-party was gathered round the fire, Sir Godfrey
telling us some story of his life abroad, and Lady Maud standing to listen, her elbow resting on the low marble chimney-piece
—it seemed to me that the " white garden lily" looked like that
flower when the sun comes by and shines upon it, making it not
only pure but thoroughly translucent with beauty and delight

I wonder, did any one else see her with my eyes ?

This morning after breakfast, Sir Godfrey Redwood asked
me to walk with him, that he might show me the conserva-
tories ; and there, sitting down under a fair orange-tree, with
the sun shining in upon all sorts of gorgeous flowers he has
brought home from abroad, he talked with me long and
seriously of the future—of my brother's future.

He says, that he intends entering public life under the new
ministry, and that Harry, now more than twenty years old,
shall be his secretary, or have a government appointment, as
may be.   The boy is able and willing to carve out his own
fortunes now ; and will be placed where he need not dread that
one word—which Sir Godfrey never uses—*patronage*.   He
will be independent, too, though not rich ; and as I said

Henry and I between us can give Aleck what he desires—
a college education, to fit him for the Church; so that, in
every way, the path before us is straight.

And here came in Sir Godfrey's generosity, which I can
hardly think of without tears.

He asked me about my health—if I were happy—if I
should not be lonely when Aleck was at Cambridge—and if,
as my younger brother's college expenses could easily be man
aged (ah! I knew how!), I would consent to give up teaching, and, just till Harry wanted me to keep his house, settle
in a pretty little cottage there was near Redwood Hall? He
said all this with some confusion and hesitation; but—let me
quite assure myself of that fact—only the hesitation of a delicate generosity to which the mere act of seeming to bestow
favors is a pain.

For me, if I were somewhat agitated, he would easily at-
tribute it to a similar cause.

I answered, that I had always lived independent, and
wished it to be so to the end;—that it was much better I
should still remain a governess. Only, as I had rather be
with those I loved than with strangers, perhaps he would use
his influence that I might stay permanently with Lady Anne.

When I said "use his influence," he half smiled; then
looked sad, and said gravely that he had no influence in the
Airlie family, except as an ordinary friend.

(Then, things are not yet quite as I imagined!) Sir Godfrey,
after a pause, continued the conversation. With true deli
cacy, he did not oppose my wish; and I shall still earn my
own bread honorably and usefully. It is far the best: an idle
life would kill me. Work, constant work, is the sustainer,
cheerer, and physician of the soul.

But that fact alters not the noble kindness of this most
noble man, kindness of which I can hardly write or speak,
but which I shall remember while I live.

After our talk we joined the others, until I came up softly into my own room, to be quiet and rest.

Henry provided for—placed where his career through life lies, humanly speaking, in his own hands; Aleck given his heart's desire : how happy my two boys will be. And how thankful, solemnly and deeply thankful, am I!

Sitting at my little Gothic window, I can see him—I mean Sir Godfrey—walking on the lawn, with Lady Dorothy and little Lady Anne. How happy he looks; happy as a man must be who diffuses happiness wherever he sets his foot. Such a man I knew he would become! God bless him— God evermore bless him! And what does it signify how far off one stands from great treasures, eternally set aside, when one knows of a certainty that the gold has not become dim, that the fine gold will never change!

" Bonnie Ladie Ann" comes this instant bounding in at my door, discomposing all my thoughts. She is a thorough little elf of mischief; nobody would ever dream she was an earl's daughter. Nothing will serve her now but that I must come into the chestnut alley, where Sir Godfrey has had put up for her a most aerial and magnificent swing ; where, moreover, he is actually going to swing her himself, and the merry, frolicsome Lady Dorothy too. They say I must go, if only to play propriety among such madcaps.

So I must just finish my journal in the afternoon.

. . . .

————

" *In the afternoon*"—these are the last words I find written down in the journal so long put aside.

Since then, many, many afternoons—many days, weeks, months—have gone by ; and out of it all I wake, as out of a nightmare dream, to live the remainder of my life—how ?— God knoweth !

I think it will do me good to write down a plain account

of the strange things which happened, beginning from that
moment—which the sight of these pages causes to seem fresh
as yesterday—when I laid them safely by, the ink scarce dry,
took the child's hand, and, almost as gay as a child myself,
ran with Lady Anne to the chestnut alley.

I had always a great love for the sight of chestnut trees in
spring.   These were very beautiful—great towering pyra-
mids of soft green, for they had not yet come into flower.   I
remember Sir Godfrey showed me a bud, and reminded me
of my once saying, in my girlish nonsense, that if I ever owned a park, I would plant it all over with horse-chestnut trees.
At which both I and they all laughed—we were merry
enough to laugh at every thing.   For me, it seemed as if a
spell were over me, some sunny reflex from my former days.
Once I quite started at the sound of my own mirth ; nay,
even Sir Godfrey Redwood turned round, and said cordially
and merrily, " Why, that's right !   You are laughing just
like Felicia Lyne."

From this strange excitement I can only account for my
doing—what in a staid old maid and a governess might seem
rather out of place—namely, that I joined in the frolic, and
suffered myself to be persuaded to take my turn with Lady
Dorothy and Lady Anne in the swinging, an amusement of
which in my girlish days I used to be passionately fond.

It made all those girlish days come back again : I can
feel it now—the wild delight of flying through the air every
minute higher and more daring, touching the leaves of lofty
boughs, which nothing touched but the birds ; sweeping backward—forward—with my bonnet falling off, and my hair
dropping over my face ; hearing Lady Dorothy clap her
hands, and little Lady Anne scream with delight.   Even
Sir Godfrey, forgetting himself, cried " Bravo, Felicia ! " entering into the scene with all the excitement of a boy.

I remember, too, that he said something about " swinging

me straight, on account of the tree"—an old withered trunk that stood near, rather in the way; and that I laughed at the notion of danger, when *he* was there.

So I was dashed on from height to dizzy height, his great strength urging me forward, till once, when his hand was on the rope, little Lady Anne cried out suddenly—

"There's Maud !"

I felt the swing sweep forward aslant, then a heavy crush ing blow—darkness—and no more.

. . . .

When many hours, nay, days, afterward, my right senses came into me again, I awoke to the knowledge, kept from me for a long time, yet gradually revealed, that I should be disfigured and crippled for life.

The only balm to this misfortune, was the consciousness *whose* hand had unwittingly caused it all.

(Writing this sentence, and confessing this thought, I feel to be selfish ; yet it was true.)

I believe Sir Godfrey Redwood was for many days almost out of his mind with grief. *He* could not feel what I did— that any thing coming from him, was to me far less bitter than had it come from any one else.   And, as even my two poor distracted boys must have seen at once, and did see— the whole circumstance was so entirely an accident.

Of course, I can not recollect any thing of the time when my life was in danger ; and every one has appeared reluctant to speak of it to me afterward.   Only, as I now and then hear, it was a terrible time to them all.   It seems very strange to think of the Redwoods and Airlies hanging, as it were, on my breath—such a frail, useless breath as mine.

—I write this account in pauses, as my strength is still not great. . . . .

It is always painful to dwell on sickness ; and in this

mournful world we ought never to give to ourselves or others
a single unnecessary pain. I shall quite pass over my long
illness ; out of which I woke, and found the harvest ripened,
and the reapers reaping, around Redwood Hall.

It was exactly like wakening into a new world. Only,
not that world into which, I pray God, I may one day
awake, to be, instead of what I am now, evermore beautiful,
active, and full of joy.

The first time I quitted my room was quite like a triumphal procession ; for all the Ladies Airlie had come down
from London to see me : indeed, Lady Maud had been more
or less at Redwood Hall the whole time. Sir Godfrey's public duties kept him much from home, which was a blessing ;
it must have been great torture to him, to come back while
I was miserably lying there. They would not let me see
him all the while.

Therefore, our first interview occurred when I was compar
atively well. I was alone when he came in—he had begged
that it might be so—and—but my heart fails me when I recollect those two hours.

" Forgiveness !"—forgiveness from me ! That, looking in
my face, which much suffering must have changed considerably and doubtless made quite old, he should have burst into
such uncontrollable agony ! That he should have kissed my
poor, thin right-hand—the only one he could kiss—and that
I should have laid it on his head—his noble head !—telling
him I was quite happy, and regretted nothing, except that I
could no longer be a governess.

He seemed to shudder at the word, and passionately as
sured me that I should never want any thing his whole for
tune could bestow—that his own sister should not be more
honored, or regarded more tenderly than I.

—I am quite sure, and was then, that the word " sister"
burst from him instinctively, as being the very impulse and

echo of his thoughts. It was well that I noted this, otherwise, from the passionate emotion of his whole manner under
the agony of such a time, I might, as has happened often to
weak women, have been somewhat led astray, so as to form
erroneous conclusions.

Afterward, when he had become more himself, and his
mother and Lady Dorothy had joined us, he insisted on taking
Harry's place, and carrying me into the other drawing-room.
I could say nothing, being very much exhausted. And so it
happened, that while he was holding me, I fainted in his
arms. I believe, for an hour, they all thought I was dead;
I wish—but no! I will not utter that sinful longing.

After I had recovered, I was left to sleep; ay, and did
sleep, heavily too, for a long time.

Waking at length, it was to an atmosphere of such twilight dimness and silence, that I hardly recognized my own
room. My brain must still have been somewhat confused, as
I remember thinking I was really dead, and lying quite still
and motionless, like a corpse, until gradually I gathered up
my ideas.

The white curtains were closely drawn, so that I could see
nothing; but I began to distinguish a soft sound of talking,
and to recollect that I had gone to sleep, with those two kind
girls—in whom it was the least of their nobility that they
were an earl's daughters—sitting by my bedside.

Lady Dorothy was speaking in a whisper, but still with
that strong energy which, as in all impulsive characters, continually gleamed through her mirth.

" I tell you, Maud, as I told him this day, *he ought.*"

" If '*he ought*,' and thinks so himself, Sir Godfrey will
probably do it: he always does what is right," was the
answer, very slow and quiet, even for Lady Maud.

" It would be right; it is what a generous man ought to
do; it is the only reparation he can make her. I told him so."

' And what did he say ?"

" Nothing ! he seemed shocked—stunned, as if he had never thought of it before. Yet it is not such a wonderful thing. If her health returns, even lame as she is, and will be always, he might have a worse wife than Felicia Lyne."

" Hush ! softer !"

But the caution was too late ; I heard all clearly now : for which, most earnestly I now thank God !

" So you think," said Maud, tremulously—" so you really think she cared for him ? He once confessed that. long ago, when he was quite a boy, he was half in love with her. And any one whom he loved or who loved him—Yes ; I am glad you told him he ought to marry her."

Then again fell around me the silence—the twilight gloom—almost like that of the grave ; but crossed by floating shadows as of another world.

In the midst of it, I heard Lady Maud softly rise, and go out ; and then I called to Lady Dorothy, said I had wakened much better, and bade her go down stairs.

Next morning I heard accidentally that Sir Godfrey Redwood had been obliged to leave hastily for town. I do not know any thing more that passed in the household : all things to me seemed a strange, dizzy dream ; and I noticed no one but Lady Maud.

The " white lily" never bent nor drooped ; but looked wanlike, as though in the coming shadow of its life's first storm

——

Two or three days after then, when I was beginning to feel myself again, I received a letter from Sir Godfrey Redwood. It contained an offer of his hand.

All in it was said nobly, frankly, truly. He told me—what I was glad to know—that he had loved me, boyishfashion, for a little while, until circumstances made our paths

so different ; and a man can not live upon a dream, as sometimes women do.   He made no allusion to my loving him, or
his loving me, now ; but merely offered me his hand, with
the promise of spending his whole life in honoring me and in
securing my happiness.

My happiness !   As if I would have accepted a whole life-
time of joy, did it cost him one sacrifice, one regret !

I answered his letter, saying, not untruly, that I had long
given up all thoughts of marrying ; and that it would be
much better for us both that he should still hold me, in the
words he had lately used, as his " sister."   There was no
need to say any more.

In so doing I took counsel of no one, told no one, except
Lady Maud.   To her I mentioned the mere facts of his letter and of mine, that she might know how nobly he had acted.   She listened quite silently, as she sat by my bedside,
only I saw, for one of the few times in her life, her falling
tears : then she left me to sleep.   I did not sleep, but lay all
night quiet and happy, happier than for many years, thinking a little of this world, but more of the world to come—of
my mother—and of God.

The next day Sir Godfrey Redwood wrote me a long, affectionate, brother-like letter, pledging himself to that affection
which I desire to keep, and believe I shall keep, to my dying
hour.

—The day after that, he came home.   Lady Maud and
my two brothers were with me when he entered.   He met
me with cordial tenderness and joy, and when his eye fell on
the " white lily"—

I need not say more, but that _that_ happened which
was sure and right to happen ;—ere the week ended, we
all knew that there would be at last a Lady Redwood of
Redwood Hall.

I have **thus** told all that has happened within this year, which has now circled round to its close.

In the early spring, Lady Maud **Airlie** will become **Sir** Godfrey's wife: and Mrs. Redwood will necessarily form a new establishment. **She** has asked me **to come** and live with her, at all events for a year or two ; **but I had** rather go home—to the quiet and comparatively humble home made for **me by** my dear Harry. I can **not** tell clearly how things **are** settled, as since I have been ill, he and Sir Godfrey do with me as they please. I only know that Harry says, " Sister, come home ;" I shall go to him, and be at rest.

With this year begins a new life, if indeed I live, **as the** physicians say I may—and as I **would** desire, though from the only reason, that my living on for a few years **longer** might save from pain him with whom **my** death **would** leave a continual **pang.** But, **in any case,** I shall write my journal **no more.**

....

" No more !"—Well ! a resolution kept for fifteen years may be considered sufficiently strong : and so now, having all but crossed the half-century of existence, I may be at liberty to finish my journal.

I don't think, though, that I ever shall find time to finish it. All the day I am as busy as busy can be ; and besides, how can **one** write with **the** nursery overhead, and hearing through the ceiling the pattering feet of such a host of little Lynes ? If Au tie can not run about the house, they can, goodness knows ! The mamma of them had need to be the sensible, energetic woman she is—Mrs. Henry Trevethlan Lyne.

I wrote down once, in strange foreboding, the old heathen

apothegm, " No man can be called truly happy until he dies."
I add to it now the Christian saying, " No man can be called
truly *unhappy* until he dies."   That is, so long as God gives
life, He also gives the possibility of enduring and even enjoying it.

I did not learn to think so all at once, and even now I
have occasional fits of depression, hard enough to bear; but
my abiding sense is that of great peace, cheerfulness, and
thankfulness.   Some people even go the length of calling the
little sitting-room, where of necessity I am much confined,
the " Bird's Nest," from its being an atmosphere so cheery,
pleasant, and warm.—Of which title I, the owner bird, am
mightily proud.

It was some years before I regained the use of my left
arm ; and even now I can scarcely manage to walk.   But
my darling Harry was to me from the first as " feet to
the lame ;" and since he married, I have gradually gained
six pairs of little trotters, all at my service from morning till
night : so I sit in as lazy state as an eastern empress.

Only, at intervals, finding it impossible to be idle, I give
up " the empress," and turn once more governess, quite in
amateur fashion, with no other salary than kisses.   With
this excuse, I gather into my bird's nest whole flocks of young
folk, not only our own tribe, but those of other people.   In
this way there came to me last week, as they do not seldom,
the little Godfrey and Anne Redwood.   I think, after all, I
love those two children best !

Lady Dorothy—poor and portionless as she was—has
gained a strawberry-leaf coronet ; but "little Lady Anne" is
still Lady Anne Airlie.   Time enough !—and except that
such a climax would be quite too romantic, save in a story—
I have now and then vague notions that when Aleck gets—
what Sir Godfrey Redwood tells me he is quite sure of ere

long, we might possibly hear of " the Dear. of So-and-so and Lady Anne Lyne."

Mentioning Sir Godfrey's name, I can but add to it- -what all the world adds—a blessing.   May that blessing follow him, as such a noble man deserves, to his life's end.

I have no more to say.

H

ALICE LEARMONT.

A Fairy Tale.

MY GODCHILD ALICE.

(A TENDER WISHES AND FUTURE HOPES,)

𝕴 Dedicate this Book.

ALICE LEARMONT.

CHAPTER I.

" I WONDER at ye, Mistress Thomas Learmont. It's no canny to do sic a thing."

" What mean ye, my gudemither ?" wearily answered the person addressed—a woman, young and gentle looking. Her figure was wrapped in a coarse mantle of Lowland plaid, and her head-dress was a humbly-fashioned imitation of that we see in the likenesses of Queen Mary Stuart. Still, fair womanhood transcends all quaintness of costume, and Mistress Thomas Learmont was very comely to behold.

" Gudemither's a coarse word ; yè ought to say ' Dame Learmont' to your husband's mither," stiffly observed the ancient gentlewoman. " But I was gaun to speak to ye anent your wark there."

" Aweel !" softly said the younger lady—a lady in form and nature, though possibly not quite " a lady born." As she spoke, the color came into her face, and she looked with eyes wherein shone a heavenly light on her handiwork—the last crowning handiwork of her mother-joy. She had been banishing the cobwebs and dust from an old oaken cradle, and hiding its worm-eaten holes with white curtains tied with green.

"Ance mair, I wonder at ye," sharply repeated Dame Learmont.

The poor young creature looked troubled. "I wish ye'd tell me your mind, my leddy. I'm but a puir peasant lassie, and dinna ken a' ye ken."

"I said that when my son married ye. But ye needna greet, Marion—let byganes be byganes," added the old lady, growing more pacified. "It'll a' come richt when I hae the bonnie bairn in my arms. And that minds me o' what I was gaun to say. Ye foolish lassie, I marvel ye daur put on the wee cradle sic braws as these."

"What's wrang, gudemither?"

"It's the green, Marion, the green;" answered Dame Learmont, in a mysterious voice. "Wad ye put ae thing that's green near your bairn, and you a Grahame?" *

"I am no a Grahame now," said the young wife, with a gentle smile.

"But there's the old blude in ye still, ye canna change that (mair's the pity);" added the mother-in-law. "And if it were not sae, do ye no ken the blude o' whilk comes your husband?"

"Na, na," sighed the young woman, absently; and her ear was bent intently to catch every footfall that might reach the dilapidated chamber where they sat.

"Your husband, Marion Grahame, comes frae ane that nae mortal grave hauds this day. Did ye never hear o' True Thomas—Thomas Learmont—Thomas the Rhymer of Er-cildoun?"

"Gude save us!" muttered Marion.

"Him that wonned into—the land ye ken o' †—for seven lang years, and came back; then was sent for by the gude

---

* Green, the fairies' color, is always fatal to be worn, especially by the Grahames.

† It is counted unlucky to mention the fairies or Fairyland by name

folk, and never seen mair. Frae him, after many generations, came his namesake, Thomas Learmont, your bairn's
father. And yet ye daur to tie the cradle wi' green !"

The old woman advanced and attempted with her feeble
hands to undo the ill-omened ribbons, when a shadow passing
the window—for it was twilight—made young Mrs. Learmont
start and scream.

"Ye're a foolish lassie, flitched wi' ony thing. It's only
Daft Simmie o' the hill at his sangs. Hear till him."

And the old woman, whose superstition seemed only to
make her more strong and fearless—even in these days confessed ghost believers are often bolder than spiritual skeptics,
who deny because they inwardly tremble to admit—the old
woman grasped her daughter-in-law's arm and made her sit
quiet, listening to the wild but not unmusical boyish voice,
singing fragments of a Border ballad :

> "High upon Hielands and laigh upon Tay,
> Bonnie George Campbell rade out on a day.
> He saddled, he bridled, and gallant rade he,
> And hame came his gude horse—but never cam he !"

"Oh, gudemither !" cried the young wife at the latter om-
inous words ; and once more she listened for footsteps, or
horse's tramp.

"The gloaming's unco dark," Marion whispered : "the
three tops o' Eildon Hill look like ane i' the mist. Isna my
husband lang o' comin ?"

"Haud your tongue, Mistress Thomas, ye're no fit for
a Border wife. My son sall come and gang as it pleases
him."

"Aweel, aweel," again patiently sighed the young creature,
and played with the ribbons of the yet empty cradle, until
the voice of Daft Simmie made her start once more.

It was other verses of the same ballad, sung in shrill tones
just under the window

"Out cam his mither dear, greeting fu' sair,
Out cam his bonnie bride, reiving her hair,
The meadow lies green, and the corn is unshorn,
But bonnie George Campbell will never return.

"He saddled, he bridled, and gallant rade he,
A plume in his helmet, a sword at his knee;
But hame cam his saddle, all bluidy to see,
And hame cam his gude horse—but never cam he!"

Hardly had ceased the song, which in the gathering darkness sounded almost like an eldrich scream—when as if in strange coincidence, the clatter of a horse's hoofs came nearer and nearer.

"It's himsel, it's himsel!" cried the young wife, as she leant out of the window, beneath which the animal apparently stopped.

He stopped—the good roan—the last valuable possession of the impoverished Learmonts—stopped of his own accord, for he was riderless!

A wild scream of despair burst from the unfortunate Marion, and she was carried into her chamber insensible.— Ay, even to a mother's throes.

Dame Learmont was of the ancient race of Border-women, fearless as the men; she uttered no shriek, even when she saw that her son was missing;—such things were common enough in those days. The descendants of True Thomas had changed from seers and rhymers into men of warfare :— Ishmaelites, whose hand was against many, and many a hand lifted perpetually against them. The mother guessed what had happened;—that in some sudden fray Learmont had been thrown from his horse, wounded or—though even her bold spirit quailed at the latter fear—dead.

"He gaed ower Eildon Hill this morn," mused she; "and at noon there cam by Willie o' the Muir, wi' Geordie Grahame, Marion's cousin, that bears her husband nae gude will. If they hae foughten there'll be bluid on the roan. I'll gang an' see."

She left her daughter-in-law's couch and went near the horse, who still stood under the window, shivering in every limb, his mouth and flanks white with foam. But there were on him neither wounds nor blood; his accoutrements were not disordered; and, except for the overwhelming terror that seemed to possess him, there had evidently come no harm to the animal. Nay, even the small burdens fastened to his back were safe; as well as a leathern pouch of money that had been thrust under the pommel of the saddle.

" Geordie Grahame or Willie Muir wadna hae passed this by," ironically said Dame Learmont. " It must be o' his ain will that my son stays. Yet's that no likely, considering his puir wife in her trouble; and this being Hogmanay nicht too—an eerie and awsome nicht to be abroad."

As the mistress spoke, some of the farm-servants trembled and looked over their shoulders, while others examined the horse's disordered mane and tail.

" Maybe, *they* hae been riding him—the wee folk. Eh, neighbors, look ye here ?" whispered one man, showing in the good roan's mane the knots which are called elf-locks, and are supposed to be plaited by the fairies, who often have a mind to ride on mortal coursers.

Dame Learmont's eyes glittered, as if she felt more pride than dread in the uncanny reputation belonging to her family.

" It's likely eneuch, ' she said mysteriously. " The ' *gude neighbors*' will be abroad this nicht, as we a' ken ; and my son Thomas bears his great Ancestor's christened name. It is maybe nae mortal wark that keeps him sae lang frae hame."

" Gude save us !" " Lord hae mercy upon us !" cried the servants in various tones of fright, eying their mistress

H*

with considerable distrust. But though she evidently had
no dislike to bear the credit of supernatural powers, still she
was not disregardful of all human means that could explain
the absence of her son. She called the farm-followers and
questioned them closely, but none could give any information.

" Ye see," the brave old lady added, driven at last to
circumstantial evidence, "nae harm can hae befa'en him
He wasna fechting, or he wad hae stickit close to Red Roan.
An' he hasna been torn frae the saddle, but has lichted doun
o' his ain accord. Na, na, sirs ; there was surely ne'er a
fray."

Her resolute voice was answered by an idiotic whine behind the crowd ; and immediately afterward **Daft Simmie**
broke out in one of his queer quavering songs—

> " There were twa lads fechtin' on Eildon Hill,
>   With a hey, and a ho, and a hoodie craw ;
> The tane the tither's bluid did spill,
>   Ho ! ho, says the hoodie craw."

"**There's meanin' in it**," whispered the servants. " There's
aye a meanin' in Daft Simmie's sangs, and he sees sights the
whilk nane ither folk can see."

But the stout-hearted mistress reproved them, and catching hold of the lad, tried to compel him to plain speech. It
was in vain ; Simmie was either too foolish or too wise. Not
another word could be got out of him, and soon the "gudemither" was summoned back from her inquiries concerning
her son to the more imminent peril of his wife.

It was just betwixt the night and the day, at the precise
hour which forms the boundary mark of the old and new
year, that the child came into the world ; a remarkable period
of birth, being the hour at which, according to the supersti-
tions of many countries, the unseen world of spiritual beings
are supposed to have most power. At any other time, the
" auld wives" might have been struck by this fact ; but now

the whole household was smitten with such deep grief and confusion, that no one noted so unimportant an event as the birth of a child to the man whom they were beginning to conjecture had been that day murdered. Truly, had it been a boy, the unhappy young mother might well have christened her new-born " *Ben-oni*"—" the son of my sorrow." But she had not even the comfort of knowing it to be a son, born to avenge his father; it was, as the indignant Dame Learmont expressed it—" nae lad-bairn : just a puir, wee, skirling lassie."

It was put into the cradle—where the green ribbons still remained—the old grandmother was too busy and excited to heed them now. There the poor little morsel of humanity lay; while Dame Learmont, now somewhat at rest respecting her duties to mother and child, began to arrange a plan for finding out, dead or alive, her lost son.

Marion hindered her little, for the poor girl had never recovered her right wits. She lay in a dreamy unconsciousness until the child began to cry out from its little cradle. Then her poor white lips found speech.

"Gie me the bairn," she murmured; "Gie me *my* bairn.'

It was touching, the emphasis on the "*my*"—the first instinct of possession. I have heard women and mothers say that this instinct, dawning at such a time, was the most delicious joy they had experienced during life.

" Gie me my bairn," again wailed the half-conscious Marion ; and the child was given to her.

"Ye needna mak sic a girning and greeting ower it," muttered the old woman ; probably embittered beyond her wont by suppressed anxiety concerning her son. " It's no anither Thomas Learmont. It's only a lassie."

Marion took no heed. She lay with her white fluttering fingers pressed near the baby's face, talking sleepily to herself

" Mither, mither, are ye there ?"

" Ay, ay, lass," answered Dame Learmont: but a moment's observation showed her that the sick girl's thoughts
were not with her at all.

" My mither, my ain mither," continued Marion, feebly ;
" I ken ye're thinking o' me now, though ye're lying cauld
under the mools. Ye are glad it's a lass-bairn ; and sae am
I. I'll call it by your ain name ; it's a bonnie name—Alice
—my bairn Alice."

There sounded something supernatural in these wanderings
of a bewildered mind. The old woman stood aside, watching with a vague awe the countenance of her daughter-in-
law, who seemed talking to the air ; and that of the new-
born babe who lay staring out into vacancy, as young infants
do ; its wide-open eyes wearing that strange look which
seems as if infants saw things which others could not see.

" It's an uncanny time ; and maybe there are uncanny
Things about them baith," said Dame Learmont to herself,
in a frightened whisper. But before her fear could increase
she was roused by the sound of many feet and voices. She
looked down into the court-yard, and there saw the people
of the farm clustered in a group round what by the light
of their lantern, seemed—no living man, but a drowned
body !

The mother's heart, hard, yet still a mother's, recoiled at
the spectacle. She strained her feeble sight ; it was well ;
for now she had strength to see that the dead man was not
clad like her son. Yet this might only be a delusion. She
had just prudence enough not to betray any thing to the
young mother, who now seemed falling into a doze; she
took the infant away, laid it in the cradle beside the bed,
and then went hastily out, leaving the door ajar.

Now here, my wise anti-superstitious reader, I must
request you to pause. What I am about to tell, you will

find quite incredible and hard to be understood. I shall **not**
stop to **argue** with you at all. I shall only say that this **my**
chronicle is a consistent chronicle of its kind, the like **of**
which, stoutly verified by the peasants, may be found in
Nithsdale, Galloway, and indeed all along **the** Scottish
Border. I do but revivify in a more complete and connected
form the fragments **of** lore attested concerning a race of
beings whose peculiarities may truly be considered to belong
to pre-historic annals.

Marion Learmont was lying quite still, in a state of entire
exhaustion, which however was rather pleasant than otherwise, as if a lulling spell had been cast upon her. Her **eyes**
were half open, and she indistinctly saw the room—a **large**
ghostly chamber dimly lighted **by the wood-fire only ;** for
her mother-in-law had taken away the lamp. She was certain that she was awake, for she noticed **the several** bits of
furniture—the oaken chair, the sole remnant of worldly gear
which she herself had brought into the family on her marriage
—the rude table and the curtained top of her baby's cradle.
She even observed the snow lying in a thin drift along the
margin of the window-panes, stealing half-melted through,
forming a large round globule of water which rested on **the**
great Bible that was placed on the window-sill.

Gradually the red embers smouldered into darkness, **and**
the shadow cast from the door standing ajar, grew **blacker**
and wider. All at once she heard a buzzing, whispering, and
laughing ; a noise not loud but very sweet. Soon the ghostly-
looking shadowy corners were full of moving light. It came
from faces peeping in at the door. Then a troop of little
creatures entered one after the other, thick and fast, until the
whole room was full of them.

They seemed at first like very beautiful children. But as
Marion looked again, she saw they were perfect little men
and women, exquisitely formed, and gracefully dressed in airy

rebes of all colors—especially green.   The youths were armed
with quivers made of bright adders'-skin, and arrows of reed.
The maidens had long yellow hair, fastened back from their
shining brows with combs of gold.   Many, both men and
women, had their heads adorned with the flower called fairy-
cap, or with white convolvuluses.   Every one of them was
fair to look at, but chiefly the first who had entered, a lady
taller than the rest, who wore a crown either of diamonds or
dew-drops; Marion thought that never was there a coronet
so glittering, lucid, and clear.

The tiny visitors had brought no visible torches, but somehow the whole room about them grew light wherever they
tripped.   And they tripped about every where, in the mer-
riest, most fantastic round, continually following the tallest
lady, who came on more softly and gravely than the rest.

Then Marion knew that these were elves, and that this
was the Queen of Fairies who had loved and carried away
her husband's ancestor, Thomas the Rhymer of Ercildoun.

It was very strange, but though she seemed to guess all
this as by a sort of intuition, she felt not in the least afraid.
The sight was so dazzling, so delicious; its glamour changed
the dark old chamber into a fairy palace.   She herself, though
seemingly without the power or desire of speech, had no sense
of physical or mental pain—no grief concerning her husband
—no terror for her child.   She lay and listened in a sort of
spell-bound delight to the little people, as they talked, danced,
and sang, glittering hither and thither like a swarm of lumin-
ous gnats.

At last the Queen of Fairies, making a large circuit round
the window to avoid the " big ha' Bible," which lay there—
came and stood beside the baby's cradle.

Now, alas! the young mother knew what her elfin majesty
was come about.   But the knowledge was vain; Marion
received it in her mind without being terrified in her heart

All human feelings or affections seemed to have grown cold in the ecstatic delight of the fairy-show.

"It's a fine bairn, and a bonnie bairn—very!" said, in quite intelligible and most enchanting accents, the lady who had been True Thomas's love. "The Learmonts have not grown uglier in all these years—that is, hundreds of years—we forgot that we are on earth just now," she continued, sententiously, as ascending gracefully an extempore staircase obediently framed of the arms and legs of fairy-squires, she reached the top of the cradle, and sat down right in front of the babe's blue eyes—which, however, were fast closed.

"What very sleepy things mortal infants are, my ladies," observed her majesty. "I wonder whether she will wake when we get her to Fairyland?"

At this some slight pang of maternal dread smote Marion's heart. She tried to cry out, but just then the fairy-lady turned upon her her diamond eyes, glittering and gay, which looked as if they never had wept—could weep—or had need to weep. Their steely brightness froze up all the tears that were pressing under the eyelids of the mortal mother, born a woman, and as a woman made to know suffering.

"Behold her," said the fairy, laughing with a sharp, clear, bell-like mirth; "she is afraid! She thinks we would harm the wee thing! Not we! No, Mistress Thomas Learmont (a fine name that, but nothing like so fine as the first man who bore it)," and the little lady heaved a sigh, which seemed so light as to be only a pause in her mirth. "No, Mistress Thomas, I'll do your child no harm; if only for the love I bear to your husband's people, especially his great Ancestor and himself—ha! ha!"

"Ha! ha! ha!" laughed the fairy troop, with a merry meaning, and pointed out of the window. There, even through the darkness, Marion fancied she saw the white waves of the Tweed foaming and dashing, and the gray mists

floating almost in human shapes over the triple summit of
Eildon Hill.

" For the love I bear your husband," continued the Elf-
queen, " I will even let you see your bairn on her birth-night
every year for three years, and then once in every seven, according as she chooses ;—a fair bargain."

" A very fair bargain !" chorused the delighted little peo
ple.

But nature in the mother's heart was stronger than even
the glamour that was over her.   Though unable to speak, she
stretched imploring hands.   The blithe troop only mocked
her, hovering over her bed like a swarm of bees, and dinning
her ears with their melodious songs.   Once she tried to raise
herself and get nearer to her sleeping babe, but invisible hands,
soft and cold, like those of dead children, held her back ; and
the fairy-lady, sitting upon the top of the cradle, laughed at
her, making elfin grimaces which sent all the rest into a tit-
ter that rung through the room like the sound of the wind
through a cluster of waving rushes.

" It's useless, Marion Learmont ; you must just lie still
and dree your weird ; and this is not the only weird that
waits ye.   Quick—quick—my people ! the gudewife will be
back soon."

While she spoke, the poor mother saw the elves take up
her child, who wakened at once.   The queen looked at her
with her great bright eyes, and instantly a gleam of strange
intelligence came into those of the hour-born babe.

" She'll do ; she's a bonnie one ; there is not her like in all
Elfland.   Haste—get her ready."

Instantly two or three motherly-looking fairies, wearing
respectable silken robes and heather-bell caps advanced, and
slipping off the child's wrappings, left it a little soft lump of
beauty, fit even for the caresses of a fairy.

" A sweet wee pet, and fortunately not christened yet ; so

she shall be altogether ours, and we will find her a name in Fairyland.

But here the mother uttered what seemed to herself a heart-piercing shriek, but which was in fact only a low murmur of "*Alice—Alice.*"

"Very well, if it so please you, my good woman; I am quite satisfied. My elves, call her Alice," answered the Queen of Fairies, bending with a grace as winning as when she met the first Thomas Learmont under Eildon-tree.

"Alice—Alice," chanted out all the "wee folk," in a chorus ravishingly sweet. It was broken by a noise far less delicious and more mundane: the sharp clattering voice of Dame Learmont. At the sound the light in the chamber vanished; there was a rustling and murmuring, which at last ended in a faint shout of eldrich laughter—then silence.

The mother-in-law coming in, found her patient in an agony of grief.

"What for do ye greet, lassie? ye ought to thank God and sing for joy."

"My bairn! my bairn!"

"Ne'er fash yourself about it; the ill-faured wean. Think o' your husband that is alive, and Geordie Grahame deid. They twa had a sair tussle for 't, Daft Simmie says, for he saw them; Geordie fell intil the Tweed, and was washit up to our door-stane. But, I doubt not, my ain laddie's safe and awa."

"Far awa, far awa," groaned the poor mother. "And my bonnie bairn's gane too."

"Ye're daft or dreaming, Marion. Here's the bit thing soun' asleep."

She rocked the cradle rather roughly, but there was no cry or stirring from within. The little cap lay turned faceward on the pillow; there were the outlines of the form, carefully wrapped up so as to resemble a sleeping infant. But what was the grandmother's horror when she lifted it up and found—no living child, but a piece of wood, rudely carved into something like humanity, and dressed in the clothes of baby Alice.

" It's ane of Simmie's images—he has been at his deil's wark, and stown away the bairn," cried the old woman, as frantically she quitted the room, to set on foot a search for the missing child.

But whether this supposition was true, or whether, as the grief-stricken mother firmly believed, the fairies had carried away her darling, certain it was that all search proved vain, and neither Thomas Learmont nor little Alice could be found.

CHAPTER II.

WHITE, and in long wavy wreaths, lay the snow on Eildon Hill. The new year was not an hour old, and yet all about the three peaks it was as bright as day. Many a hardy mountain ram started in its fold, and trembled to hear the silvery ringing of fairy bridles resounding in the night air.

Great sport was the Fairies' Raid. On they came—a goodly troop, flashing along the high-roads, over the hedges, and through the plowed fields; on elfin nags—black, chestnut, gray—whose hoofs left no mark on the smooth snow. Yet what with their prancing and singing and laughing, the fairy folk made as much noise as a company of living horsemen. But it was like sounds heard in a dream, that fade the instant one awakens. And many a dreamer in Melrose that night heard such sounds, wondering whence they came.

"Heigho!" said the Queen of Fairies, as she reined in her palfrey at the spot where the triple-peaked hill divides. "Heigho! for my bonnie green wood, where I met True Thomas! It's all hewn down. Hardly would I know the upper world again. Very provoking! that people will plow and till, and turn waste-lands into meadows. They look much prettier as they are, do they not, Counselor Kelpie?"

This was addressed to the water-sprite of that name, an ugly creature, half-man, half-brute, who had crept out of the shallows of the Tweed to fawn at her majesty's feet.

"Ay, ay," he answered; "and for my part, if folk keep on growing so prudent and clever, building bridges and boats I will never get a living soul to drown."

"Ha, ha!" laughed the queen. "But, good Kelpie, have you kept safe the treasure I lent you—the youth that slew his fellow in an evil fray, and so fell into the fairies' power?"

"He is safe," answered the Kelpie, in a voice hollow as the waters rising in a well. "He lies in an underground cave, through which my river oozily creeps. He will sleep there until his wounds are healed; and there will not even be one wet lock in his yellow hair when you find him resting by the streams of Fairyland. But, oh! queen; if you would but have let Kelpie have him!"

"Could not, my ancient friend! Quite impossible. His great ancestor is growing tiresome now, and we want a new mortal in Fairyland. Besides, soon will come the seventh year, when we must pay the teind to hell."

A low wail broke from the fairy troop at the mention of this, the sole shadow on their perpetual joys—the tribute of one of their number exacted by the Arch-fiend every seven years.

But the pause was only momentary; for the elfin-race have an existence entirely soulless, free from human grief, affection, or fear. Soon again were the silver bridles ringing merrily up the white hill-side.

"Where is my changeling? Where is the child?" cried the queen, suddenly stopping.

"Here, gracious majesty! A weary burden it is too; human babies are so helpless and so fat."

And a fairy-lady toiled up; bearing before her on a palfrey the unlucky infant, who lay pale, cold, and half dead; a weight perfectly enormous for the elfin-steed to bear.

"Kanitha, guardian of the fairy youth, your salary shall be increased to four golden rods a year, if you do your duty by my small friend here. What ho! Alice, open your eyes."

The queen, dismounting, amused herself with poking her dainty fingers under the pale eyelids of the mortal babe, and

playing with its frozen limbs, white as the snow on which
they lay.

"Madam," observed a sage elf-lady, "it is a fact scarce
worth bringing under your highness's notice, but nevertheless
true—that earthly mothers are so foolish as to pay attention
to their babes—swaddling them warmly—hugging them in
their arms, and giving them nourishment from their own
breast. We never think of such trouble in Fairyland.
Nevertheless, unless something is done for this babe, your
majesty will be disappointed in your sport, for the little thing
will slip away in that curious fashion which mortals call
dying. It's a trick they have."

"How very unpleasant," said the queen. But she had
not time for more, when suddenly the chanticleer of some
honest Tweedside farmer began to cry aloud ; and far down
Melrose village appeared dim lights creeping about like
glow-worms. The world—the hard-working patient, much
enduring, yet happy world, was waking again to its New
Year.

"We must begone, elves ; we must begone !" Snatching wee Alice in her own regal arms, the Queen of Fairies
stamped, once, twice, thrice. Immediately the hill side was
cloven, and a dark gate opened itself before her. Thither
she passed with all her train. The earth closed behind them
—leaving not a trace along the mountain heather, not a footstep in the snow.

But far—far, through the underground passage went the
merry elves, up and down, along and across ; past valleys,
plains, and mountains ; through black and thundering rivers,
by smooth lakes, and over seas. The little babe in its deathly
stupor saw nothing of this : it lay immovable—its eyes sealed,
until at last they opened on a green bank in Fairyland—
Fairyland, which was like earth in its gayest aspects ; a
region of perpetual, unvaried pleasure ; a clime where there

was neither summer nor winter: a day which knew neither
noon nor night; a sky in which was never seen either sun
or cloud. So live the fairy people; an intermediate race,
created for neither earth, heaven, nor hell.

Alice Learmont came to life again there. The little
limbs stretched themselves out, the eyes opened, and the first
sound she uttered was that with which we mortals enter
into the world, and which we must utter at intervals, until
we cease to suffer and to breathe together—a cry of pain and
anguish.

It was quite new to fairy ears. All the little people stopped theirs, and bounded about in disquiet; doubtless thinking
their mistress had brought a most unpleasant element into
the elfin society. And when the unhappy changeling rolled
its heavy head about, and helplessly stirred its fingers, they
began to mock and sport with it, as being a creation so very
much inferior to themselves.

" This will not do," said her elfin majesty, with dignity, " I
had another intent in entering the door which Dame Learmont
so kindly left ajar for me. I wished a babe, new-born, unchristened, who might receive with our teaching something
of the elfin nature, and so be content always to stay in Fairyland. For,"—and her majesty shrugged her fair round
shoulders, beautiful, though laden with gossamer wing-like
appendages that might have been considered unbecoming in a
mortal—" for it is a curious and altogether unaccountable
fact that these human folk are never satisfied; and even my
True Thomas has a hankering after the troubles of earth
sometimes. As for his descendant, this wee lady's father—
I vow I shall scarcely be able to keep him a year of his own
free will.

" Oh! oh!" exclaimed the sympathetic elves, in token of
their wonder and indignation.

" Now, my subjects, see what I intend to do; we'll turn

this coarse bit of humanity into a creature something like ourselves. Behold!"

She touched the infant's head with her sceptre, a silver lily—and soon the inanimate meaningless features grew into the beauty of sense and consciousness. The eyes became quickened to distinguish objects, the lips seemed perfecting themselves into **speech.** It was the face of a grown person, or of a child prematurely wise.

"Ha! ha!" laughed the elf; she seemed to do nothing **except laugh. "But we must** have a body to match."

She passed her hand down the weak, shapeless limbs, **and** they expanded into delicate form. The little girl stood upright on her feet, a tiny, old-fashioned figure—less beautiful than the **elves,** for, though fair enough, she was no fairer than she **would.have been had she grown up** as Alice Learmont of Tweedside;—a miniature woman, but, as her expression showed, gifted with little more than the understanding **of a child.**

"Well my changeling, **how** do you feel? what do you **want?"**

"I'm hungry," said the little mortal.

"Eh! she's a low-born lassie after all," cried the Queen of Fairies, turning up her roseleaf of a chin; "take her away, and feed her **with** milk from the fairy cows. I **must go** see after my grown mortal, my braw young Thomas Learmont."

A merry life they led in Fairyland, where a day lengthened out to the pleasures of a year, **and** a year glided **past as** easily and happily as a single day. Alice Learmont was as one of them; sprung at once from babyhood to maturity—at least the only maturity the fairies ever knew; **for** their existence was like that of perpetual childhood, without its sorrows They suffered not, because to feel is to suffer, and they never felt; all their life was sport, **and all their sport was unreal**

glamour.   Nevertheless, they were merry elves, and the little
child who would else have spent its first year of babyhood
sleeping on its mother's breast, was the very cynosure of all
elfin eyes.

"So, you seem satisfied enough with yourself, my little
Princess Royal of Fairyland," said Kanitha, the fairy peda-
gogue-ess ; "You have looked at your large image long enough
in that stream.   Truly, you are growing quite a coarse child
of earth, and very like your mother."

"What is a mother ?"

"A thing, my little lady, to be all that I am to you—in
the way of feeding and rearing you.   But you will see for
yourself to-morrow, for it is your birth-day, and our merry
mistress will send you home for an hour."

Alice began to cry.

Now crying was an original and hereditary accomplishment
which the little mortal had, and which was quite unknown
in Fairyland.   Whenever she set up a wail—which she did
in true baby fashion—the elves immediately stopped their
ears and skipped away.

Therefore, before the changeling had screamed for a minute,
she found herself lying alone amidst the remnants of the feast
and the musical instruments of the dancers.   Even a vocal
concert that was being carried on in a large water-lily leaf,
had ceased : the performers, six aquatic elves, and their tutor,
an ancient frog, having dived under the bulrushes, in agony
at being outdone in their own profession by a mere amateur.

Alice lay and sobbed—it might have been until evening,
but there is no twilight in Fairyland—no dawn, nor close of
day ; all is one unvaried brightness—a changeless song—a
shadowless picture.   As the child lay pulling the daisies—
that as she pulled them sprouted again—trying in how musical tones she could cry there fell across her a tall dark shade.

Now the.elves are small and have no shadow—therefore this stranger could not have been of their race. And when **he spoke it** was not in the speech **of** Fairyland, but with an accent quite new to Alice. Yet it thrilled her with an instinct of pleasure.

" Wherefore greet **ye, Alice L**earmont ? Hae ye ony sorrow ?"

" What is sorrow ?—I do not know. I'm crying to amuse myself," **answered** the little creature, as she looked boldly up at her questioner.

He was a tall man—past middle age—of grand and stately mien. His lips, close set, seemed as if they rarely opened ; for it was on them **that the** kisses of the **Fairy** Queen had left the wondrous spell that they could utter nothing but truth. He was the wondrous Seer—the Prophet who never foretold falsely—the Bard before his age—Thomas of Ercildoun.

Many generations had passed, since, following the mysteri**ous hart** and hind which came as **his** summoners, True Thomas had vanished from earth ; and yet he still abode in Elfland, with the same aspect that he had worn when dwelling at Ercildoun and walking on Eildon Hill.

" Did ye never hear tell o' sorrow, Alice ? Then **the** Learmonts o' this day are aye happier than in my **time.** But I mind that ye were a new-born wean, just snatched frae mither's breast. Ye'll gang back to earth **the morn**!"

His voice was pensive, and the light of his eye sad ; but **Alice gamboled about, as** unheeding **as a** young fawn of the wilderness.

It **was the hour** when all grew quiet and lonely in Fairyland—for the elfin people were abroad working their merry wiles on the midnight earth. At that time Alice was always used to fold up her little limbs and go to sleep like a flower—for only flowers slept in Elfland. Thus drooped she

I

regardless of the presence of the stranger, and indifferent to
his anxious speech. He watched her a long time silently, and
then tried to arouse her.

"Waken, Alice Learmont! it's brief time that I hae for
speech wi' the youngest o' my race. Tell me, bairn, how
things are in my ain countrie? Rins the Tweed clear as
over, and does the sun glint as red ower bonnie Melrose?"

He sighed, but Alice only laughed "I know little about
it, old man; will you leave me to sleep?"

"Sleep?" said he, "sleep?—when ye are gaun hame to
your mither, and your father lies sae near that ye might hear
the soun' o' his breathing—every breath a sigh! Lassie,
lassie, look ye here!"

He lifted the child in his arms, and carried her to a river
side. There, bedded in the weeds and rushes, lay a stalwart
form, deathlike, yet alive. Water efts and bright-tinted fishes
were sporting over the large limbs; blue forget-me-nots
grew up and twisted themselves in natural garlands among
the yellow hair. The decaying garments were dropping
off from the manly chest, which yet heaved in regular suspi-
rations. He who thus lay, motionless yet living, bound by
elfin spell, was the younger Thomas Learmont.

"I'm wae to see ye, my son," softly said the Rhymer
"Why will ye gainsay them that it's vain to gainsay?—
It's no hard to live here in Elfland."

The youth turned and muttered, as if in sleep—"I canna
loe strange women, and I wad fain gang hame to my wife
Marion."

Thomas of Ercildoun sat down and covered his face with
his robe, in sorrow, perhaps even in shame.

Meanwhile the sportive infant leaped from him, and pad-
dling among the rushes, climbed up and sat astride on the
form of the spell-numbed man, crowing aloud with glee.

"Alice, the 'gude neighbors' hae made ye like themselves,"

said the old Seer, mournfully. " Else ye wadna be sae light
o' heart beside your puir father, nor when ye are sune to be
creeping to your mither's breast."

" Is that as pleasant as playing among the flowers, or
dancing in the grand halls here ?" cried the little changeling,
making queer grimaces, and comporting herself in all things
like a soulless elf. The Rhymer lifted his voice in anger,
when a low murmur of reproach arose from the younger
Thomas.

" It's just a puir bit wean, a twalmonth auld ! Alice,
gang back to your mither, and then she'll mind o' me."

The little child paused a minute, as if some natural instinct, awakened by her father's voice, were at work within
her. But soon she relapsed into her gambols, and then,
pausing to listen, clapped her baby hands.

" They are coming—the beautiful elves. I'm away, oid
man, away to my playmates."   .

Thomas the Rhymer looked up. There were clouds of
dust, and behind them a gallant company—the same that in
the days of his youth he had seen pass along the greenwood
side. It was, he knew, daybreak on earth, and the " good
neighbors" were speeding back to Fairyland. He stole away
from his descendant, in alarm and shame, lest his compassion
should work him ill ; and went forth to meet his elfin-
mistress, for whose sake he had forsaken earth and all its ties
for evermore.

CHAPTER III.

I TELL ye, gudemither, it was nae dream. I saw her—I felt her—my bonnie doo—my sweet lassie—my ain bairn ! She was wi' me this ae nicht—ay, i' these arms."

So sobbed out Marion Learmont, as she sat in breathless sorrow beside her wheel, by which she and her husband's mother earned their daily bread—two desolate women.

" The Lord keep ye in your wits, dochter, and forgie ye ae fancies ! Puir lassie, ye're a widow and childless, like my ain sel. For it's ower certain that your gudeman was drowned in the Tweed—and Daft Simmie—de'il take him ! has stown awa' your bairn. Ye'll ne'er see tane nor tither mair."

" Gudemither, I will !" said the girl solemnly. " There's mony a ane brought back frae the wee folk ; and my bairn's alive, for I hae seen her not four hours syne."

The old woman shook her head, but there was something so earnest in Marion's manner that she seemed rather less incredulous.

" Tell a' the truth, lassie. It'll do nae harm."

" It was i' the mirk o' night, just afore moonrise ; I waukened, sabbin' because o' a dream I had, that my puir bairn was sleeping at my side ;—and I felt a wee bit cheek, saft and warm, creepin'—creepin' till me ! It was a wean gudemither ! It was my ain Alice !"

" Gude guide us !"

" She lay here at my breast, wi' her sweet lips close, and drank, and drank—or it seemed sae. I tell ye, this ae nicht I hae gi'en mither's milk to my dear bairn."

" It's a' the wark o' the Evil Ane," whispered **Dame** Learmont. " But, Marion, lass, in what form gaed she **awa** ! In a flash o' fire, nae doubt ?"

" Ye speak ill, gudemither," cried **the young** creature, tried past her patience, " It's nae deil's wark—it's the wee folk that hae changed my bairn, as I tell't ye."

The old **woman shook her head** with **incredulous** pity. She did not **like that** any who were not strictly of the Learmont blood **should** attain to the honors of fairy intercourse. **Still, as** Mistress Thomas persisted, she grew more acquiescent.

" Maybe, Marion ; but then the bairn could be naething but a wee deil—a changeling."

" I tell ye she was my **ain** bairn."

" The new-born wean ye scarce set e'en on **?**"

" Na, na ; but a bonnie lassie—a twalmonth auld, **as she** wad be this day ?"

" Ance mair," **said Dame Learmont,** mysteriously, " ance mair, I ask—how did she gang ?"

" I dinna ken," sobbed Marion. " I **was** sleeping soun', **and** she slippit awa' frae my arms like a snaw-wreath, and was gane.   Wae's me for my bonnie, bonnie bairn!"

Thus sorrowed the forsaken mother, more, perhaps, **as a** mother than a wife ; for certainty, the slayer of **hope, is** oftentimes the healer of despair—and she, as well as **the** whole country side, believed that Thomas Learmont **had** been drowned in the Tweed and washed out **to sea.   But** nothing ever shook Marion in her statement that she had seen her babe carried away by fairies. And when the strange **story** which she told on the first anniversary after her loss was repeated the next year and the next, people began to look on her with awe and respect, not unmingled with a sort of dread

On the third New-year's eve the young widow—as she be

lieved herself to be—was sitting in the large room which in the days of the Learmonts had been the well-furnished farmer's kitchen. It was now desolate enough, for the two women—relicts of the last two of the race—were very poor. On this winter-night, Dame Learmont, sick and ailing, had been taken to the charity of some far-away kin; but Marion refused to quit her home. There she sat, heavily turning her wheel by the light of one half burnt fagot, shivering with cold, listening to the howling of wind and rain; or perhaps—so strangely thrilled was her mother-heart—listening for some other sound which she hoped would come.

"I winna try to sleep," she said to herself. "I'll bide, and see what this year brings."

So she sat and harkened, but heard nothing save the burring of her wheel and the noise of the storm without, until between twelve and one, the hour that marked the boundary of the old and new year. Then, in a pause of the rain, Marion fancied she heard a faint knock at the door.

"Come ben," she said, thinking it was a neighbor belated, and sorrowful that the hour of her accustomed joy had passed by.

"I can not come ben, unless ye open to me."

It was a child's voice; yet at once sharper and sweeter than a child's. Could it come from those soft, but always dumb lips, that had clung to her bosom yearly at this time?

Trembling, Marion tottered across the room, and unlatched the door. There in the bleak night, stood a little shivering child, dressed in a tattered cloak, with its arms all bare and drenched with rain. Alas! it did not look like her fairy child: but, nevertheless, the kind woman drew it in.

"Puir wee lassie, what gars ye stay out sae late? Hae ye nae minnie at hame? What for do ye greet sae sair?"

But the child made no answer, for no sooner had she been lifted over the threshold, than her crying was changed into a shout of laughter. The old rags dropped from her, and she stood in the centre of the dark, miserable room, a lovely three-years' child, dressed in the shining robes of Fairyland.

"It's my bairn, it's my bairn," cried the mother; as regardless of the wondrous glitter and supernatural aspect of the visitor, she ran to clasp her. But the little thing flitted from her, and escaped.

"Are ye no my ain? Will ye no come to me?" sobbed Marion in an agony. But Alice only laughed the more, and gamboled about the house without noticing her.

"Alice, Alice," shrieked the mother, following.

"Ay, I'm Alice. What do you want?"

This was all the child said, and continued her play. But the mother had at length heard the sound of her daughter's voice. The little one had even for the first time answered to the name "Alice." It was joy enough, and too much; Marion Learmont fell on her knees, and weeping, thanked God.

While she murmured her prayer, the changeling's wild sports and laughter were momentarily hushed; and a faint, sweet shadow of earth stole over the elfin brightness of her countenance. She came up softly, and said—

"What are you doing that for?"

"For thankfu' joy, that He may bless ye and save ye, my bairn," cried Marion, ceasing her prayer in the delight of embracing her child. But no sooner had she risen from her knees, and tried by tender force to hold her darling fast, than Alice slipped away, and laughed, and mocked, and played strange elfish antics, until even the mother's self was terrified. She began to weep, not now for joy, but for very sorrow The changeling only jested the more.

"How dull and queer you seem, big, dark-looking woman of earth! and what coarse clothes you wear, and what an ugly place this is! Where are your pretty gold tables, and shining clothes, and beautiful dancing-halls?"

"I hae nane, my bairn ; I am but a puir woman, that live my lane in poortith and care. But I wadna grieve, gin I had but ye, my dochter !"

And once more Marion tried to draw to her arms the bright being who looked a child and spoke like a denizen of Fairyland. For a minute or two Alice staid, seemingly amused by the novelty of caresses.

" What are you doing to me ?" she cried.

"I haud ye fast, my darling ; and I gie ye ae kiss, and anither—and anither," answered the mother, fearlessly pressing her lips to the soft hair that was bound with the garlands and redolent of the perfumes of Elfland. I loe ye, my bairn ; I loe ye !"

" What does that mean ?"

" Do ye no ken ? Did ye never hear o' love in Fairyland ? Oh, then come hame, Alice ; come hame !" sighed the mother, in passionate entreaty. But perpetually the bright creature escaped her clasp.

For an hour, which seemed a moment, yet an age, Marion Learmont watched the gambols of her elfin child flitting about the desolate house. Awe-struck, she crouched beside where the fire had been, and heard strange shouts of invisible laughter echoing Alice and mocking herself. At last, the house seemed to grow stiller, and Marion felt a drowsy oppression creeping over her. The changeling, too, as if tired out with play like a mortal child, had laid herself down, and suffered the mother to fold her in her arms. Thus secure, Marion yielded to irresistible weariness and fell asleep.

In the cold dawn she woke, but it was to stretch out her empty arms and moan. The child was gone. All over the house was silence, solitude, and gloom. Only, tinkling in her brain was a sort of musical rhyme, which seemed like a tune heard in dreams or just in the act of waking, and re-

membered afterward.   It had little connected meaning ; yet
still the mere words clung tenaciously to her memory—

> " Prayer o' faith is an arm o' airn ;
> —Whilk will ye hae, spouse or bairn ?"

While amidst her frantic lamentations, the wife of Thomas
Learmont paused to think over this rhyme, the first ray of
daylight glinted into the room, and rested on a relic belonging to her husband's family.   It was a portrait blackened
with smoke and age, yet now the face seemed to grow defined,
even lifelike.   She could have fancied that the eyes turned
toward her with a human expression of pity and gentle sad-
ness.   And she shuddered, remembering what awful tales
were told of that picture—the portrait of her husband's wondrous ancestor, Thomas the Rhymer.

She closed her eyes in terror, nor opened them again till,
in broad daylight, she saw it was only a picture on the wall

1*

CHAPTER IV.

FAR up the Eildon Hill there were footmarks in the New year snow: small light traces, as if some poor barefooted child had been there wandering through the night. But when the marks reached the Eildon Tree, they vanished suddenly and were no more seen.

The mortal child was once more in her home in Fairyland. She awoke, as if out of a sleep or trance, and found herself lying on the green-sward, in the warm light of that sunless day. She stretched her limbs with delight, and drank in the pleasant air.

"Oh! this is happy," she said, and began once more to revel among the flowers. She was alone, but that mattered little in Elfland, where all sought their own pleasure, and such a thing as sympathy was unknown. It troubled her when she saw coming over the valley toward her, that tall Shadow, grave and pale, who ever met her after her yearly visits to earth.

Alice tried to escape, and hid herself among the willows of the stream; but her laugh betrayed her, when looking down, she saw a brave sight and a merry—at least, so the elf-child thought.

There was the figure of the spell-bound man, the sport of all Fairyland for three years. He had half broken from his enchantment, and lifted himself out of the water; his long yellow hair and beard flowed down upon his breast, mingled with rushes and water-reeds; his eyes were still closed, but his face, unlike that of a drowned man, was bright, ruddy, and lighted with hope. Nevertheless tears quivered in the heavy lashes as the child approached.

"Wherefore grieve ye, my son?" said Thomas the Rhymer, as with slow footsteps he followed Alice to the river side.

" I see wee feet near me, the feet that are yet white frae
the snaw on Eildon Hill."

" And why listen ye to ilka sound, my son?"

" I hear a blithe voice ahint me, the voice that spak wi'
her yestreen.   Oh, Marion, Marion!"

The tones died away in a wail, as the young Borderer's
head sank upon his breast.

True Thomas gazed upon his descendant, and the pensive
repose of his own features was overshadowed.   "Gin I had
been like ye, a leal lover and faithfu' spouse, I hadna wonne
into Fairyland.   My puir bodie wad be lying saft aneath the
Tower o' Ercildoun, and the saints in paradise wad keep my
saul.   But what's dune is dune.   Even ye, my son, your ill
deed maun be punished; yet for a' that, ye sall gang back
safe to bonnie Melrose, and live happy, though in poortith and
toil.   For, as I hae foretold lang syne,

'The hare sall hirple on my hearth-stane,
    There'll ne'er be a Laird o' Learmont again.'"

So spoke he, with a grave sweetness, becoming the lips that
never lied.   At his words, strong shudders convulsed the
frame of young Thomas Learmont.

"Oh, it's hame that I wad be; hame, hame!" he moaned;
and his moaning went up to the pale sky, and his trembling
shook the glassy waters of Elfland.

Alice crept away, as if she feared or disliked the sight of
emotion, a thing to her unknown.   She went merrily to
watch beside the golden gates of the enchanted vale until the
fairy train returned.

Thomas the Rhymer sat and watched too.   His harp lay
at his feet—the same harp which had echoed in the Tower
of Ercildoun; sometimes he touched a chord or two, chanting
fragments of his own poem of " Sir Tristram," once so re

nowned, the very name of which is now scarce remembered along Tweedside. As he sang, his face shone with the calm and solemn beauty of middle age, which two centuries had left unchanged ; only that over all was a vague sadness and unrest which came at times, when earthly memories marred the even tenor of his elfin joys.

He had not long sat waiting, when from afar was heard the bridle-ringing that heralded the Queen of Fairies and her court. True Thomas laid down his harp and smiled.

" Ah," he said, musingly ; " 'tis a sweet sound ; I mind it weel. Blithely sung the mavis on Huntley Bank ; the grass was saft and green, and the gowans wat wi' dew. Oh, but ye were a May meet for a young man's luve, my bonnie Elfin Queen ?"

So spoke he, and behold afar the gallant train. In the midst of it, riding on her dapple gray palfrey, all in her green kirtle set with beryl-stone, he saw the lady of his love—even as she appeared to him the first time out of the greenwood by the hill side ; and his grave eye kindled like that of an aged poet at the memory of youthful dreams.

But the fairy lady was not given to dreaming. Merrily rode she on, her palfrey's bells ringing at every step ; a mingling of silver bells and silver laughter. Lightsome and heartless was the glitter of her eyes, and gayly swept she the Rhymer by, like the changed goddess of many a young bard's worship.

He followed her with aspect thoughtful indeed, but not love-lorn : he had no more lives of earth to peril for a moment of passion. Slow and grave was his step as he entered the elfin ring.

" Ha ! my True Thomas, hither you come at last : is it for news of the bonnie banks of Tweed and the gray tower of Ercildoun, where the white owl sits beside the ' hoodie craw' ? Would my bold Thomas wend thither again ?"

" Never mair, never mair !" sighed he : " But I wad fain hae speech wi' ye, my ladye and my queen."

" Say on, only sigh no more, it torments my merry elves. And we have been having a blithesome raid, up and down in the snow ; scaring and leading astray folk that have been abroad keeping their New-year ; ha ! ha !

'Lord what fools these mortals be !'

as sings a young English poet, whom I would say for sure had been in Fairyland, only he paints me so little after received tradition, and so much out of his own fancy, that I hardly know my own likeness. Eh, my elves ! shall we send home our ancient Rhymer, and go to Avon's banks to steal sweet Will ?"

" Ye sport and jest, my ladye and love," said True Thomas, sadly ; "ye heed not that the year's began—the seventh year. When its second morn appears, ye'll see the Evil Ane wend up that sloping road to claim the teind to hell."

Terror—the sole terror they knew—seized the fairy-folk ; the dances ceased, and the gitterns and lyres, falling from elfin-hands, began to wail of their own accord.

"Who fears ?" said the Queen. " Let the teind be paid ! I have a fine stout mortal fattening under Kelpie's hands, in the river near. Ha, ha ! my young Thomas Learmont will serve my turn well."

" Nae harm can touch the lad," answered the Rhymer, sternly. " He has a wife at hame wha prays for him nicht and day, to Ane that here we maunna name. I foresee that this same year a mortal will be won away frae Elfland."

" You grow bold in speech, my knight of old !"

" I speak wi' the lips that canna lee."

The queen looked as abashed and angry as it was possible for a fairy to look. " I marvel, True Thomas, that your vision extends no further, and that though you are grown old and ill-favored with two centuries of life, you do not see your noble self wending that fated road."

And she pointed to a downward slope blackening in the distance, from which all the elves turned their eyes, for they knew it was the gate of hell. On the other hand rose the thin cloudland of Paradise! while between both, like glistening fantastic towers with fair landscapes between, was seen the land of Faery.

The Rhymer gazed around, and turned to his mistress. "Do ye mind, my queen, the day ye laid my head on your knee, and showed me thae three sights? For your luve I wonned frae earth, and I hae tint heaven: but hell will ne'er open her mouth for me. I maun bide here in Faery for evermair."

"And grieve you at that, True Thomas?" smiled the winning elf, assuming the aspect by which she once wiled the youth away from Huntley Bank.

"I grieve not," murmured he; while his eyes glittered with a passion before which the mirth of Fairyland sank spiritless and tame—"I wad dree it ower and ower for siccan joy!—"

He sank kneeling at his lady's feet, and for a brief space, thought of earth no more.

But soon there came flitting near him little Alice, whispering—

"There's the man with the bonnie yellow hair moaning out—'*Hame, hame;*' and it frights my butterflies in the meadow—my bright fishes in the stream. I can not sleep or play for listening.—Entreat our mistress to send him 'hame.'"

So True Thomas changed from elfin wooing to entreaties for his descendant.

"Oh, the trouble you mortals give me!" cried the Queen of Fairies. "There are too many of you here: you will produce quite a revolution in our government. But for all that I can not let my handsome prisoner go. He began an evil fray and fell into the Tweed, hard fighting, he and his adversary together. The tide swept Geordie Grahame down while I stood by and laughed, for I knew that the other was mine."

"But no for aye. It's lang syne, yet Marion Learmont's saut tears fa'. She prays; and there's Ane that will hear. Send the young man back to earth, my gentle elfin queen."

" Ay, and then give back my fair changeling, too?—impossible! One or the other I must keep. So lie thee down, True Thomas, at my feet, and let us harken to wee Alice's songs."

But wee Alice, standing by, looked half-thoughtful still.

" The man is moaning yet. He wearies me. Let him go back to earth, and keep me in his stead always."

The Rhymer smiled, with the glad sense of a poet who beholds that noblest sight—a generous deed.

" My bairn—the dear earth blude is in ye yet: ye wad tine a', and win your father!"

" Father," repeated the child, carelessly ; " it is a strange word—I know it not. And what is earth to me? I spent a weary night last night, wandering there over snow and brier I would rather stay in Fairyland."

" But ye gaed hame, my bairn—hame to sweet Melrose ? ye sat by the ingle-side that was your father's ? ye crept close to your mither's knee ?" eagerly cried Thomas of Ercildoun.

" It was a gloomy place, dark and cold. There was a woman there, doleful to see. She never smiled, or danced, or sung, but only wept. It wearied me. I would rather stay in Fairyland."

" Then stay, my merry changeling," cried the delighted queen. " Not an elf in my kingdom shall live so blithely as you.—By all means stay."

" For seven years, nae mair," said the Rhymer, earnestly. " My ladye and queen, ye hae me by my ain will, for that

I first sought your luve, and not ye mine. Ay, and again I were fu' fain to tine my saul for your beauty's sake. But ilk ither mortal man, woman, or wean, ye may keep seven year and nae mair."

"My True Thomas, your earth-born honesty is very inconvenient in Fairyland. Nevertheless, away with the burly Border Squire ; and come, my bright Alice, and my lightsome eives, let us to our sports again."

That night, when the lights were out in all Melrose, and the new moon shone dimly on the snow—when the young Marion sat weeping by her fireless hearth, where even the cricket's song had ceased in the cold and silence—there came a step on the threshold—a voice in the darkness—a strong, close, passionate clasp, that she felt, yet saw not. But when the moonlight glinted palely in, she knew the noble height, the broad stalwart breast, the yellow hair.—It was the dead alive—the lost found.

Yet even on that joyful night, when marvels hardly seemed to be such, since love was ready unquestioning to receive all, many a time Marion would droop tearful on his neck, sighing out—

"Oh, hus and ! our bairn, our bairn :"

CHAPTER V

"Come ben, come ben, my bairnies a'!" softly cried a mo
ther—not a young mother now, as she stood by the ingle-
side, and threw on a fresh fagot, which merrily lighted up the
dusk of the winter night.

An old woman, bent and withered, cowered over the blaze,
and childishly watched it glittering between the joints of her
skeleton fingers.

"It's a rare fire, Marion," mumbled she : "we hae na
had the like o't for mony a New-year. Wow! but it's unco fine !"

"Aweel, gudemither, gin ye're content?" answered Mistress Learmont, half sorrowfully. "Yet, I'se warrant it has
been 'muckle siller and muckle dule,' sin the day the gudeman was awa' to serve the queen in Edinburgh. Eh! callants, I fear me ye'll no see your daddy this braw New-year."

So said she to the two sturdy bare-legged laddies that came
from the next room, toddling to the welcome fire. A third—
the eldest apparently, entered from without doors, bringing in
plenty of snow upon his shoeless feet and flaxen hair. For he
too was a "yellow-haired laddie," a true son of the Learmont
race. He was his father's very image ; a great fellow, whose
bulk almost belied the round, innocent face of six years old.
The other two were fat, sunburnt, roly-poly creatures—twins.
The last born, a delicate looking child who could just stand
alone, and whose sole speech was the dumb language of blue
eyes—was crawling about the floor—making vain efforts to
get nearer to the beautiful blaze.

They were all boys, these later blessings sent to comfort

Marion Learmont after her woes. There never came another daughter.

Every human being must change, more or less, in seven years. Mistress Thomas Learmont was a douce, matronly body now. She could chatter, and she could scold, though not often ; for she was of a sweet nature always. But she had to be both father and mother to her boys, in the absence of the gudeman, whom chance had lifted to comparative prosperity, as archer of the guard to Queen Mary. Mere infants as they were, there was their race's fierce spirit in the lads, so that poor Marion had sore trouble to manage them at times.

They had not been long gathered round the fire, when a domestic storm arose.

" Hey, Habbie, what are ye yaumerin' for ? Haud your ill tongue, Jock ! Wee Sandy, come and tell your minnie what ails ye. Oh, laddies, laddies, what'll I do wi' ye a'?"

" Why dinna ye wish the ' gude neighbors' wad tak them, and send ye back your ae dochter ?" grumbled the old woman. " I'd gie a' these ill-faured callants for ane bonnie lass-bairn."

" Ye didna think sae ance, gudemither. Gin ye had, maybe my puir Alice had been safe at your knee. Now, ye'll gang to your grave, and me too, wi' ne'er a dochter to close our e'en."

Marion sighed bitterly. Strange it seemed, and yet was not strange, that amidst the cares and joys which followed after, the mother never forgot her first-born. Year by year, as Alice's birth-night came round, she grew thoughtful, and watched with anxiety ; but never again, in any shape, vision, or sound, did the changeling appear. At last a sacredness like unto death stilled the pain of this heavy loss ; many other children came to comfort the bereaved mother—yet the wound was never thoroughly healed. Constantly, when the boys were to her cold or rough, as boys will be, she would sigh after the one lost blessing, which, like all vanished joys seemed dearer than any of the rest.

She sat by the ingle ; and, rocking on her knee the gentlest of the tribe, the little year-old babe, whose looks sometimes reminded her of Alice—gave herself up to sad thoughts, which on this New-year's eve seemed to come thicker and faster than ordinary.

"What for do ye greet, minnie ?" cried one after the other of the bairns, gathering round her ; for childhood's heart is always tender, and the wildest boys are often the most moved at sight of trouble.

Marion uncovered her eyes, to see Habbie and Sandy with great thunder-drops of tears in theirs ; while Hugh, the bold eldest, stood in an attitude of defiance, as if ready to challenge some invisible foe who had made his mother weep. Even the wee thing at her lap lifted up his sweet looks in troubled won-derment, and nestled closer to her, bringing unconscious comfort.

"Ye're gude bairns a'," said the mother tenderly, as she caressed them by turns. "But, oh ! ye arena my Alice—my ae dochter—that I will see nae mair!"

The children had often heard of their sister Alice, and had questioned about her with childish awe. With them she had grown into a sort of myth, to be thought of with grave faces, and spoken of softly. They had even set up a kind of rude service to her—children often have the oddest instinctive notions of worship. Many a tiny bowl of milk, or rosy-cheek-ed apple, was left on the "door-stane," or carried to some thicket on Eildon Hill, or placed at four cross-roads, in the vague hope that "Sister Alice" would somehow come and partake of it. And as, of course, the dainty frequently van-ished, they would come home feeling sure that "Sister Alice" had indeed received their gift.

Now, when they heard the rare mention of her name, they became silent and grave. Only Hugh, who being next eldest to the lost one, thought himself peculiarly privileged, took courage to say—

"Mither, dinna ye greet for Sister Alice; and I'll gang and speer for her ower the hale warld."

The mother shook her head.

"But I will, mither," cried the fearless boy. "What like is she?—When gaed she awa?"

It was a bold question; for Marion had feared to tell the whole story of Alice's disappearance to her young children, and had left their speculations thereon vague and dim. But, somehow, to-night her heart was opened and her tongue loosed.

"Bide ye here, callants, and I'll tell ye. What like was she?—she was the sweetest wee lady, jimp and sma'—wi' een like Willie's here, but oh, sae bright! She was ta'en awa on this nicht, the nicht she was born, just ten year sin-syne. She came back ance—twice—ilka new-year, and then nae mair. Ah, laddies, she came nae mair!"

"And whar is she noo, mither?"

"She's in a braw, braw land, blithe and gay, amang folk that it's no gude to speak o', my bairns."

"Then they're no gude ava," cried Hughie, boldly. "Maybe they'll gar her forget her minnie and us. I'll gang and fecht them a'!"

Marion laid her finger on her little son's lips, and, with the other hand, was about tremblingly to make the sign of the cross—but stopped, remembering what that good man John Knox had said, when last he preached under the shadow of Eildon Tree. Scarcely had she collected her thoughts and resolved not to fear, when through a pause in the blast which seemed suddenly to have risen, shaking the whole dwelling, she heard a sound that was neither wind nor storm.

"Eh! siccan a sight!" shouted the daring Hugh, who had rushed to the window. "Sax braw white horses dragging a thing like a wain, only bonnier far; wi' sic grand folk intilt, and mony mair ridin' ahint the lave."

"Surely, it's a coach, that fine new wain your daddie saw. Maybe the queen herself is there. Oh, bairnies, rin and hide!"

"I'll no hide," said Hugh. "I wad like to speak to the queen. Folk say she's a bonnie leddy."

Without more ado, this bold young scion of the humbled Learmont race unbarred the door, and walked out. Marion trembling followed. The coach and attendants had apparently driven away, for she saw them not, though she fancied she heard the sound of retreating wheels. There was only a faint glare, like that of invisible torches, cast on the road; and there she saw her son, escorting a brilliant little lady, who seemed neither quite a woman nor yet a child.

One frenzied hope darted through the mother's heart, but quickly it faded when Hugh rushed in.

"Mither! here's a bonnie wee leddy, sent frae the queen."

"Frae the queen? wi' news o' your daddie? Ah, she's kindly welcome," said the mother, but still she drew back in disappointment.

Hugh ran gallantly to the aid of his lovely guest, who hesitated at the threshold.

"Come ben, my wee leddy," said he, eagerly, apparently not in the least abashed either by her fair presence, or by her gold and jewels and gay robes.

"I can not come in, unless you lift me," murmured the dainty creature, in tones like a silver bell.

Hugh sturdily gathered up all the strength of his childish arms and carried her over the door-sill, into the very middle of the floor. There she stood—a beautiful vision, making all light about her, as though her very garments shone. But, gradually, the glitter paled off, and she seemed nothing more than a very small, elegantly-formed lady, magnificently clad but with the face and manner of a child.

Despite its change, and against the utter improbability of the thing, the mother fancied she knew that face. Trem blingly she advanced to the guest.

" Wha may ye be, my sweet wee leddy ?"

" I was not to tell my name."

" Wherefore cam ye ?"

" The queen sent me." And whatever questions were put the only answer that could be won from the little damsel was still the same—" The queen sent me."

Her sudden appearance and dazzling mien spread such an admiring awe over the little circle that they felt no power to question her ; but in their intercourse the little lady altogether took the initiative.

She flitted about the house, peering into every hole and corner with most amusing pertinacity. She played with the children and pulled them about, more with curiosity than interest ; and at last having fairly bewildered them all with her beauty, her willful ways, and her perpetual chatter in a tongue which at first seemed to them strange and court-like, but gradually became intelligible and more like their own— she called for something to eat.

It was supper time ; and the mother had been preparing bowls of porridge, turning every now-and then, with an incomprehensible yearning, to watch the movements of their guest ; yet evermore repelled by something in the fair creature's mien which told that her hopes were delusions, that it was impossible this could be her Alice—her child.

" I want some food," again cried the visitor, impatiently.

Marion got ready the children's messes. She set out five instead of four portions, and placed the first and largest before the stranger.

" Will ye eat wi' my bairns? ye're dearly welcome," said she, tenderly.

The little lady tasted the porridge, and threw it aside with

a gesture of disgust. " It is not like my food ; give me some
better."

It was strange, but the words and look went like an arrow
to Marion's heart.

" I haena ony better," she said, sadly. " Gin ye come to
puir folk's door, ye maun live as puir folk live."

The little damsel laughed, more carelessly than angrily ,
and with hungry looks suffered Hugh to place her bowl once
more within her hand.

" Bide a wee," whispered Marion, as she was about to begin. " My bairns, say your grace afore meat, as ye hae been
taught."

One after the other the boys—in this at least well-lessoned
—folded their hands and said a few words of prayer. At the
sound, the new-comer began to tremble and grow pale ; at
'ast she set up a loud cry—

" Oh, it hurts me—it hurts me !"

" What, my sweet lassie ?"

" Oh, my heart—my heart !" and she began to weep.

Hugh started up, but the mother put him back, and threw
her arms, brown and hard with labor, round the silken-robed
child.

" Tell me, in the great Name ye ken o', wha may ye be ?"

The girl struggled with difficulty to speak. " I'm Alice—
Alice Learmont ; let me go back to whence I came."

" I winna let ye gang, my ain bairn, my dochter !" cried
the mother, snatching her close, and sobbing over her.
" Come near, laddies, haud her fast—fast ! She's your sister
Alice."

Amazed, the children clung round ; some admiring her
bright clothing, and others half-frightened at the wild elfin
beauty of her face, for she was now smiling again.

But the mother wept still.

"Is it your ain sel', my dochter ?" cried she, fondling the

pretty creature who nevertheless every now and then tried to escape out of her hands. " Eh, but ye're grown a winsome lassie, your hair sae shining, and your skin sae white ! I wad-na hae kent my wee Alice, my ain dear bairn !"

" Indeed ?" said the little maiden carelessly, as she re-arranged her tossed hair, and smoothed her crumpled gear, too bright and gaudy for the touch of common mortal hands; " Was I ever in this ugly dark place before ?"

" Do you no mind o' that ?" said the mother, sadly , " Hae ye forgotten your ain mither ? Ye're a braw, braw leddy now, but ye were ance a puir bit bairnie in these arms."

Alice smiled with an air of indifference, and turned from the worn and pensive looking mother to the children, who, young, rosy, and fair, seemed more like herself and her elfin companions.

" Are these my brothers, and will they play with me, as the little fairy-children do in the land where I live ?"

" Eh, whar is that land ?" asked bold Hugh, the first who had dared to address their magnificent new sister.

" I know not, but it must be a long way off, for it's a country so much prettier than this." And she went peering about into dark and dusty corners, and curled her sweet lips in a half-scornful indifference at every thing she saw.

" Do you always live here ?" said Alice, when at last she and the rest had become more sociable ; " Where are your golden halls, and your silver dining tables, and your sweet music ? And why don't you laugh and dance—in this way ?"

Immediately she began to float and bound, with an air so ravishingly graceful and joyous that she seemed like a creature of light compared with the other children, who watched her in dumb wonder, Hugh especially.

" Is it thus ye live in your land ? Eh, but I never see'd sic a bonnie ploy !"

" And **how do** *you* amuse yourself?" asked Alice, with dignified condescension.

" When it's simmer, I rin about the braes, or amang the **corn**-rigs wi' the shearers ; **i'** the mirk winter days I haud **the** pleugh ; and then a' the spring-time I gang **wi'** the bit lammies on the hill. **I'll** show ye thae lammies, gin ye'll bide wi' us, Sister Alice."

She seemed amused and pleased, and her sweet winning looks stole **the** very **heart of the** affectionate boy. He went boldly **to his sister,** kissed her mouth, and hugged her close, **saying, " I'm** unco glad ye're come, Sister Alice ; but gin ye **hadna** come o' your ain will, I wad hae fought for **ye and** brought ye hame. Ye sall never gang awa mair."

" Never gang awa mair ?" cried Alice, mimicking him, **as** she stole slily out of his **embrace, and once more began** dancing about the floor.

The children forgot their supper in watching her, half with **shy wonder,** half with delight ; **so** graceful, so blithe was she, **so** utterly free from thought **or** care. But the neglected **mother sat** in a corner apart and mourned.

More than once she came to her child, and with piteous tenderness looked into those blue eyes whose brightness was never shadowed by one cloud of regret, **or** emotion, or love.

" Are ye no my Alice?" she would say, imploringly ; " **and** haena ye ae kiss for your ain mither that bore ye ? **Ah, lassie !** what wad I gie for ane wee wordie, **just** ' Mither,'— **naething** mair."

Alice shook her head, and laughed. " It's a new word ; I don't understand it." And then she went back to her sports among her brothers.

Merry sports they **were,** and with much wonderment she sometimes paused to listen to Hugh's harangues, very sensi- **ble for** his years.

" Ye're our ae sister, and we aye liked **ye** weel, though **we**

K

never saw ye. Why did ye no come hame ? Mither used
to greet for ye ; she aye loed ye aboon the lave."

Alice turned a curious glance to her mother. " What does
loving mean ?" she asked.

Hughie was puzzled. At last he tried a practical illustra-
tion. He wrapped his arms round his fairy-like sister, and
kissed her with childish fondness, which she did not repulse,
though she took it coldly and wonderingly.

" It means *that*," said he, " an' it means that I'll tak tent
o' ye, and I'll carry ye when ye're wearied, and treat ye weel,
and no beat ye—as I beat Habbie and Sandy ; I'm your ain
brither, and I loe ye, Alice dear !"

Alice paused in her frolics, and putting her tiny hand ameng
Hugh's curls, looked as if her eyes were drinking in from his
some strange new lesson of human affection. But, turning,
she saw in a tiny mirror her own fair image ; suddenly bursting away, she danced up to it, and became absorbed by pleasure at the sight of her glittering frock and her silver shoes.

The night wore on ; the old grandmother had gone to her
rest long ago, and knew nothing of the strange visitant who
had so fascinated the children. But at length even they grew
weary ; while the little elfin maiden still frolicked, her brothers dropped away one after the other—and came, in the wearied, peevish mood that very young children have, to take
shelter by their mother's side. Mistress Learmont soothed
them, and folded her arms around them, though in the troubled bewilderment of her own mind she did not attempt to
put them to bed. Whatever she did, or wherever she moved,
her eyes never quitted her beloved first-born, whom now she
left to her own devices, and tried to caress no more.

Hugh was the last to leave his sister, but even he came to
the ingle-side at length, rubbing his eyes, and looking dull
and melancholy.

" She's no like a real lassie. She's unco' fair and unco'

gleg, but she'll no be our ain sister," said he disconsolately,
as he gathered himself up on the hearth, and laid his head
wearily on his mother's knee. The twin-laddies were already
dropping to sleep beside her, and wee Willie had nestled close
into her bosom. Marion kissed them all round, tenderly and
with tears.

While she did so, she was aware of the approach of her
eldest child, who glided softly into the circle. Alice's eyes
were downcast, and there was a strange sadness in her as
pect.

" *Mother!*" she said, and Marion could have shrieked
with joy at the word. " Have ye got never a kiss for me ?"

" My bairn ! my bairn !" she cried, but could not rise for
the other sleeping children that clung round her. She stretched out her hand and drew her daughter into the circle. Slowly, neither with impulse nor with hesitation, Alice came.
Her bright face was rather grave, and there was a softer
expression in her sparkling eyes. She let her mother fold
her close to her breast ; and lay there quietly, though without any caresses.

But for the mother herself, her joy was unutterable and
without bounds. It forced itself out in sobs and tears, which
fell on the neck of the fairy child. Alice recoiled.

" I do not like that ; the tears wet me. Why do you
cry ?"

" For joy, my dochter. But I winna do't gin it grieves
ye." And Marion tried to smile and be merry, though her
heart was so full that the mirth seemed but an idle show.

Alice leaned on her breast with a quiet contented look—a
look subdued almost into earthliness—until the night wore on,
and the light on the hearth faded. Then she drew herself
away restlessly.

" It's very dark and dull, and I'm cold, mother."

" Come closer and I'll warm ye, my bairn ; I hae dune

that, mony a nicht, to thae wee lads your brithers, that were
born amid poortith, and cauld, and care."

Alice looked frightened, and shivered more and more. "Is
this what they call living on earth, mother ? If I had lived
here among ye, would I have been hungry, and cold, and
dressed in ugly clothes like you and my brothers there ?"

"I fear me, it wad hae been and will be, my Alice !"
sighed the mother. "But we'll tend ye close, and loe ye sae
dear—oh sae dear !"

In vague fear, the poor woman strained her daughter to
her breast. Her coarse garments frayed the tender skin, her
look and speech were almost rough in their passionate intensity. Yet the deep love in her eyes would to one who could
feel and respond to it, have atoned for and sublimated all.
But such a common-place, every-day thing as *love*, was quite
unknown in Fairyland.

Alice, half-frightened, half-annoyed, crept a little way farther from her mother. She had hardly done so, when a cock
crowing loudly from the farm broke upon the night's silence.
The children were all asleep ; Marion herself, despite her
struggles against it, felt herself overpowered as by a hazy dream. Just as the cock crew, she heard clearly, rolling nearer and nearer, the sound of wheels which had heralded her daughter's coming. She knew instinctively that
it was the signal for Alice's being snatched from her once
more.

She could not cry out or speak ; her tongue seemed bound.
She only turned her imploring eyes to the little elfin-maiden,
and saw with agony unutterable that the warning, to her so
dreadful, had brightened her daughter's face with joy.

"They're coming ! I will soon be back in my merry home.
Fare you well, good mother," cheerfully cried Alice, as the
wheels stopped, and a brilliant light glimmered through the
black window and under the chinks of the crazy door 'Fare

you well," she repeated, as with a sudden spring she bounded
out of her mother's desperate hold.

Marion's tongue was loosed ; she uttered a shriek like that
we sometimes utter in dreams. To herself it seemed the very
rending of her soul ; but it was in reality a mere sigh, not
loud enough to wake the infant who slumbered on her knees.

She felt the little maiden turn and pat her cheek for a
moment, escaping quickly and softly, like a bird out of the
hand.

" Don't cry, mother ; it makes you look not pretty, and it
hurts me. But I can't stay here ; I must go back to my
beautiful home."

There was a light tap at the door, which was merely latch-
ed. Now Marion knew that the fairies could only enter
through a door left open, or opened unto them. She tried to
rise, but could not. Then she made frantic signs to Alice to
bolt and bar the entrance, but in vain.

Another tap came ; for the daughter was pausing to look in
mingled wonder and doubt on the agonized countenance of
her mother. A third summons—and then, with her own
hands, the changeling opened the door.

A flood of light—a multitude of airy beings filling the
gloomy house, and Alice herself, blithe and beautiful as any,
flitting among them all !

It was but for a moment ;—then the vision began to fade,
and the mother knew that her child was departed. With a
vehement cry she called upon the one Name which all beings,
of whatever race, must obey.

The fairy-train paused, and Alice was left standing on the
threshold, her eyes wandering between the lowly home within
and the brilliant pageant without.

" What do you want with me ?" she said. " Must I stay
and live here in this house ? It is so dark, so dreary. Yet
my mother---"

She stood irresolute, looking at the little group among whom for one hour she had lain, encircled by caresses, and learning for the first time that there was a sweeter thing even than the perpetual pleasures of elfin-land. A little, too, she seemed moved by the despair with which the dumb, spell-bound mother stretched out imploring hands.

"Choose, Alice, choose," chanted the elves from without, as the glitter of their invisible torches flashed upon her, lighting up her fair countenance and her amber hair.

She turned; their elfin glamour was cast over her, and every rising emotion of earth and earthly tenderness was stilled.

"Farewell!" she cried; and without casting one more look at the dark cottage—the little brothers who lay sleeping where they had played with her—the poor mother, whose dumb anguish was all in vain—Alice passed from the threshold and disappeared.

ALL days and all years are alike in Fairyland. One after the other they glide, like waves in a river of which the current never changes. And though there are among these lightsome beings elves young and old, save that the infirmities of age are unknown; though as veracious chroniclers have asserted, they continually marry and replenish their community with elfin babes—still their existence flows on in a perpetual monotony; and their unreal pleasures remain always the same.

Four winters had the snow gathered and melted on the crest of Eildon Hill, since Alice vanished from her mother's cottage, on that last New-year's morn. But summers and winters make no count in Elfland; and it seemed to the changeling as if she had only been gone four days.

No extraneous power can change the eternal laws of nature, and, despite the will of the Queen of Fairies, the little stolen mortal had grown up to be a maiden of fourteen years. She was still tiny enough for an earthly damsel; but she walked the soft sward of Fairyland, casting a gigantic shadow which quite alarmed her elfin mates. Even the queen herself, who bore the stamp of royalty as the tallest of her race, and who in past times had actually prided herself on being able, standing tiptoe, to gird with her emerald girdle her earthly love, the Knight of Ercildoun—even the queen began to be indignant that her young handmaiden was an inch or two above herself, and was growing, she strongly suspected, very nearly as fair.

" Look at her, my True Thomas," her majesty observed

(for with true royal caprice, or from scarcity of stolen mortals she had of late gone back to her old love)—" Look how mundane she is, far too tall and round ; and her step is so heavy, it would crush half-a-dozen of my pet grasshoppers. Nay, she has even got a most unpleasant earthly gloom on her face ; as doleful as yourself, my knight, when you begin to dream of the old tower where the owls hoot, and the corbie builds."

True Thomas sighed.

" Would you go back to earth again ?" mocked the queen, in her pretty willful way ; " My sister majesty on the throne of Scotland is as fair, as love-winning, and—so you would say —as fatal in her love as myself. "Oh, it was a bonnie blaze that one night scared my elves who dwell underneath the Calton Hill ! and truly there is no moonlight riding over the plain of Langsyde for the ugly corpses that lie bleaching there ! Eh, would you go back to earth, my gallant Thomas ?"

The Rhymer's head fell on his breast. " For me," said he, mournfully ; "for me there is nae return. And I wadna see the black, black nicht that's fa'ing, and maun fa', ower my dear Scotland. But it's after mirkest nicht that glints the dawn.—I see't, I see't ! Years on years maun pass, and ne'er a queen's foot sall fa' on Scottish heather. And then ane comes—a Leddy wi' saft sma' tread ; wearing a marriage-ring that's dearer than her crown; hearing bairns' voices at hame, sweeter than a' the clavers o' daft crowds.—Ah, she's the Queen for bonnie Scotland !"

" Hold your tongue, True Thomas," said her Majesty, rather unceremoniously ; " no one here ever thinks of to-morrow ; it is only you stupid mortals who bring the unpleasant word 'future' into Fairyland. Look, as I said before, at your descendant there ; see her eyes, so clouded and grave ; can it be that despite my care the old Learmont leaven has reached her blithe spirit ?"

The Rhymer lookal. Alice was walking slowly down the river-side, **the** same river which meandered through **Fairy-land, rising** and disappearing, how **or** whither none could **trace.** She had neared the place where the water lilies grew thick, and where they had once twined their long stems round the form of the mortal captive who lay there three years bound, afar from sweet Melrose. Some recollection seemed to possess **the** changeling, **for** she staid in the same spot where she **had** then staid to look at her father. Sitting down by the bank, she played with the water plants and dip-ped her fingers in the stream. It went on singing over the pebbles with a melancholy monotonous flow, just like earthly rivers. Indeed, it seemed the only earthly sound in Fairyland

Alice listened, and slowly there came a deep strange pen siveness to her eyes.

" What hear ye, Alice ?" said Thomas of Ercildoun, com-ing nearer ;—for her volatile majesty of Elfland had suddenly descried a lovely specimen of entomology sailing down the **river-side, and** had summoned all her court on a dragon-fly **hunt :** leaving her mortal lover to dream on the green bank alone. " Why harken ye to the stream wi' sic a waefu' heart ?"

Alice looked up. " My heart ! is it so ? is this weight **on** my heart what my mother called *care* ?—**Then, I did net** understand the word !" said she, musingly.

" It is even sae. Were ye thinking o' your mither ?"

" I do that sometimes, now, when I get dull and weary. It is so weary to be always gay—and then I was born on earth, and not in Fairyland."

So said **she, very** gently, and with an altered tone of wo-manly thoughtfulness. Either the fairies' power had grown weaker, or the mother's prayers stronger ; but there was cer-tainly a change coming over the child. Having spoken, she again bent her head to the water, listening.

K*

" What hear ye ?" repeated Thomas, eagerly.

" I hear the murmur of the river, and other sounds that it brings with it, seemingly from a long way."

" And thae sounds are unlike aught here ? There's weeping and wailing, and saft sighs, and tears that fa' sweeter than kisses ? I ken them weel ; it's the sounds of earth that float alang wi' the earth-risen stream," cried the Rhymer, as he stooped and laved his hands and brow. " Oh, bonnie river, come ye frae the Tweed ; or frae my ain bright Leader, that rins by Ercildoun ? Oh, sweet water ! whar did ye spring, and whither do ye flow ?"

His heart seemed bursting with those words, but very soon his aspect grew calm, and he again asked Alice what she heard.

" I can hear naething of earth mysel," he said ; " never, sin' the day I shut my ear to ilka voice but that whilk led astray. But ye were stown awa, a puir bairn that kent nor gude nor ill. Listen, Alice, and tell me."

" I hear great lamenting along the river-brink—screams of children in terror—and people shouting about some one being drowned. And now there's a choking cry—ah ! I know who *that* is ! It's Hughie, my bonnie brother, so kind and so brave ! I must run—I must run !"

With an impulse, quite strange and unaccountable in Fairy-land, the earth-born maiden started off and flew along toward the source of the river ; skimming almost like a bird over bush and brake, through green bank and morass, wherever the windings of the stream led. She thought not of her companion ; she never looked behind ; on she went, guided by the sound which she seemed still to hear—the gasping sobs of a drowning child.

As Alice proceeded, the face of the country changed. The sunny plains of Elfland became grim rocks, through which the river flowed with angry bursts and moans. At last the thin rift of blue overhead altogether vanished ; she found her self in a cavern hung with oozy water-plants, and rugged with basaltic fragments.

Alice knew she had passed from the domain of the merry earth-elves to the gloomy abode of the Kelpie, the water-demon, whose pleasures were only in the working of ill. . There he sat, the grim creature—not beautiful, like the Queen of Fairies and her train—but foul and ugly to behold. His face and brawny shoulders were those of an old man, the gray wild hair drooping down like withered sedge; but underneath, half in and half out of the water, his form was like that of a huge river-horse. He had a harp of reeds beside him, upon which he played sweet music to allure his prey; and ever amidst his playing, he reared, snorted, and plunged, hoarsely laughing between, in a tone mockingly human.

So uncouth and fearsome a creature was he, that the child would have crept away in terror, but that far hid in the darkness of the cave, floating hither and thither upon the dark waters, she saw the glitter of yellow hair. It looked like the form of a drowned boy swaying to and fro on the surface.

A strange emotion possessed the changeling-maiden;—a feeling stronger than the desire for pleasure, or mirth, or sport —an emotion that drew her out of herself and toward another. The one night in her mother's cottage flashed upon her like a dream, not of weariness, but of sweetness. She hardly knew what she was doing, but somehow she murmured all the home-names, scarcely noticed at the time. While so doing, the waves stirred the face of the drowned child and turned it toward her. It was that of the eldest and most loving of her brothers—Hugh !

He lay, his bonnie face pale, but composed and sweet as if safely pillowed at home, instead of being tossed on those hungry waves. His fingers still tightly grasped his blue bonnet and his shepherd's staff, as though it were in fording some current that the Kelpie had overtaken him. He had grown into a sturdy boy, but the frank beauty of his mien was the same as when Alice had twisted her fingers in his curls, and looked for the first time in a brother's face.

She remembered it all—and how in the merry games of Fairyland she had often paused and wished for Hughie to come and say the sweet words—never said or thought of by the lightsome elfin race, " *I love you.*" She longed to reach him, and hear them over again.

" Hughie, brother," she whispered over the waves, but in vain : she dared not come nearer the fierce Kelpie, who sat and played in dignified gravity, never looking toward the mortal who was invading his domains. And farther—farther every minute, the river was drifting the helpless form of the drowned boy.

Alice paused a moment ; her bare feet trembled in the cold water, and among the sharp rocks ; then, acting on an impulse unknown before, she waded in—deeper—deeper, until her footing slid from her. She had never heard of death ; yet as she felt her breath failing, some strange formless horror seemed to encompass her. Nevertheless, she tried to grasp the yellow hair, and to cling closer to her brother ; as if, whatever happened, she would be safer and better thus. Then all sensation ceased.

She woke on the greensward of Fairyland, with Hughie tightly clasped in her arms, and over them bending the grave countenance of Thomas of Ercildoun.

The seer looked from one to the other of the children ; but Alice noticed only Hughie, who still lay as if asleep.

" Oh ! wake him, wake him," she cried : and a new tone of human pain thrilled through her smooth accents of Fairyland.

" He'll waken soon, and then he must gang far, far awa, or e'er 'tis morning on earth, and the queen comes hame to Fairyland. Haste ye, Alice ; kiss him ance, twice, and then bid him farewell

"I will **not** let him go; I want to keep him to play **with—my own, own** brother!"

"**An'** ye wad keep him—a fair christened wean, in this ill place, while his mither grieves the leelang day? Ye wad gar him forget his hame, and a' that's gude, to bide here in Elf-land? And when the seventh year comes roun', and they pay the teind to hell—he's sae fat and fair, and weel-liking · oh! wae's me for the lad!"

This and more the Rhymer urged; but little did Alice **heed, or at least seem** to heed. She smiled and laughed in wild **elfin** pleasure, as slowly Hughie opened his eyes. **But not a** word he said, except one bitter cry—" Hame—hame—I maun gae hame."

Alice led him every where, and showed him the fair **land-scapes** and the banquet hall—but he took no pleasure therein.

"Oh, let's gae hame," he said perpetually. "It's a bra·v land, but it's no like hame. Sister Alice, I daurna bide wi' ye.'

His sister listened, and her bright face was troubled with thought. "Must ye go, Hughie?" she said, now for the first **time** learning how sweet it was to share a pleasure that did not centre in herself alone; learning, too, a little of that pain of parting, without which the happiness of affection were as unreal as light without shadow.

"Must ye go?" she repeated, sadly. As she spoke, **it was** already dawn in the world, and the ringing **of the fairy** bridles was heard afar, beyond the golden gates **of** Elfland.

Alice grasped her brother—who now **or** never must be saved to return to earth. "You will not stay then, Hughie dear? **Ah** well! it's best not. They're oftentimes weari-some—all the feastings, and dances, and pleasures. **Go** back **to** our mother, and **bid her** remember me."

Half sadly the little maiden spoke; but there was no time to talk more—for flashing through the golden gates came the fairy cavalcade.

"We must be gone," said Alice. "I know the earthward
way;" and wrapping her arms round her young brother, she
drew him into a brake of fern. She gathered a bunch of
fern-seed, which, plucked on earth at St. John's Eve will
make the wearer invisible—and set it in Hughie's bonnet.

Then she took him by the hand, and led him secretly
toward the entrance of Fairyland. As they went out, they
saw, standing behind them with sad eyes, him who never
might pass those gates to his beloved country—Thomas the
Rhymer of Ercildoun.

"Is it far we hae to gang? and will ye gang wi' me
Sister Alice?" asked the boy.

"Ay," said Alice; "as far as may be."

So these children took together their strange journey. It
was all amidst darkness; there was neither sun nor moon.
Sometimes a pale, weird-like auroral light glimmered above
them, showing each the other's face, dim and wan. At other
times they went through mirk ways, seeing nothing, but hearing awful sounds like forests of trees soughing wildly, or
waterfalls dashing, or seas roaring, close by. Again, they
seemed to wade through deep rivers as red as blood; and
then their feet slid along great masses of ice, or sank in black
morasses. Alice always led the way, silent, but holding fast
her brother's hand.

Hughie went on, not in his usual daring mood, but heavily
like a boy in a dream. At times his feet lagged on the toilsome road, and he began to moan; then Alice would pause,
and try to teach herself those things which women of earth
learn instinctively, and have to practice all their life—how to
bear with and to comfort the afflicted. It was a new lesson,
but very sweet.

On they went, over river and plain, mountain and valley,
until at last they came to a cavern ending in a great doorway
fashioned of green stone. Through its crevices glided a pale

ray, like daylight, or like moonlight upon snow. By this
glimmer they saw indistinctly the latter part of the way they
had come ; a steep path, rising, as it were, out of the depths
of the earth.   Between them and the light were these gigantic doors.

Hughie sat down before them, and wept : " Ah, Sister
Alice, I will never reach hame !   I'll lay me doun and dee."

But Alice showed him a cranny in the stone, through
which came a broad beam of light—and bade him peep
through.

" Tell me, what see ye, Hughie dear ?"

" I see a long, white snaw drift, braid and still.   We're on
a hill-tap, and the morn's blinking out i' the east, and the
cocks are crawing afar.   There's the Abbey o' Melrose !   Oh,
Sister Alice, we're close at hame !"

He set up a shout of joy which made the black vault ring '
and stretching his hand through the tiny hole, gathered some
of the snow—the blessed snow which lay upon earthly
plains ! and put it to his parched lips.   For he was weary
and worn, poor child ; while Alice looked as fresh and fair as
she had done in the haunts of Fairyland.   But while he
smiled, she sighed.

" Yes, you will be soon at home, Hughie.   Are you glad
to go ?"

" Ay, unco glad !   I'll rin doun the hill-side, and ower the
brig, and creep in at the byre, for the ha' door's steekit fast
an' gin our mither comes to milk the kye, I'll loup intil her
arms.   Then I'll ca' Habbie, and Sandy, and winsome Willie,
and we'll a' be blithe thegither.   Come, Sister Alice," added
he, advancing to the heavy door, " tirl the pin, and let's
awa !"

" Away, then," said Alice, sadly ; and fare you well, my
bonnie brother that I will never see more !"

He hardly heard her, so eager was he in looking for the in

visible fastening **of the door.** The moment his fingers touched it, it opened of its own accord, wide enough to admit **of**
the boy's passing. He leaped through in **an** instant.

" Come awa, quick, sister !" cried Hugh, stretching out his
hand from the other side.

" I can not. They stole me, an unchristened child ; **I may**
not return **to** earth, unless they please. See, brother, the
gates are closing, and crushing me. Ah, hold them back !"

For a minute the boy's fearless hands did as she bade ; the
brother and sister clung together **and kissed** one another sorrowfully **through the** opening that was momently diminishing
between **them. Then the great** green doors closed with a
hollow clang, and **not a** trace remained **of where** they had
been.

Hughie sat and wept, all alone, on the snowy hill-side.

CHAPTER VII.

"Awa wi' your father, my bonnie sons; I wadna ye suld bide at hame wi' a puir sick doited body like mysel. Though it's wearie wark, lyin' here my lane ;—but may be it's no for lang."

The words, faint but patient, began cheerfully, and ended in a half-audible murmur. Mistress Learmont leaned back on the couch that was made up for her near the ingle-side, and looked fondly yet sorrowfully on her three tall lads, now fast outgrowing boyhood. There were but three, Hugh and the twins. Winsome Willie, the youngest, had been covered up to sleep in the green kirkyard of Melrose—one of those lost darlings who are destined to live in household-memory, endowed with the beauty of perpetual babyhood.

The triad of brothers left, Hugh, Halbert, and Alexander —though from the Scottish habit of diminutives, rarely enough did they win that full-lettered dignity—were near of an age and near of a height; fine bold fellows, exalting the honors of the Learmont name through all the country round —ay, even though they were but plow-boys and herd-laddies For to that low estate had their fortunes dwindled at last, when Queen Mary, needing no court nor guard, pined away in Tutbury-hold, and her archer, Thomas Learmont, returned to his old home. The next generation bade fair to merge the race of the old Knights of Ercildoun into mere tillers of the field and keepers of flocks and herds. Dame Learmont now dead and gone, was the last that ever owned that honorary title.

" It's no for lang—it's no for lang," repeated the mother, as scarce reluctantly the lads obeyed her and went out, leav-

ing her with a servant-lassie. "It's sair to bide, though,
while it lasts. A twalvmonth and mair I haena stirred
frae this ingle-side. It was i' the winter time, ye ken, lass,
that I fell sick ; and now the winter's here ance mair. Eh ?
what day is't, Meg ? Meg Brydon, I say !"

But the faint voice scarcely reached the careless young damsel, who stood watching the corner of the kailyard—it might
be for the sake of enjoying that pleasant sight, a red winter
sunset; especially as the foreground object was Jock the shep-
herd-lad leaning against a dyke and whistling amain.

"Wae's me !" sighed Mistress Learmont, as she ceased
the vain call, and sank down once more on her uneasy pillow
"It's aye the same, and sae 'twill be till I am laid under the
mools. Braw, sons I hae, and a husband leal and kind, but
they're no like a dochter. Ah ! I mind when I was a lassie,
and had a mither o' my ain—a puir wee wifie she was, sick
and dowie, for she had ay a dour life o' mickle wae—I mind
how ane day, when I was sitting by her, and she near her
end, she said, ' Marion, ye hae been a gude bairn to me, a'
your days ; I ken nae what ye're ettled to be, nor how ye'll
gae through this wearie warld ; but, Marion, your mither
leaves ye ane blessing, better than a'—May ye hae a dochter
like yoursel !"—But I hae nane, and never will ! Oh !
Alice, Alice, wherefore did ye gang ?

Thus, bitterly moaning to herself over her never-healed loss,
the mother lay. Meg Brydon had stolen out to Whistling
Jock, leaving the door a little way open.—The sharp winter
air blew in upon the sick woman.

"Meg, can ye no come and hap me better ? it's sair cauld.
Ye dinna speak; ye canna be fashed wi' a puir sick body.
Oh, dear Meg, be kind till me, just for a wee whilie—I'll ne
trouble ye lang. What, ye're gane ? Aweel, it's nae wonder—I'm no your mither, lass. But, oh, gin I had my ain
dochter ! Alice, Alice !"

The heart-wrung cry was suddenly stopped. While she called, Marion saw, or fancied she saw, looking in at the frosted window-panes, a face, which by the dim light of fading day seemed that of a young woman. But there was a likeness in it that made a thrill of awe come over her—a likeness unseen for twenty years.

She said to herself—"It maun be that my end is near; and that my mither is come back—come frae the grave to 'tak me hame,' as she said. Aweel, I'm ready; I downa care to bide langer. But oh, mither, gin I had, like ye, a dochter to close my een! Oh! that she were here—my bairn Alice!"

While she was speaking the face had vanished; but with her latter words it reappeared. Sweet it was, and tender in aspect, wearing that fair and angelic look always given by golden hair. Well might the sick woman have mistaken it for a vision from the land of the blessed! But as its eyes met hers, they took a human look, almost amounting to grief. Marion began to doubt.

"It's like her, yet it's no hersel—It's nae spirit for it stands dark atween me and the sky. Is it my bairn, that I wished might bear my mither's likeness? Is it my bairn that I haena seen for seven years? Alice, Alice!"

"I am here, mother," was the answer, heard indistinctly through the open door.

Marion uttered a great cry. She tried to raise herself, but her limbs were powerless.

"In the name o' God! my dochter, come ben!"

Alice stepped over the doorway, and came in.

She stood in the middle of the room, a maiden of seventeen years. Her features had sharpened out into distinct form and thoughtful beauty. She was neither like her mother, nor her father—except in the color of her hair; but bore the likeness which Marion had so desired when she gave her

first-born the name of Alice—her own mother's name. So
strong was the resemblance, that, when the girl stood, still
afar off, in her white clothing, with her hands loosely folded
together and her eyes bent tenderly forward, the sick woman
looked at her daughter with a sort of awe, as if there had still
been some reality in her first fancy, and Alice were indeed a
vision from the dead.

"Are ye my bairn?" she whispered solemnly. "Are ye
flesh and blude—*my* flesh and *my* blude—my ae dochter that
I bore?"

Alice approached, and stood at her mother's feet.

"I am your bairn. Will ye take me, mother, for this
night? I was so wearying to come home."

"My bairn—my dear Alice—my lassie true and kind!"
cried the mother, stretching out longing arms. But in vain,
for her strength was gone.

"I canna reach ye," she said piteously. "I'm sair changed
and weak. I do naething but murn and murn a' the day.
Ye maun tak your puir auld mither to your arms, Alice, for
she canna tak ye in hers."

Alice looked surprised, anxious, grieved, at the worn face,
and the gray hairs which had come before their time. For
though Mistress Learmont was not old, the cares and sorrows
of her life, its poverty and its toil, had made her seem like a
woman far gone in years. Her beauty had faded; all except
the one charm that she could not lose—the mild patience
which sat like a glory in her eyes. It touched Alice as something new—something never seen in Fairyland. It subdued
her so, that she, in all her loveliness of unclouded youth, came
near, and bending down lowly, knelt before her sick mother,
and threw round the shivering frame her shining arms.

"Are ye come back, my dearie? come back for gude and
a'?" whispered Marion, giving herself up to the uncontrollable
joy.

Alice sighed; ay, a real sigh, **the** first the mother had **ever** heard **on** her lips. " Nay, we will not speak of that. **1 am** here **now.** They let me come the minute the sun set, because my longings made their power weak. Are you glad to see me, mother ?"

" Glad, my bairn !" echoed Marion in a tone that was sufficient answer.

Her daughter looked **round**, half-curiously, yet with a mingling of interest. " It's the same place I see, the room where I and my brothers played so merrily. Where's Hughie, mother ?"

" He's gane wi' the rest to follow the pleugh, or fetch the kye hame ; or maybe he's awa to some ploy or ither. **He's a** pawky lad—our Hugh."

" Does he mind of me, mother ?"

" Ay ; often thae callants **talk o' wee Alice that** was **wi'** them seven years syne ; and ance when Hughie was missing on the hills for a day and a nicht, he cam hame saying he **had been dreaming that he fell intil** the Tweed, and that his sister Alice saved him. **He kent nae mair.** But 'twas unco strange."

Nothing did Alice say, for she knew that those who return from Fairyland have no clear remembrance of aught that has happened to them there. Only thinking of her brother **Hugh** and of that wondrous journey, she smiled pensively.

In her smile the likeness she bore grew stronger. **Marion** watching her, saw it. She took **her** daughter's face between **her** hands, and said,

" Look sae ance mair, Alice ! Ye're *her* very picture. I didna see't till this day, when ye're grown a woman, grave and dowie like. **Ye hae** her een, and her bonnie bree wi' **the** hair lying soft aboon ; only yours is bright as gowd, and hers was like threads of siller—my puir auld mither ! But I'm glad ye're like her, Alice ; I'm unco glad !"

Her voice was trembling **through tears ; her** words, feeble, "maundering," and long drawn out, bespoke the wandering fancies of sickness. When she ceased, her head sank back exhausted on the pillow.

Alice stood wistfully regarding that—to her—strange new sight—disease and pain.

"What ails you, mother? What can I do for you?" she asked, more by the human and womanly instinct within her than by any deeper feeling.

"I'm very sick, Alice; and I hae naebody to tend me. Oh, gin ye'd gie me a drink, and bathe my bree, and kame my hair," she moaned, looking imploringly at her daughter.

Alice rose up, and went about the house, not as in years before, with flaunting childish mien, but with the grave light footsteps of maidenhood. She went—all in her bright clothing, still redolent of the odors of Fairyland; she brought the light, and got ready the cool drink—doing things which she had never done before, but which her earthly nature instinctively taught her.

"Ah, it's sweet, sae sweet," murmured the sick woman. receiving, for the first time, the cup from her daughter's hand. "Ilka thing tastes gude frae ye, my lassie, as my ain mither was wont to say to me lang syne. God help thae puir auld bodies that hae ne'er a dochter!"

Alice smiled, and in her cheek, always so clear, rose a transparent flush of pleasure—pleasure quite different to what was so called in Elfland.

Her mother, a little revived, sat up in her bed, and looked at her once more; it seemed as if she could never tire of such gazing, which absorbed all thought, but of the present.

"Ye're a sweet lassie, Alice—and fair to see. But I dinna like thae braws—they're no fit for a puir man's bairn," said she, touching the glittering robes, armlets, and jewels, or what seemed such—with which her daughter was adorned Alice looked vexed.

" Aweel, my dearie, I wadna grieve ye. Only it gars ye seem as if ye were a grand leddy, and no my ain dochter ;— whilk, maybe, is but the truth," added she, sadly.

Alice sat a minute in thought ; then, without speaking, she went to the corner where thick in dust hung some of her mother's garments, long unworn through sickness. She stripped off all her shining gauds, and dressed herself in these coarse clothes, which, while somewhat hiding her form, made her look sweeter and fairer, because more like a mortal maiden.

" Ah ! I ken ye now—ye're my ain, my ain," cried the mother embracing her. " Ye'll loe me—and tend me—and never, never part frae me !"

The girl sighed, but made no answer ; and began quietly to fulfill all a daughter's offices toward the sick woman. She bathed her face, and taking off her cap, let down the hair already turned to gray. Alice paused, with the locks in her hand.

" Are you very old, mother ? Will you never be young and fair-looking any more ? Do all people that live on earth grow feeble as you ?"

" In time—my bairn—in time ! But it's naething. I was a bonny lass mysel, ance—when I married your father, and even when I brought ye into the warld. But I forget a' that. It's sweeter to be an auld wifie, and hae a bonnie dochter smilin' near. Then, a body isna feared for growin' auld."

Her cheerful look, as she leaned forward and let Alice comb her gray hair, was almost like the smile of young Marion Learmont, when, seventeen years before, she sat tying the fatal green round the cradle of her expected babe. Her overladen heart heaved a sigh of entire content ; and again and again she drew Alice closer, to look into her young face, and admire the maidenly beauties of her form. In this maternal love was an exulting pride, almost as strong as that with which

a young man watches the dawning perfections of his mistress
—a pride which none can know or understand but a mother
who beholds her only daughter woman-grown, and feels her
own youth restored in the fair completeness of what was once
a frail baby-life trembling at her breast.

An hour passed in this deep serenity of joy; and then Meg
Brydon came creeping in, eyeing with shame and discomfiture
her forsaken mistress.

"Gang your gate, Meg," said Mistress Learmont, cheerfully. "I will need ye nae mair; I hae my ain dochter,
that's come hame this nicht. Look ye here, Meg Brydon :—
isna she a bonnie lass?"

But Meg, frightened at the apparition of the fair creature
that sat beside Mistress Learmont's bed, and remembering
all the tales of the stolen Alice, took hastily to flight. The
mother and daughter were left together, as before.

"We'll be our lane the hale nicht, maist likely," said Marion
to her child. "It's New Year's night, ye ken, and your father
and the three callants are down at Melrose, keeping Hogmanay. I forbade them to bide at hame—douf and dowie
wi' me. But, my Alice, I kenn'd na then I wad hae thee!"

So amidst long talk and sweet pauses of silence, the night
passed away. Then, for the first time, Alice heard the
things pertaining to simple earthly lore ; of precious home-
bonds ; of afflictions softened by tenderness ; of trials made
holy by patience ; of human sorrows, that go hand-in-hand
with human joys ; of evil enhancing good ; of wrong creating
forbearance ; and long-suffering, ever present love, reigning
triumphant over all.

These many things did Marion Learmont teach unto her
daughter, though so unconsciously, that any stranger listening
would have said that it was merely an " auld wife clavering"
to a young girl about former days, and her own past life, together with the events of her family. Nothing wonderful

she told—only that history which belongs to every household
and every individual, in all times ancient or modern, of which
the **text,** adduced either as example or warning, perpetually
is, or ought to be, these words—the honey of the world's bitter cup—" *My little children, love one another.*"

It might be about ten o'clock, at night when the solitude of
Marion Learmont and her daughter was broken by **voices at**
the door without.

Alice trembled, and instinctively clung to **her mother's**
hand.

" Oh, hold me fast; just a little while longer," she whispered
eagerly.

" What for do ye fear, my lassie ?   It's naebody but your
ain father, and your brithers three ; **stand and let them see**
ye, my dochter."

With a sweet and bashful grace, her face yet pale from the
unexplained terror, Alice stood—a vision of beauty—before
her rough **sire and her three wild brothers.**   They were ut-
terly confounded.

" What's this, Marion ?" said the late archer of Queen
Mary's guard, stooping his yellow locks, now growing grizzled
and thin, near his ailing wife, and trying to lower his **strong**
voice so as not to jar upon her feeble ear.

"It's our Alice, our first-born. She's come hame. **Gie her**
your blessing."

" Eh, our Alice that was stown **awa ?" said Thomas Lear-**
mont, who, like all recovered mortals, was utterly oblivious
of the past, and bore no memory of the stream **in** Fairyland,
or the little elfin daughter that used to visit him there.
" Alice come back ! **Sure, lass,** I'm unco glad to see **ye !"**

He took her in his sturdy arms, and his hearty parental kiss
resounded over the whole house.

" Whar hae ye been, ye foolish lassie ? ye hae caused us
mickle **dule.** Ye suld hae came back **for** your puir mither's

sake that needs a lass-bairn to tend on her, instead of thae big callants and mysel, though we aye do our best. But ye'll fare better now, Marion woman!"

He patted his wife's shoulder with his huge hand, and she looked up tenderly at him. Times were changed with them, and they were changed too—except in the affection which on both sides had lasted, and would last, until the end.

Meanwhile the three lads had hung back, oppressed with the uncouth shyness peculiar to their age. Only Hugh among them took courage to lift up his eyes and speak to sister Alice. He had grown a sturdy fellow, less bonnie, perhaps, than in childhood, but with the promise of becoming a Learmont worthy even as True Thomas of a Queen of Fairies' love.

His sister came and looked up in his face—a decided looking up, for she was a wee creature always, quite elf-like in proportion, when standing beside her big brother of thirteen years old.

"Hughie, dear! won't you speak to me?"

Hughie cast his eyes upon her shyly, but tenderly, "Ay, I'll do that—I mind ye now, sister Alice, and a' the things I dreamed about ye; and," he added mysteriously, "I ken ye hae been wi' the gude neighbors, and I hae sought ye in ilka green ring, and aye at Hallowe'en, but I couldna find ye. Ye're found now! Oh, but we'll keep Hogmanay, fine!"

As a mild way of expressing his feelings, Hughie tossed up his bonnet in the air, and executed a brief fragment of a reel, which drove Habbie and Sandy out of the reach of his legs with great precipitation.

"Ye're richt, lad," said the father, turning round with a loud cheerful laugh. "Auld wife, it's our blithest New Year yet, and we'll keep it brawly; sitting here wi' a' our bairns round us!"

"Save ane," whispered the mother, "wee Willie, that's sittin' this ae ni;ht in heaven at His feet."

Thomas Learmont took off his bonnet, so did the lads ; and there was silence in the house for a minute. It was a pause consecrated to the memory of the one lamb lost out of the flock to be gathered into the safe fold of the Great Shepherd.

Then began the merriment of Hogmañay—kept as merrily in those olden days as now. Parents and children gathered round the fire, which, for this occasion only was piled up with faggots that would have done honor to the time when the wine ran red, and the hospitable ingle blazed perpetually in the Tower of Ercildoun. The young Learmonts sported, shouted, and danced ; but whenever the uproar grew too wild, Alice's gentleness fell like dew upon the other three, softening rudeness or contention, coming among her troop of brothers to be what a sister can always be, the healer of discord, the soother, the refiner.

All these things she had learned, partly by nature—her mother's nature, which was inherent in her ; and partly by the sudden instinct, developed at once, during the few hours when she had lain listening to that mild speech which first put all a daughter's emotions into her heart.

She was very happy too. Ay, though on this memorable night when she began to feel altogether like a maiden of earth, she grew hungry—and the food was coarse ; weary—and was startled by her father's loud laugh, so different from the lulling melodies of Fairyland ; though oftentimes her brothers' noisy play jarred upon her delicate senses, and their rough caresses half-frightened her—still, she was happy. She had learnt for the first time the great secret of all human happiness—family love.

The hour came, the eerie time between the night and the day, between the past and coming year—the hour which had brought Alice into the world. As the clock chimed, Thomas

Learmont took his first-born and only daughter in his arms and blessed her; while the parental love, which is an instinct in a mother, but in a father is usually the growth of years, and dependent on external sympathies, rose to his heart, and fell in drops from his manly eyes.

Then her mother kissed her fondly, and afterward her brothers did the same—awkwardly and shyly, as all brothers do, at the age when the testifying of household affections seems to them undignified—in fact, a positive sin against the independence of boyhood. All said, "God bless thee, Alice— our Alice!" and she felt that she was indeed one of them, ready to share all things with them, through good and evil ;— that the solitary delights of Elfland were desired by her no more.

"Now, gang to your bed, my dochter," said Mistress Learmont tenderly, when, the New Year having fairly commenced, the three lads were dispatched to sleep and quiet- ness, during the only portion of the twenty-four hours that they ever were quiet. "But yet I canna tine ye for an hour."

"Oh, do not, mother," sighed Alice, while the olden shadow of fear troubled her face. "Hold me fast—fast; let me not go."

"Ay, the lass is skeared. Nae doubt; the place looks drearie like—bide ye wi' your mither, Alice," said Thomas Learmont kindly, as he rolled himself in his plaid and lay down at the outer door.

So Alice, exhausted with a joy that made her feel weak and trembling like any earthly maiden, crept gladly to the maternal breast.

She had not slept there long, when she was wakened with the dawn glimmering into her eyelids. Very soon that dim ray was swallowed up in one far brighter. The whole house was filled with light, and thrilled with delicious music

Alice knew it well. The sweet summons reached her as one of doom. It was the fairy people come to take her away.

Shuddering she listened, and with an instinct natural and child-like, yet alas! to her so new, tried to wake her mother. But Marion Learmont slept soundly, with a sweet smile on her worn face, which in this happiness seemed almost to have renewed its youth. She slept as if a deep spell was upon her, blinding her to her child's peril. Only in sleep she held her arms so tightly wound round her, that Alice felt a kind of safety in their fold. From thence the poor maiden looked out and watched the elfin people gathering round the bed.

"Come, Alice; come, pretty Alice," sang they, amidst their gambols. "Are you not weary of these coarse laidly mortals? Come back to us, quick!"

"Oh, let me stay a little longer," implored the girl. "I am so tired of dancing and singing. I had rather bide at home."

"Hey ho!" laughed out the Elf-queen, stepping lightly into the ring, "this is something quite new. What has come over my young hand-maiden? She would like to stay in a wretched tumble-down dwelling where the rain always comes in and the smoke never goes out; and to live with such people. too! Entering the door, which he left open to stretch his feet through, I had to step over such a lumbering carcass of a mortal. Faugh! is my young Thomas Learmont come to this? a thing with grizzled hair and coarse hands!"

"He is my father, my kind good father," cried Alice.

"And that woman there, how ugly; why, I could lay my little finger in each of her wrinkles."

"My mother, my own mother that I love!" Alice answered, as she turned and pressed her young lips to every furrow marked in the withered brows.

The elves set up a shout of derision.

"Nay, Alice," said the queen, her silvery laughter making

a pleasant under-tone of melody, " this may be all very well
for some common tastes, but not for a descendant of my True
Thomas, who gave up all for me.   Ay, all ! though the Tower of Ercildoun was a home rich and fair, while this is a poor
cottage ;—though he was held the noblest knight in all Scotland, while you are just a farmer's lass.   Be wise, simple one ;
come back to former ways and former delights."

    At her signal the elves began to dance the old delicious
measures which Alice remembered well.   So strong was the
enchantment that she had need to close her eyes and stop her
ears lest she should be allured against her will.   Had it not
been that her mother's arms were so closely locked around
her, perhaps she would even have leaped forth and joined the
rout of frantic pleasure.

    All at once it paused, melting into delicious soul-enticing
music, through which was only heard the voice of the Elf-
queen, murmuring " Alice, come."

    She lifted her head and said firmly, " I will not come."

    There was a loud and angry wail, like that of the wind
tearing the trees, a rolling like thunder, and in these sounds
the music died.

    " Do as you list, foolish mortal," Alice heard uttered in a
sharp sarcastic voice by her side, though she saw nothing.
" It matters not to us, for you will soon be ours.   It is daylight and we must be away to Fairyland ; while those arms
still hold you safe from our power.   But by the next twilight
when the shadows fall grey behind Eildon Hill, ha ! ha ! aa !
—Foolish Alice, foolish Alice, when this is the seventh year
—and a mortal fair as you will please the Fiend well.   Ho, ho !"

    A shout of angry laughter shook the roof ; the elves van-
ished, and the whole house lay silent in the dawn.

    Mistress Learmont woke, and tremblingly felt for her
daughter.   Her beloved Alice lay in her bosom, quite still
and pale with open eyes watching the sunbeams creep along

the floor.   It was the first time Marion had ever seen that face in daylight—the first time Alice had ever beheld the sun —the warm, healthy, labour-inspiring, earth-risen sun.

" Is this morning ?" she said, softly, turning her eyes, full of strange pensiveness, on her mother.

"It is, my bairn ; God be wi' ye on this braw New Year.''

Alice was silent.   She scarce understood the blessing ; it belonged to a lore not taught in Fairyland.   Soon afterward she said, still keeping her thoughtful look—

" Mother, how long do you call a day—from twilight to twilight ?"

" It's unco short now, frae sunrise to sunset ; we hae scarce time for the wark that maun be dune."

" Nor I," said Alice, sadly.   " Mother, may I rise ?"

She rose accordingly ; and Marion Learmont beheld her daughter moving about the house like other mortal daughters, ready to fulfill all the duties that it behooved her to learn. Very pale and clear Alice's features looked in the bright daylight.   There was even a wan unearthly aspect about her— a weariness and painful repose.   All the day she comported herself thus ; doing whatsoever became her station, and doing it in a manner that seemed as if she had been used to it all her life.   Only when the neighbors came in to stare at her, and some marveled at her wondrous grace, and some jested bitterly about Thomas Learmont's lost daughter, who had come back they knew not from where, Alice would shrink away and hide herself by her mother's side, where alone she seemed to find entire content and rest.

It was a dull winter day, and the forenoon had scarcely passed, when black rain-clouds grew heavy over Eildon Hill. As they darkened, evermore Alice's sweet face darkened too. She would pause continually in her light labor or her pleasant talk, and look sorrowfully at her mother, as if she could not find speech to tell her pain.   As the afternoon closed in

and the mid-day meal being over, the father and brothers went
back to their toil—Alice, sitting with her mother, grew continually sadder and sadder.   Nevertheless, she went about
the house, heaped fagots on the fire, prepared food, and did
every thing for the sick woman's comfort, just as if she herself had been going away and wished to leave every thing in
neat order, so as to be comfortable for the one she loved.

She took one other precaution, before she came and sat
down at her mother's side ;—she bolted and barred the doors,
leaving no entrance from without.   But she did it with a
despairing look, as though she knew that all was in vain.

About dusk Marion Learmont fell asleep ; but waking
soon after, asked for water.   Alice brought her a pitcher-full.

"Ah, not that, my bairn ; I wad like a draught frae that
bonnie burn ye see," said she, with feverish longing.   "It's
no mony steps frae this, and it rins ower pebbles sae fresh and
clear.   Alice, will ye gang ?"

Alice sighed, as though knowing all that would follow from
this request, so meekly and unconsciously made.   But there
was no resisting the mother's desire.   She took up her pitch-
er, and went.

She came back again, very pale, with quick wild steps.
There was a sound following her, like the soughing of an
angry wind, though nothing could be seen.

Hurriedly the girl put the cup to her mother's lips.

"Drink, mother, drink, and then kiss me ; for I must go."

"Whar, my lassie ?"

"Far away, far away, with those you know.   They drag
me, they constrain me.   Mother, I can not stay !"

Her voice was almost a scream, and she writhed like one
struggling with invisible hands.

"Oh, remember me, mother, and I'll remember you !   And
ah ! keep Hughie safe, that he comes no more into their
power, where I stay miserable and against my will '

" Then ye sall be saved, my bairn," cried the mother, rising from her first numbed terror into supernatural strength. ' He that gave ye to me—He that is the keeper o' your saul—is greater than they that haud ye fast. He winna leave ye tc perish. He will help your mither to save ye. How maun I do't? Tell me, Alice, my ae dochter—my first-born, sent by God!"

As she uttered the great Name, a wild and mournful cry arose. With it was mingled Alice's voice :

" Ay ! save me, mother. Stand at the four cross roads, on the eve of Roodmass, when we all ride. Ye'll see me. Snatch me, and hold me fast, and have no fear. Oh ! save me, mother, mother !"

It was only a voice that spoke—nothing more. Alice had melted out of sight. Her cry of " Save me, save me !" died away in distance and silence ; and the mother heard nothing —felt nothing—but the bitter winter wind blowing through the open door.

CHAPTER VIII.

FAR far through all the black depths of the underground world, did the elves bear their changeling maiden ; now, for the first time, an unwilling and sorrowful prey. Feeble and exhausted she was too, even like any mortal girl, worn out by weeping and regret.

" Now, Alice, thou art the most foolish damsel on earth," said the blithesome queen, who had not feeling enough to be either angry or revengeful. " To think of your desiring to remain behind, and crying your sweet eyes blind because the thing was impossible. Look, how near shines the golden gate ; soon we will be once more in Fairyland."

But Alice wept on.

" I never knew such a provoking little mortal. Don't go on dreaming, Alice. Look at this stream we have to cross."

The girl looked mechanically. Well she knew the shallow river, which, with many another, she had waded through again and again, while the light elves skimmed along the top. But, while in the midst of its current, she cast her eyes down, shuddered and screamed : she saw it as she had never seen before—a river of blood !

" What, you dislike that !" said the Queen of Fairies " Really, how very particular my handsome maiden has grown ; worse by far than the Knight of Ercildoun, whom I led hither. It is only the blood spilt on earth which drips down to Fairyland. We have no objection ; it makes our streams a brighter color, that is all. Come across, my little maid."

In an agony Alice struggled to the shore, unharmed, save by a few red drops that clung to her robe.

"It is the blood of Geordie Grahame, slain by your father the day you were born," observed the queen, carelessly. "But no matter, the next stream we cross will wash it out. Ay, and you may drink of that," she continued, as Alice lay exhausted beside another rivulet, which ran clear and sparkling, though with a perfectly silent flow.

Dying with thirst, Alice dipped in her hollowed hand, and put it to her lips, but the water was salt and bitter.

"Drink, silly maiden ! It is only the tears shed on earth, coming down hither. Mortal women—and your mother especially—help to keep the river continually flowing. Prythee, Alice, do not add to the wave."

"Ah me !" cried Alice, "and it is through blood and tears that I must pass, and have passed, to reach the land of pleasure !"

No more she spake, but fell heavily on the ground, so often traversed with delight, but which she now with opened eyes saw to be a delusive and a thorny way.

"Oh, these mortals, these mortals !" petulantly exclaimed the Queen of Fairies. "But take her up, my elves, and bring her safe through the golden gate ; it is quite impossible that our peace can be disturbed by an earth-born creature's lamentings outside the portals of Fairyland. Once within there, she will of course be content , and we will have a few extra feasts and junkettings. The glory of our kingdom is concerned ; for, my subjects, the fact is"—and her majesty shrugged her shoulders—"we may not keep any thing human long, if altogether against its will. As my Knight of Ercildoun foretold, we may have to give her up at last but we'l keep the creature as long as we can."

Having delivered herself of this dignified harangue, to the which the bells of her palfrey rung applause, the queen spurred on, and entered the fair gates of her kingdom.

There, silently leaning against the portals which he might never pass, sometimes looking wistfully through their transparent net-work, sometimes striking momentary chords on the harp that hung always at his side, stood Thomas of Ercildoun.

His countenance brightened when he saw the queen—his adored ever; though like many another bard, he had worshiped no reality but only the dream of his own poet-heart.

"Are ye come back, my lady and love?" said he, advancing; "and hae ye brought young Alice Learmont?"

"Ay, at last; and not content with a whole night and a day on earth, she wanted to abide there constantly. She is as discontented as you are sometimes, my knight, only with much more cause, since she has never a true-love here in Fairyland."

The Rhymer looked with glittering eyes at the small elfin form that wreathed itself about him in sprite-like, child-like vagaries. Even in her caressing moods, the fairy-lady had an inconstant, butterfly air; there was nothing in her of the quiet tender woman-nature which will cling to what it loves, because it loves, and, loving can not choose but cling. Yet very witching—in any shape—was the Rhymer's love!

He watched her, still overcome by the glamour which had never entirely passed away. But at last his eye turned to where Alice Learmont lay in a state of death-like unconsciousness which quite puzzled the elves. They were trying all means to awake her; some buzzing about her in the shape of bees, others putting on the tiny feathers of birds, and warbling close in her ears; and the rest shouting her name, their call sounding like dim echoes heard among woodlands. But there she lay, white and motionless, save for the slow tears

that came stealing under her eyelids. Her bitter grief was **upon her** still.

It penetrated the mortal nature of the Bard of Ercildoun.

"Let me gang till her," said he to the queen. "She comes o' my blude—the earthly blude that throbs **in my** heart still. Like can comfort **like.** I'll ask at the lassie **wherefore** she grieves sae **sair."**

"Away **with you, True** Thomas ; only take heed"—and the queen shook her dainty finger warningly—" I can not spare any more mortals of the Learmont race, after him **that truly** was well spared, the great burly archer of Melrose."

She flitted away, her elves careering after her in **merry** whirls on the grass, or in airy eddies like dust-clouds leaving the coast clear for Thomas the Rhymer and hi. descendant.

He approached Alice softly, nay reverently ; for he saw in her the traces of that earthly suffering **which** from himself **had for centuries passed away.** Pensive he was, but the faint shadow **on his** brow was nothing to Alice's utter despair. She lay and wept like one **who** would not be comforted.

He called her by her name, but **she** answered not. Then **in** a tone gentle as a woman, he said—" My dochter !"

Alice started up with **a great cry**—" Who calls me thus ? Oh, mother, mother ! have you come after me all the **way to** this cruel land ?"

But she saw nothing except the green grass, **and the hazy** shadowless trees standing up in their places, while underneath them, as upright and as still, stood the Rhymer.

"It is no **your** mither that speaks," said **he.** "It is **my ain sel, that ye ken weel—your** Ancestor, Thomas Learmont of Ercildoun, that mony hundred years syne wonned away to Fairyland, and was never seen mair."

Alice came nearer, and there was life and interest in her **eyes.** "Are you from Tweedside, a mortal, and of my kin ?'

" Ye heard a' that—lang syne."

"I heard, but heeded not. I scarce heeded any thing till yesternight, when I hearkened to my mother. Oh, mother, mother! will I never hear your voice any more?"

"Did she tell ye aught concerning me?" asked the Rhymer, eagerly. "Or is my name clean forgot amang my ain folk and i' the land I lo'ed sae weel?"

Alice put her hand to her brow. "Wait till I think of what she said. Ay, it is clear now." And she looked up in his face steadily. "You were the Knight of Ercildoun; and you left every thing—home, parents, young wife, and inno-cent babe—to go with a beautiful lady into Fairyland for seven years. Then you came back, and lived as a good knight should. At last she summoned you—the Queen of Fairies—and you went away again—forever Oh! how could you go, having once come back to the dear earth?"

The Rhymer sunk his head, murmuring, "I canna tell. It was to be, and it was sae."

"And how returned you? Ah, show me the way. Teach me how to go back to my dear mother and my brother Hugh."

She flung herself at his feet, embracing them in her agony of entreaty.

"Ye ken there's but ane way," said the Rhymer, gently: "to bide here till spring dawns on the earth; and at the time o' Roodmass the fairies ride. Gin your mither loe ye still, ye may be saved, Alice Learmont. Gie thanks to her that yestreen ye didna tine your saul," added he in an awful whisper.

Alice looked up, trembling.

"Ye kentna that while ye lay saft i' your mither's arms, there cam up that black road the Evil Ane, him that goes about like a ramping and a roaring lion. He took back nae mortal, but an elf, as the teind to hell. Ye're safe, my bairn, gin your heart fail not, nor your mither's luve."

While the seer spoke, the solitude of the wood where they sat was broken by the entrance of the fairy-troop. Little heed the elves took of the mortals, being absorbed in their own delights. They came on with songs and laughter, and sat down to golden banquet-tables, that sprang out of the ground like mushrooms. Alice, half dead with hunger, thirst, and exhaustion, looked on, but came not nigh. The feast ended, they broke forth into mad revelries : music that allured the very soul, and dances that whoever saw must needs dance after—were it through bush, bramble, or brier.

Alice pressed her eyelids forcibly down to shut out the sight—once so familiar—which she felt was controlling her senses, and luring her back beyond recall.

"Oh, mother, mother !" she murmured, and strove to think of the dim cottage, and the sick bed, and her who lay there, moaning her heart away for the loss of her child. But still the fairy spell was too strong, and drew the girl's feet nearer and nearer to the enchanting scene.

"Oh, keep me back," she cried, turning to what seemed her only stay—him who had once been a mortal like herself. But still the words were words only ; continually she moved nearer and nearer to the dazzling rout.

Thomas the Rhymer looked after her with doubtful eyes. "It maunna be," said he thoughtfully ; "a' that I hae tint, I hae tint ; but this lassie, sae tender and sae fair—Alice Learmont !" added he, calling her by her earthly name, with a severe and firm voice.

The maiden paused, even though her feet were just touching the magic ring.

"Whar are ye gaun ? Hae ye forgotten your mither ?"

Alice paused, sighed, and stood irresolute.

"Will ye be saved ?" said the Rhymer.

"I can not—I can not ! their power is too strong for me,' sobbed Alice ; "yet, oh, my mother !"

At the word, Thomas of Ercildoun drew her to the brink
of a little rivulet that crept through the wood; just a slender
rill, coming from the one river of earth that flowed through
Fairyland. He dipped his fingers in the water, sprinkled
her eyelids, and made on them a sign, in his days held most
sacred, and still reverenced as a memorial of holy things—
the cross. Then he bade her open her eyes and see.

Alice saw—but oh, with what changed vision!

All the fair wood, alive with flickering leaves and waving
plants, had become a forest of bare lifeless trees. The foliage
had dropped off the boughs, the flowers had withered where
they grew. There was no beauty, no pleasure therein; nothing but discordant voices, and a dead blank of sight and
sound.

Shuddering, Alice ran forward to seek her old companions,
ay, any companionship at all in the desolate place. But the
banquet-hall had faded into ruins; the dainties were only so
many withered leaves; the golden tables nothing but fungi
and ugly incrustations of blasted trees; the gay draperies
around mere spider-webs, flittering to and fro in the gusty
wind.

The girl would have shrieked, but the same spell which
had opened her eyes had sealed her lips for the time. Vainly
she looked round for Thomas the Rhymer; he had disappeared. She wandered along the paths she knew, yet sometimes doubtful of her way, so changed was every thing, until
she reached the dell where the Queen of Fairies kept her
favorite court.

" Welcome, welcome, Alice!" shouted the elves in the distance. But their voices, once so sweet, now sounded discordant as ravens hooting from a crumbling tower. And, coming
nearer, the maiden beheld them clear.

Oh, horror! There was a ghastly, loathly hag sitting on
a throne, laughing loudly through her toothless lips, her yel

low shrunken limbs peering ugly beneath foul rags that were **disposed** as jauntily as if they had been rich clothing. There **was a court** of withered worn-looking creatures, that in their uncomely age imitated the frolics of youth. All things about them were pale and unsubstantial, jaded, comfortless, and drear. Yet they seemed not to know it, but in all this wretched guise played the same antics, and with their cracked hoarse voices sang the same songs, which had once been so enchanting. Every thing was as it had ever been—only from it the glamour was gone.

"Ye see the truth now," said a mournful whisper in Alice's ear ; and the Rhymer stood behind her.

"And do you see it thus ?" asked the shuddering girl

"Maybe, not sae fearsome as it is in your een. For I am ane o' them, and we maun a' cheat ane anither, until the end ; but I ken weel that whate'er it *seems*, it *is* even sae."

So saying, with a mechanical footstep, neither hurried nor slow, he went into the magic ring and lay down at the feet of the ghastly queen—who, under whatever guise he beheld her, was doomed to be his object of worship evermore.

But Alice, shrinking away with terror and disgust, hid herself in the solitary wood. There she staid for days and weeks; lying on withered fern, and feeding scantily on **ber**ries that came from seeds of earth drifted along by the earthly rivulet. Perpetually there came by her portions of the elfin shows, which had once seemed so pleasant, but were now so foul. She joined them not ; in misery, and repentance, and pain, did she bide her time, until the season of the Fairies' Raid came round.

One **evening, when she** sat on the brink of the stream— **which alone of** all the sights in fairyland, kept its freshness **and** beauty—she saw drifting by one of those branches covered with soft woolly leaf-buds, which, appearing at Easter, are to this day called palms.

As she looked, Thomas of Ercildoun, whom she had not
seen for long, appeared at her side, watching likewise the little bough.

"Alice," said he, "ye hae received your sign. It is spring
time on the bonnie meadows o' Tweedside.   When the next
gloaming fa's, it will be the Eve o' Roodmass."

He had scarcely spoken, when the gathering summons stir
red up all the dwellers in Fairyland. On they came, cluster-
ing in throngs round the entrance gate, collecting what had
once seemed their gallant nags and palfreys, but which now
Alice saw to be only hemp-stalks, and bean-wands, and withered boughs of trees, on which the skeleton leaves, waving
and rustling, made what had appeared the glitter of golden
housings and the music of bridles ringing.

Hoarsely resounded the universal call, for on this, the first of
the two grand yearly festivals, no one, elfin or mortal, might
be absent from the Fairies' Raid—except him, who coming
of his own will, had lost the power of revisiting earth.

Slowly he followed, lingering until already the first of the
pageant had passed through the gates, and Alice, the last of
all, waited with eager longings until she herself was allowed
to depart.

The Rhymer stood watching her with sorrowful yearning.

"Fare-ye-weel, Alice ; I see a' things clear.   Mither's
luve is strong, and mither's prayers stronger.   Ye pass the
gate that ye will enter nae mair.   Fare-ye-weel!"

Alice trembled with joy.   She prepared to go ; bathed her
naked bruised feet in the little stream, and drew round her
the poor rags that had once seemed the gaudy robes of Elfin-
land.   Still, ere she left she turned round with kind tears to
the Rhymer, her Ancestor.

"My father, can I do aught for you ?   Should I reach safe
the dear earth—our earth—is there no power—no prayers
that could avail ?"

He shook his head mournfully. "Na, na! the time is past. Gin I were ever found on the fair earth, it wad be but as a heap o' white banes crumbling i' the kirkyard o' Melrose. That a man sowed, he sall even reap: I maun dree my wierd, until the warld's ending. Hereafter, there's Ane that maun do as His mercy wills wi' my erring saul."

Ceasing—he folded his hands and cast down his eyes, so majestic yet so sad. His descendant had no more to urge.

Once more only the Rhymer spoke, but in a low voice, and humbly even as a mortal penitent. " Alice ae word. When a' chances as it will chance, gang ye to the chapel by Ercildoun, and look out for a gray stane I raised, aneath the whilk I thocht that I and mine were to sleep. There'll sure be there my son Thomas, and ane that was aye a gude wife to me. Alice, say ten masses for their sauls."

So said he, not thinking of the centuries that had swept away all traces of the living and the dead alike, nor that mere tradition kept alive the name of Thomas of Ercildoun.

Alice made him little answer, for she hardly understood his meaning, and her whole heart and thoughts were flying earthward, in longing and in love.

One by one, the fairy train passed out from the gate, and last of all, the mortal maiden passed out likewise.

"Fare-ye-weel, Alice," sounded behind her like a sigh ; and looking back, she saw the Rhymer standing, dimly visible through the ragged mould-encrusted bars which had once seemed gold. His harp had fallen on the ground, his arms were folded on his breast, and his eyes that could not weep, were bent forward with the mournfulness of a yearning never to be fulfilled. "Fare-ye-weel," he repeated once more ; then turned himself, lifted up his beloved harp, and went back for ever into Fairyland.

CHAPTER IX.

IT was early spring over all the Border-country. The gowans in the pasture fields began to lift up their tiny heads, and the willows that grew in the windings of the Tweed put on downy buds, which the farmers' children call "geese and goslings." A few young lambs were tottering in the folds, and once or twice, when the noon was very warm and mild, a laverock had been heard singing high up in the still blue air, above the abbey-turrets of Melrose.

There was a woman, very pale and weak, but no longer sick—sitting under the shelter of the monastery walls. Every day when the weather was mild, she crawled out and sat there, anxious to gather up her strength to the utmost; and so she had done for weeks and months. Very quiet and composed she was; full of that serenity which is given by a firm purpose deep buried in the heart. This purpose—so intense and resolved, had imparted strength and health even to Marion Learmont.

She sat, a little way from the place where wee Willie's last cradle was made; lifting her head to the warm afternoon sunshine, and drinking in the pleasant air. Meg Brydon kept not far off; sometimes twisting flax diligently—sometimes stretching her lazy length upon the graves.

There they remained, hour after hour, until the sun began to sink behind the hills; and from the near Abbey, the few remaining monks of Melrose, were heard chanting their feeble and unregarded vespers. For now the old religion of the Stuarts was dying away in all the land, and John Knox's preachings **were every** where heard instead of matins **and** evensong.

" Meg," said Mistress Learmont, suddenly calling.

The damsel appeared, from a gossip at the abbey-gate.

" It's near the gloaming," said Marion, in a tremulous and rather excited tone. " Gang whar ye will, gude **Meg;** I'll just daunder hame my ain sel ; I'm gey strong the noo. See !"

She rose, and with the aid of a stout hazel-stick, marched steadily forward a few paces.

" **Ye** needna fash yoursel, lass," said she kindly, when Meg, whom so good a mistress had at last made a careful and devoted servant, tried to assist her steps. " Na, na; **I'll** e'en gang my lane : I maun do't," she added in a whisper **to** herself. " And He wha had on earth a mither o' His ain, will guide a waefu' mither this ae nicht."

She gently put her hand-maiden aside, and walked on alone. Only having gone a little way, she turned, and called back Meg, saying—

" Gin I'm ower lang o' comin', tell the gudeman he needna fear. I'll be about wark in the whilk a Greater Ane than either husband or bairn will tak tent to me, and see that **I** come to nae harm. And Meg," she added, for the second time turning back to give directions. "•Dear Meg, **be an** cident lass, and see that a' things are keepit braw for the gudeman and thae wild callants, until the time that I come **hame.**"

Her words, so serious and gentle, had a deeper meaning than Meg could **fathom.** She was half inclined to **follow,** but something in her mistress's aspect forbade. She staid behind, and Marion Learmont went on alone.

—Past all her neighbors in Melrose **town ;** past house after house, where the old wives sat knitting or spinning, and the children played in the gloaming, the mother went. **Nc** one spoke to her on the way ; it seemed so strange to see the lone sick woman walking thus, that many thought it was Marion Learmont's wraith. And even those few who believed it was herself, saw such a wondrously steadfast and absorbed expression in her face, that they were afraid to stop and address her. So on she went, leaning on her hazel-staff, with her mantle thrown over her head and stooping form ; and in her left hand nothing but a little Book, which during her sickness a young minister, a follower of John Knox, had taught her to read. She left the town soon, and reached the open country. It was already so far dusk, that the sheep along the hill-side and in the fields looked like white dots moving about ; while every where was heard the tinkle of the bells, and the whistle of the shepherds coming home.

Marion distinguished a voice she knew and hid herself by the dyke-side, until those who were approaching had passed by. It was her husband and her three sons, returning from their daily labor on their farm. There came into her heart a terror—a longing, lest perchance she should never see them again, these dear ones—though by a natural yet mysterious instinct not held so dear as the one lost, who by her must yet be saved.

She dared not speak to them, lest they should overrule her plan ; but she watched them with eager eyes, and followed them a little distance, stealing along under the shadow of the dyke and of the rowan trees that grew beside. She listened to their merry and unconscious voices.

"Eh," said Hughie. "I hear a soun' o' footsteps close by."

"It's naething but a bit maukin loupin' out of a whin-bush Are ye feared for the like o' that?" answered the father laughing.

"I'm no feared, father ; but it's the eve o' Roodmass when there's uncanny folk abroad," whispered the boy.

" Then we'll e'en **gae hame, lads, for** the gudewife's **sake**
She's easy fleyed, and **she has** aye a waefu' heart to bear.
We maun tak tent o' the puir mither."

" Ay, ay," echoed the sons, **moving forward** bravely and
quickly, and were soon out of sight.

The mother **herself** stood by the road-side, shedding many
and mingled tears. **But still her courage failed not, nor did**
she shrink **from her purpose.**

Very soon she came to a place where four roads met ; **a**
spot renowned throughout the whole neighborhood as being
"**uncanny.**" Tradition had faded concerning it—whether it
was the scene of midnight murder, or of more harmless elfin
tryste. Or perhaps the natural ghostliness of the place **added**
to its ill name. It was an open moorland, **except where a**
row of tall firs stood up, black sentinels, right against the sky ;
the wind in their tops keeping up a distant soughing peculiar
to trees of that species. **There is** not a more eerie sound in nature, than **the breeze passing** through the high dark branches
of a fir-wood.

Marion leant against one of **the** stems, exhausted, but not
afraid. The gloaming was fast melting into night; **the**
gloomy, cloudy night of early spring, when after the brief
hour of sunset all things frequently seem passing again into
dreariness and winter cold. The lonely woman began **to**
shiver where she stood ; and **a** heavy rain-cloud **gathering**
over the moor, fell down in showers, drenching **her even**
through her close mantle. All the moor vanished in haze ;
there **was neither star nor** moon. She could discern nothing
except the near **trees,** which in the mistiness around oftentimes seemed to stir **and** change their places, like great giants
walking about in the **night.**

And yet—even yet—the mother was not afraid.

She had waited a long time ; **so** long that she could have
thought the night almost **past, except** that she knew **the**

moon would rise at midnght, and it had not risen yet
Every thing was quite dark.

At length she saw a bright light dancing across the moor
at the eastern horizon.

"It is but the moon-rise," Marion said, and her heart grew
colder than ever with disappointment and fear. "Wac's
me! my hope is gane. Alice, Alice, I hae tint ye for evermair!"

Thus she, lamenting, hid her eyes from the light that grew
broader and deeper, though no orb appeared to rise. When
Marion looked again, there was a long stream of radiance
glittering across the moor; and faintly approaching came another music than that of the wind in the fir-tops. It was—
as a Nithsdale woman, who once heard the like, used to ex-
press it—"like the soun' o' a far awa' psalm."

Marion Learmont, even amidst her joy, trembled at the
crisis that was approaching; for she knew that what she now
saw and heard was the Fairies' Raid.

She crouched down behind the tree, muttering sometimes
the unintelligible Aves and Credos of her ancient faith; and
then again bursting out into the heartfelt prayers taught by
John Knox and his brethren. Alternately she clutched the
Bible, or, forgetting herself, made the familiar sign of the cross
Mingled and strange were all her religious forms; but there
was one thing that could not err, the intensity of devotion
in her heart. And never once did she take her straining
eyes from the sight on which was concentrated all her energy,
courage, and hope.

Nearer and nearer came the light, and separated itself into
individual forms. Never had Marion Learmont seen such a
glittering show. The elves rode one by one, men and
women alternately. Their steeds, of all colors, were capar-
isoned with gold and jewels, that sparked at every motion.
They themselves were as fair to behold as when the young

mother had seen them gathering in her chamber, on that fatal night of Alice's birth. She noticed as before their green kirtles, and their yellow hair, that while they rode streamed behind in a long train of light.

For the mortal mother beheld the elves but as mortals do, until they have abode in Fairyland long enough to learn that all this show is but outward glamour, nothingness, and vanity.

The cavalcade neared the tree, and Marion watched in agony for the first that should pass by. It was an elf, taller than the rest, whom she knew to be the Queen of Fairies Afterward, scores upon scores of elfin-horsemen rode near her; but the mother's eye lingered upon none. No doubt had she in her search;—through all that disguise she could not mistake her own child.

Each after the other, the whole train passed by, until there remained but one—who rode slower than the rest; and neither by voice nor merry gesture urged her palfrey on. She sat, amidst all the brilliant show of her attire quite passive and silent. Only as her horse was sweeping past the cross-roads, she turned and leaned sideways showing distinctly her pale face and eager eyes. It was Alice herself.

Quick as lightning—strong as though she had never been sick—the mother leaped forward and dragged her child down from the palfrey. Instantly it melted away, and lay, a withered bramble bough, in the middle of the path. A loud wail ran across the moor;—the fairy pageant vanished, and all was perfect silence.

For several minutes this hush lasted; during which neither mother nor daughter spoke. Marion was conscious of nothing save that she held in her arms her living, breathing Alice. After a little she loosened her clasp, trying to look in her daughter's face

M

"Ah, hold me fast—let me not go," murmured the girl, in terror.

And even while she spoke, there gradually arose across the moor a whirlwind of unearthly sounds—loud voices, screams, and laughter. It came nearer, eddying round on every side, dinning in Marion's ears so close that she started, as though strange things were clutching at her—but nothing was visible.

"Hold me fast—fast," was all Alice's cry.

"I *will* haud ye fast, my bairn that I bore," the mother answered, firmly. And so they stood, clinging together in the midst of that eldritch rout, the more fearful that it was only heard, not seen.

The blackness of the night changed a little, and the great round moon rose up from the edge of the moor. As soon as it gave sufficient light to distinguish objects, Marion gained some comfort. But her terror returned, when in the shadow cast by the bole of the opposite fir trees she saw something leaning. It was a human form, the very image of herself, except the face, which was hid.

"Turn your cloak, mother, and it will vanish," whispered Alice.—"But oh, do not let go your hold of me."

Marion did as her child desired, and the illusion melted away.

This was the first of the elfin spells, through the fierce ordeal of which the mother passed that night The next trial was far more horrible to bear.

Suddenly, in her very arms, the soft form of Alice seemed changing to that of a wild beast. "Hold me close, and I'll do ye no harm," screamed the voice, which alone was human. And still the brave mother held fast her own, until again she felt the warm maiden-flesh beating against her bosom.

After that, through every horror that elfin malice could plan, amidst transformations uncouth, loathsome, or terrible, did Marion Learmont keep her treasure close embraced. Sometimes she seemed to enfold a goblin shape, or had a slimy serpent crawling on her breast, or clasped with her bare arms a red-hot bar of iron ; but through each change, foul or frightful, the mother knew and held fast to her own child. Many another mother through all human t ials has done the same !

At last the sky, which except just at moon-rise had been overcast all night, was brightened at the east with a streak of yellow and pale green. The elfin clamour began to die away in the dawn.

" Bide a wee, bide a wee," sighed the exhausted mother, as after the last transformation her daughter lay almost like a corse in her arms. " While I hae life I winna tine my bairn."

Ere she ceased speaking, there came a sound like a clap of thunder, mingled with howlings that might have risen from the bottomless pit. All around where Marion stood was flame, and it was a living flame that swayed to and fro in her arms.

" Hae pity on us, oh God !" shrieked the mother aloud. Instantly the thunder ceased, the jet of flame sank down, and Marion held to her breast her young daughter, who lay there, pallid, trembling, cold—and naked as when she had come into the world, a helpless babe.

" Throw your mantle over me, and then I will be safe and all your own," feebly said Alice.

The mother did so, taking off some of her own garments and wrapping her child close. Then all the eldritch sounds died away in distance ; the light broadened across the moor, and all the earth lay in the stillness and freshness of day-break

Marion and her daughter sank down together, and leaning against the fir tree's bole, kissed one another and wept. Suddenly, in one of the topmost branches was heard the twittei of a waking bird.

"It is a' true, and ye're my ain—thanks be to the gude God !" cried Marion, in a choking voice. " Let us arise, my dochter, and gae hame thegither."

Across the yet dark fields they took their way, the mother leaning on Alice's arm. They passed through the silent town of Melrose, where all were still fast asleep—tired fathers resting after their work, and mothers lying with their little children round. But there was never a mother like this mother !

Not a creature they met in all the street, or beyond it, until they came to their own door. Then, creeping along the side of the byre, Marion Learmont saw something which seemed through the misty morning-light to be a human form, all fluttering in gaudy-colored rags. And a cracked voice, that might have been sweet when young, and still had a kind of wild pathos, startled her by its old familiar sounds, now unheard for many years. It sang a fragment of meaningless rhyme, which yet had a certain method in it :

> "Simmer and winter baith gae round,
> Spak the mither wren to her bairnies three ;
> Tint was tint, and found is found,
> I'll hap my heid saft in my ain countrie."

" It's Daft Simmie come back, him that was hunted far and near for stealing my bairn. He's at his sangs again. Wonderfu' are the ways o' the Lord !"

And her thoughts went back to old times, remembering how all things had worked together for good, until her heart was mute for very thankfulness.

As her feet touched the doorsill, the sun rose upon the earth ; she turned a minute to gaze at the brightening Abbey-tower and the three summits of Eildon Hill, and all the land around, wakening up into the glory of a new day. Then she looked at Alice, who stood near, her unearthly beauty chastened into that which was merely human—the loveliness of love itself.

"My ain bairn, my ae dochter! that was dead and is alive again—was lost and found!" cried Marion, falling on her neck.

She rested there a little space, then took her daughter's hand, and with great joyfulness they two then went together into the house.

THE END

VALUABLE AND INTERESTING WORKS
FOR
PUBLIC & PRIVATE LIBRARIES
PUBLISHED BY HARPER & BROTHERS, New York.

☞ *For a full List of Books suitable for Libraries published by* Harper & Brothers, *see* Harper's Catalogue, *which may be had gratuitously on application to the publishers personally, or by letter enclosing Ten Cents in postage stamps.*

☞ Harper & Brothers *will send their publications by mail, postage prepaid, on receipt of the price.*

BOSWELL'S LIFE OF JOHNSON, Including Boswell's Journal of a Tour to the Hebrides, and Johnson's Diary of a Journey into North Wales. Edited by George Birkbeck Hill, D.C.L., Pembroke College, Oxford. *Édition de Luxe.* In Six Volumes. Large 8vo, Half Vellum, Uncut Edges and Gilt Tops, with many Portraits, Fac-similes, etc., $30 00. *Popular Edition.* 6 vols., Cloth, Uncut Edges and Gilt Tops, $10 00.

THE JOURNAL OF SIR WALTER SCOTT, 1825–1832. From the Original Manuscript at Abbotsford. With Two Portraits and Engraved Title-pages. Two volumes, 8vo, Cloth, Uncut Edges and Gilt Tops, $7 50; Half Calf, $12 00. *Popular Edition.* One volume, Crown 8vo, Cloth, $2 50.

STUDIES IN CHAUCER: His Life and Writings. By Thomas R. Lounsbury, Professor of English in the Sheffield Scientific School of Yale University. With a Portrait of Chaucer. 3 vols., 8vo, Cloth, Uncut Edges and Gilt Tops, $9 00. (*In a Box.*)

PHARAOHS, FELLAHS, AND EXPLORERS. By Amelia B. Edwards. Illustrated. 8vo, Cloth, Ornamental, Uncut Edges and Gilt Top, $4 00.

INDIKA. The Country and the People of India and Ceylon. By John F. Hurst, D.D., LL.D. With 6 Maps and 250 Illustrations. 8vo, Cloth, $5 00; Half Morocco, $7 00. (*Sold by Subscription only.*)

MOTLEY'S LETTERS. The Correspondence of John Lothrop Motley, D.C.L. Edited by George William Curtis. With Portrait. 2 vols., 8vo, Cloth, $7 00; Sheep, $8 00; Half Calf, $11 50.

MACAULAY'S ENGLAND. The History of England from the Accession of James II. By THOMAS BABINGTON MACAULAY. 5 vols., in a Box, 8vo, Cloth, with Paper Labels, Uncut Edges and Gilt Tops, $10 00; Sheep, $12 50; Half Calf, $21 25. (*Sold only in Sets.*) Cheap Edition, 5 vols., 12mo, Cloth, $2 50; Sheep, $3 75.

MACAULAY'S MISCELLANEOUS WORKS. The Miscellaneous Works of Lord Macaulay. 5 vols., in a Box, 8vo, Cloth, with Paper Labels, Uncut Edges and Gilt Tops, $10 00; Sheep, $12 50; Half Calf, $21 25. (*Sold only in Sets.*)

HUME'S ENGLAND. History of England, from the Invasion of Julius Cæsar to the Abdication of James II., 1688. By DAVID HUME. 6 vols., in a Box, 8vo, Cloth, with Paper Labels, Uncut Edges and Gilt Tops, $12 00; Sheep, $15 00; Half Calf, $25 50. (*Sold only in Sets.*) Popular Edition, 6 vols., in a Box, 12mo, Cloth, $3 00; Sheep, $4 50.

THE WORKS OF OLIVER GOLDSMITH. Edited by PETER CUNNINGHAM, F.S.A. 4 vols., 8vo, Cloth, Paper Labels, Uncut Edges and Gilt Tops, $8 00; Sheep, $10 00; Half Calf, $17 00.

THE RISE OF THE DUTCH REPUBLIC. A History. By JOHN LOTHROP MOTLEY, LL.D., D.C.L. With a Portrait of William of Orange. 3 vols., in a Box. 8vo, Cloth, with Paper Labels, Uncut Edges and Gilt Tops, $6 00; Sheep, $7 50; Half Calf, $12 75. (*Sold only in Sets.*)

HISTORY OF THE UNITED NETHERLANDS: From the Death of William the Silent to the Twelve Years' Truce—1548–1609. With a full View of the English-Dutch Struggle against Spain, and of the Origin and Destruction of the Spanish Armada. By JOHN LOTHROP MOTLEY, LL.D., D.C.L. Portraits. 4 vols., in a Box, 8vo, Cloth, with Paper Labels, Uncut Edges and Gilt Tops, $8 00; Sheep, $10 00; Half Calf, $17 00. (*Sold only in Sets.*)

THE LIFE AND DEATH OF JOHN OF BARNEVELD, Advocate of Holland. With a View of the Primary Causes and Movements of the "Thirty Years' War." By JOHN LOTHROP MOTLEY, LL.D., D.C.L. Illustrated. 2 vols., in a Box, 8vo, Cloth, with Paper Labels, Uncut Edges and Gilt Tops, $4 00; Sheep, $5 00; Half Calf, $8 50. (*Sold only in Sets.*)

GIBBON'S ROME. **The** History of the **Decline** and Fall of the Roman Empire. **By** EDWARD GIBBON. **With** Notes by Dean MILMAN, **M. GUIZOT,** and Dr. WILLIAM SMITH. 6 vols., in a Box, 8vo, **Cloth,** with Paper Labels, Uncut Edges and Gilt Tops, $12 00; Sheep, $15 00; Half Calf, $25 50. **Popular Edition.** 6 vols., in a Box, 12mo, Cloth, $3 00; **Sheep, $4 50.** (*Sold only in Sets.*)

A DICTIONARY OF THE ENGLISH LANGUAGE. Pronouncing, Etymological, **and** Explanatory: embracing Scientific and other **Terms,** Numerous Familiar Terms, and a Copious Selection of Old English Words. By the Rev. JAMES STORMONTH. The Pronunciation Revised by the **Rev. P. H.** PHELP, M.A. Imperial 8vo, **Cloth,** $5 00; **Half Roan, $6 50; Full Sheep,** $6 50.

A MANUAL OF HISTORICAL LITERATURE, comprising Brief Descriptions **of the most Important Histories** in English, French, **and German, together with** Practical Suggestions as to Methods **and Courses of Historical Study,** for the **Use of Students,** General **Readers, and Collectors of** Books. By CHARLES KENDALL ADAMS, LL.D. **Third Edition,** Revised and Enlarged. Crown 8vo, Cloth, **$2 50.**

ART AND CRITICISM. Monographs and Studies. By THEODORE CHILD. Richly Illustrated. Large 8vo, Cloth, Ornamental, Uncut Edges and Gilt Top, $6 00. (*In a Box.*)

THE SPANISH-AMERICAN REPUBLICS. By THEODORE CHILD. Illustrated by T. DE THULSTRUP, FREDERIC REMINGTON, WILLIAM HAMILTON GIBSON, W. H. ROGERS, and **other** Eminent Artists. Large 8vo, Cloth, Ornamental, $3 50.

ILIOS, the City and Country of the Trojans. **A Narrative of the Most Recent Discoveries** and Researches made on the Plain of **Troy. By** Dr. HENRY SCHLIEMANN. Maps, **Plans, and Illustrations. Imperial** 8vo, Illuminated Cloth, $7 50; **Half Morocco, $10 00.**

TROJA. Results of the Latest Researches and Discoveries on the Site of Homer's Troy, and in the Heroic Tumuli and other Sites, **made** in the Year 1882, and a Narrative of a Journey in the Troad in 1881. **By Dr.** HENRY SCHLIEMANN. Preface by Professor A. H. **Sayce.** With Wood-cuts, Maps, and Plans. 8vo, Cloth, $5 00; **Half** Morocco, $7 50.

HISTORY OF THE UNITED STATES. By RICHARD HIL-
DRETH. FIRST SERIES: From the Discovery of the Continent
to the Organization of the Government under the Federal Con-
stitution. SECOND SERIES: From the Adoption of the Federal
Constitution to the end of the Sixteenth Congress. Popular
Edition, 6 vols., in a Box, 8vo, Cloth, with Paper Labels, Uncut
Edges and Gilt Tops, $12 00; Sheep, $15 00; Half Calf, $25 00.
(*Sold only in Sets.*)

RECOLLECTIONS OF PRESIDENT LINCOLN and His Ad-
ministration. By LUCIUS E. CHITTENDEN. With Portrait.
8vo, Cloth, Uncut Edges and Gilt Top, $2 50; Half Calf,
$4 75.

MEMOIR OF THE LIFE OF LAURENCE OLIPHANT and of
Alice Oliphant, his wife. By MARGARET OLIPHANT W. OLI-
PHANT. 2 vols., 8vo, Cloth, Uncut Edges and Gilt Tops, $7 00.
(*In a Box.*)

EPISODES IN A LIFE OF ADVENTURE; or, Moss from a
Rolling Stone. By LAURENCE OLIPHANT. 12mo, Cloth, $1 25.

HAIFA; OR, LIFE IN MODERN PALESTINE. By LAURENCE
OLIPHANT. Edited, with Introduction, by CHARLES A. DANA.
12mo, Cloth, $1 75.

CONSTITUTIONAL HISTORY OF THE UNITED STATES
from their Declaration of Independence to the Close of their
Civil War. By GEORGE TICKNOR CURTIS. Two Volumes.
Vol. I., 8vo, Cloth, Uncut Edges and Gilt Top, $3 00.

OUR ITALY. An Exposition of the Climate and Resources of
Southern California. By CHARLES DUDLEY WARNER. Illustrated. 8vo, Cloth, Uncut Edges and Gilt Top, $2 50.

LONDON LETTERS, and Some Others. By GEORGE W.
SMALLEY, London Correspondent of the *New York Tribune.*
Two Volumes. Vol I. Personalities—Two Midlothian Cam-
paigns. Vol. II. Notes on Social Life—Notes on Parliament—
Pageants — Miscellanies. 8vo, Cloth, Uncut Edges and Gilt
Tops, $6 00.

LIFE AND LETTERS OF GENERAL THOMAS J. JACKSON
(Stonewall Jackson). By His Wife, MARY ANNA JACKSON.
With an Introduction by HENRY M. FIELD, D.D. Illustrated.
8vo, Cloth, $2 00.

POLITICAL HISTORY **OF** RECENT **TIMES** (1816-1875). With Special Reference to Germany. By **WILLIAM** MÜLLER. Translated, with an Appendix covering the Period from 1876 to 1881, by the Rev. **JOHN** P. **PETERS,** Ph.D.   12mo, Cloth, $2 00.

THE **LIFE** AND **LETTERS OF** LORD **MACAULAY.** By his Nephew, **GEORGE** OTTO **TREVELYAN,** M.P.   With Portrait on Steel.   2 vols., 8vo, Cloth, Uncut Edges and Gilt Tops, $5 00 ; Sheep, $6 00 ; Half Calf, $9 50.   *Popular Edition,* two vols. in one, 12mo, Cloth, $1 75.

THE EARLY HISTORY OF CHARLES JAMES FOX.   By **GEORGE** OTTO **TREVELYAN.**   8vo, Cloth, Uncut Edges and Gilt Tops, $2 50 ; Half Calf, $4 75.

WRITINGS AND SPEECHES OF **SAMUEL** J. **TILDEN.** Edited by **JOHN** BIGELOW.   2 vols., 8vo, Cloth, Uncut Edges and Gilt Tops, $6 00 per set.

MEMOIRS **OF** JOHN ADAMS **DIX.**   Compiled by his Son, **MORGAN DIX.**   With Five Steel-plate Portraits.   2 vols., 8vo, Cloth, Uncut Edges and Gilt Tops, $5 00.

THROUGH THE DARK CONTINENT ; or, The Sources of the Nile, Around the Great Lakes of Equatorial Africa, and Down the Livingstone River to the Atlantic Ocean.   149 Illustrations and 10 Maps.   By H. M. **STANLEY.**   2 vols., 8vo, Cloth, $7 50 ; Sheep, $9 50 ; Half Morocco, $12 00.

THE CONGO and the Founding of its Free State, a Story of Work and Exploration.   With over One Hundred Full-page and smaller Illustrations, Two Large Maps, and several smaller ones.   By H. M. **STANLEY.**   2 vols., 8vo, Cloth, $7 50 ; Sheep, $9 50 ; Half Morocco, $12 00.

HISTORY **OF THE** ENGLISH **PEOPLE.**   By **JOHN RICHARD** GREEN, M.A.   With Maps.   4 vols., 8vo, Cloth, $2 50 per vol. Volumes sold separately.   Complete sets, Sheep, $12 00 ; Half Calf, $19 00.

THE MAKING **OF** ENGLAND.   By **JOHN RICHARD** GREEN. With Maps.   8vo, Cloth, $2 50 ; Sheep, $3 00 ; Half Calf, $4 75.

THE CONQUEST OF ENGLAND.   By **JOHN RICHARD** GREEN. With Maps.   8vo, Cloth, $2 50 ; Sheep, $3 00 ; Half Calf, $4 75.

A SHORT HISTORY **OF** THE ENGLISH **PEOPLE.**   By **JOHN RICHARD** GREEN, M.A.   Revised and Enlarged.   With Colored Maps and Tables.   8vo, Cloth, $1 20.

THE LAND OF THE MIDNIGHT SUN. Summer and Winter Journeys in Sweden, Norway, Lapland, and Northern Finland. By PAUL B. DU CHAILLU. Illustrated. 2 vols., 8vo, Cloth, $7 50; Half Calf, $12 00.

CYCLOPÆDIA OF UNITED STATES HISTORY. From the Aboriginal Period to 1876. By BENSON J. LOSSING. Illustrated by 2 Steel Portraits and over 1000 Engravings. 2 vols., Royal 8vo, Cloth, $10 00; Sheep, $12 00; Half Morocco, $15 00.

PICTORIAL FIELD-BOOK OF THE REVOLUTION; or, Illustrations by Pen and Pencil of the History, Biography, Scenery, Relics, and Traditions of the War for Independence. By BENSON J. LOSSING. 2 vols., 8vo, Cloth, $14 00; Sheep or Roan, $15 00; Half Calf, $18 00.

PICTORIAL FIELD-BOOK OF THE WAR OF 1812; or, Illustrations by Pen and Pencil of the History, Biography, Scenery, Relics, and Traditions of the last War for American Independence. By BENSON J. LOSSING. 8vo, Cloth, $7 00; Sheep or Roan, $8 50; Half Calf, $10 00.

ENGLISH MEN OF LETTERS. Edited by JOHN MORLEY. The following volumes are now ready:

JOHNSON. By L. Stephen.—GIBBON. By J. C. Morison.—SCOTT. By R. H. Hutton.—SHELLEY. By J. A. Symonds.—GOLDSMITH. By W. Black.—HUME. By Professor Huxley.—DEFOE. By W. Minto.—BURNS. By Principal Shairp. —SPENSER. By R. W. Church.—THACKERAY. By A. Trollope.—BURKE. By J. Morley.—MILTON. By M. Pattison.—SOUTHEY. By E. Dowden.—CHAUCER. By A. W. Ward.—BUNYAN. By J. A. Froude.—COWPER. By G. Smith.—POPE. By L. Stephen.—BYRON. By J. Nichols.—LOCKE. By T. Fowler.—WORDSWORTH. By F. W H. Myers.—HAWTHORNE. By Henry James, Jr.—DRYDEN. By G. Saintsbury.—LANDOR. By S. Colvin.—DE QUINCEY. By D. Masson.—LAMB. By A. Ainger.—BENTLEY. By R. C. Jebb.—DICKENS. By A. W. Ward.—GRAY. By E. W. Gosse.—SWIFT. By L. Stephen.—STERNE. By H. D. Traill.—MACAULAY. By J. C. Morison.—FIELDING. By A. Dobson.—SHERIDAN. By Mrs. Oliphant.—ADDISON. By W. J. Courthope.—BACON. By R. W. Church.—COLERIDGE. By H. D. Traill.—SIR PHILIP SIDNEY. By J. A. Symonds.—KEATS. By S. Colvin. 12mo, Cloth, 75 cents per volume.

Popular Edition. 36 volumes in 12, Cloth, $12 00; Half Leather, $21 00.

HISTORY OF THE INQUISITION OF THE MIDDLE AGES. By HENRY CHARLES LEA. 3 vols., 8vo, Cloth, Uncut Edges and Gilt Tops, $3 00 per vol.

THE MIKADO'S EMPIRE. Book I. History of Japan, from 660 b.c. to 1872 a.d. Book II. Personal Experiences, Observations, and Studies in Japan, from 1870 to 1874. With Two Supplementary Chapters: Japan in 1883, 1886, and 1890. By W. E. Griffis. Copiously Illustrated. 8vo, Cloth, $4 00; Half Calf, $6 25.

A SHORT HISTORY OF THE ENGLISH COLONIES IN AMERICA. By Henry Cabot Lodge. With Colored Map. 8vo, Half Leather, $3 00.

THE LAND AND THE BOOK. Biblical Illustrations drawn from the Manners and Customs, the Scenes and Scenery, of the Holy Land. By William M. Thomson, D.D., Forty-five Years a Missionary in Syria and Palestine. In Three Volumes. Copiously Illustrated. Square 8vo, Ornamental Cloth, per volume, $6 00; Sheep, $7 00; Half Morocco, $8 50; Full Morocco, Gilt Edges, $10 00.
    Volume I. Southern Palestine and Jerusalem.—Volume II. Central Palestine and Phœnicia.—Volume III. Lebanon, Damascus, and Beyond Jordan.
    Also, Handsome *Popular Edition* in Three Vols., Cloth, $9 00 per Set; Half Leather, $12 00. (*Sold only in Sets.*)

THE INVASION OF THE CRIMEA: its Origin, and an Account of its Progress down to the Death of Lord Raglan. By Alexander William Kinglake. With Maps and Plans. Six vols. 12mo, Cloth, $2 00 per vol.; Half Calf, $22 50 per set.

FIFTY YEARS AGO. By Walter Besant. With a Portrait and Characteristic Illustrations by Cruikshank and others. 8vo, Cloth, $2 50.

THE TSAR AND HIS PEOPLE; or, Social Life in Russia. Papers by Theodore Child, Eugène Melchior de Vogüé, Clarence Cook, and Vassili Verestchagin. Illustrated. Square 8vo, Cloth, Uncut Edges and Gilt Top, $3 00.

THE CAPITALS OF SPANISH AMERICA. By William Eleroy Curtis. With a Colored Map and 358 Illustrations. 8vo, Cloth, $3 50.

JINRIKISHA DAYS IN JAPAN. By Eliza Ruhamah Skidmore. Illustrated. Post 8vo, Cloth, Ornamental, $2 00.

LIFE OF BISHOP MATTHEW SIMPSON, of the Methodist
Episcopal Church. By GEORGE R. CROOKS, D.D. Illustrated.
8vo, Cloth, $3 75; Gilt Edges, $4 25; Half Morocco, $5 25.
(*Sold by Subscription.*)

SERMONS BY BISHOP MATTHEW SIMPSON, of the Methodist Episcopal Church. Edited by GEORGE R. CROOKS, D.D.
8vo, Cloth, $2 50.

LITERARY INDUSTRIES. By HUBERT HOWE BANCROFT.
With Steel-Plate Portrait. Post 8vo, Cloth $1 50.

CURIOSITIES OF THE AMERICAN STAGE. By LAURENCE
HUTTON. With Copious and Characteristic Illustrations.
Crown 8vo, Cloth, Uncut Edges and Gilt Top, $2 50.

STUDIES IN THE WAGNERIAN DRAMA. By HENRY E.
KREHBIEL. Post 8vo, Cloth, $1 25.

HISTORY OF MEDIÆVAL ART. By Dr. FRANZ VON RE-
BER. Translated and Augmented by Joseph Thacher Clarke.
With 422 Illustrations, and a Glossary of Technical Terms.
8vo, Cloth, $5 00.

HISTORY OF ANCIENT ART. By Dr. FRANZ VON REBER.
Revised by the Author. Translated and Augmented by Joseph Thacher Clarke. With 310 Illustrations and a Glossary
of Technical Terms. 8vo, Cloth, $3 50.

OUTLINES OF INTERNATIONAL LAW, with an Account
of its Origin and Sources, and of its Historical Development.
By GEORGE B. DAVIS, U.S.A. Crown 8vo, Cloth, $2 00.

CYPRUS: its Ancient Cities, Tombs, and Temples. A Narrative
of Researches and Excavations during Ten Years' Residence
in that Island. By L. P. DI CESNOLA. With Portrait, Maps,
and 400 Illustrations. 8vo, Cloth, Extra, Uncut Edges and
Gilt Top, $7 50.

THE ANCIENT CITIES OF THE NEW WORLD: Being
Voyages and Explorations in Mexico and Central America,
from 1857 to 1882. By DÉSIRÉ CHARNAY. Translated by J.
Gonino and Helen S. Conant. Illustrations and Map. Royal
8vo, Ornamental Cloth, Uncut Edges, Gilt Top, $6 00.

A HISTORY OF **OUR** OWN TIMES, from the Accession of Queen Victoria to the General Election of 1880. By JUSTIN M'CARTHY, M.P. **2 vols.,** 12mo, Cloth, $2 50; Half Calf, $6 00.

A SHORT **HISTORY** OF **OUR OWN TIMES,** from the Accession of Queen Victoria to the General Election of 1880. By JUSTIN M'CARTHY, M.P. 12mo, Cloth, $1 50.

A HISTORY OF THE FOUR GEORGES. By JUSTIN M'CARTHY, M.P. In Four Volumes. Vols. I. and II., 12mo, Cloth, $1 25 each.

THE FRENCH REVOLUTION. By JUSTIN H. McCARTHY. In Two Volumes. Volume I. Post 8vo, Cloth, $1 50.

THE FRENCH REVOLUTION OF 1789, as viewed in the Light of Republican Institutions. By JOHN S. C. ABBOTT. Illustrated. 8vo, Cloth, $3 50; Sheep, $4 00; Half Calf, $5 75.

THE HISTORY OF NAPOLEON BONAPARTE. By JOHN S. C. ABBOTT. Maps, Illustrations, and Portraits. 2 vols., 8vo, Cloth, $7 00; Sheep, $8 00; Half Calf, $11 50.

NAPOLEON AT ST. HELENA; or, Anecdotes and Conversations of the Emperor during the Years of his Captivity. Collected from the Memorials of Las Casas, O'Meara, Montholon, Antommarchi, and others. By JOHN S. C. ABBOTT. Illustrated. 8vo, Cloth, $3 50; Sheep, $4 00; Half Calf, $5 75.

THE HISTORY OF FREDERICK THE SECOND, called Frederick the Great. By JOHN S. C. ABBOTT. Illustrated. 8vo, Cloth, $3 50; Sheep, $4 00; Half Calf, $5 75.

THE ORIGIN OF THE WORLD, according to Revelation and Science. By J. W. DAWSON, LL.D., F.R.S., F.G.S. 12mo, Cloth, $2 00.

MODERN SCIENCE IN BIBLE LANDS. By Sir J. W. DAWSON, C.M.G., LL.D., F.R.S. Maps and Illustrations. 12mo, Cloth, $2 00.

THE STORY OF THE EARTH AND MAN. By J. W. DAWSON, LL.D., F.R.S., F.G.S., Principal and Vice-Chancellor of McGill University, Montreal. With Twenty Illustrations. *New and Revised Edition.* 12mo, Cloth, $1 50.

THE STUDENT'S SERIES. Maps and Ill's. 12mo, Cloth:
FRANCE.—GIBBON.—GREECE.—ROME (by LIDDELL).—OLD
TESTAMENT HISTORY.—NEW TESTAMENT HISTORY.—STRICK-
LAND'S QUEENS OF ENGLAND. — ANCIENT HISTORY OF THE
EAST.—HALLAM'S MIDDLE AGES.—HALLAM'S CONSTITUTIONAL
HISTORY OF ENGLAND.— LYELL'S ELEMENTS OF GEOLOGY.—
MERIVALE'S GENERAL HISTORY OF ROME. — COX'S GENERAL
HISTORY OF GREECE.—CLASSICAL DICTIONARY.—SKEAT'S ETY-
MOLOGICAL DICTIONARY. — RAWLINSON'S ANCIENT HISTORY.
$1 25 per volume.
LEWIS'S HISTORY OF GERMANY.—ECCLESIASTICAL HISTORY,
Two Vols.—HUME'S ENGLAND.—MODERN EUROPE. $1 50 per
volume.
WESTCOTT AND HORT'S GREEK TESTAMENT, $1 00.

JESUS CHRIST IN THE OLD TESTAMENT ; or, The Great
Argument. By W. H. THOMSON, M.A., M.D. Crown 8vo,
Cloth, $2 00.

STUDIES OF THE GREEK POETS. By JOHN ADDINGTON
SYMONDS. 2 vols., Square 16mo, Cloth,$3 50 ; Half Calf,$7 00.

A HISTORY OF CLASSICAL GREEK LITERATURE. By
J. P. MAHAFFY. 2 vols., 12mo, Cloth, $4 00 ; Half Calf,$7 50.

A HISTORY OF LATIN LITERATURE, from Ennius to Boe-
thius. By GEORGE AUGUSTUS SIMCOX, M.A. 2 vols., 12mo,
Cloth, $4 00.

MY AUTOBIOGRAPHY AND REMINISCENCES. By W. P.
FRITH, R.A. Portraits and Fac-similes. 2 vols., 12mo, Cloth,
$1 50 each.

WHAT I REMEMBER. By THOMAS ADOLPHUS TROLLOPE.
2 vols., 12mo, Cloth, $1 75 each.

MODERN ITALIAN POETS. (1770–1870.) Essays and Ver-
sions. By WILLIAM DEAN HOWELLS. With Portraits. 12mo,
Cloth, $2 00.

SYDNEY SMITH. A Sketch of the Life and Times of the
Rev. Sydney Smith. Based on Family Documents and the
Recollections of Personal Friends. By STUART J. REID. With
Steel-plate Portrait and Illustrations. 8vo, Cloth, $3 00.

CARICATURE AND OTHER COMIC ART, in All Times and Many Lands. By JAMES PARTON. 203 Illustrations. 8vo, Cloth, Uncut Edges and Gilt Tops, $5 00; Half Calf, $7 25.

GEORGE ELIOT'S LIFE. Related in her Letters and Journals. Arranged and Edited by her Husband, J. W. CROSS. Portraits and Illustrations. In 3 vols., 12mo, Cloth, $3 75; Half Calf, $9 00. *Popular Edition:* Cloth, $2 25; Half Binding, $2 00.

THE FALL OF CONSTANTINOPLE. Being the Story of the Fourth Crusade. By EDWIN PEARS, LL.B. 8vo, Cloth, $2 50.

COLERIDGE'S WORKS. The Complete Works of Samuel Taylor Coleridge. With an Introductory Essay upon his Philosophical and Theological Opinions. Edited by Professor W. G. T. SHEDD. With Steel Portrait, and an Index. 7 vols., 12mo, Cloth, $2 00 per volume; $12 00 per set; Half Calf, $24 25.

TENNYSON'S COMPLETE POEMS. The Complete Poetical Works of Alfred, Lord Tennyson. With an Introductory Sketch by Anne Thackeray Ritchie. With Portraits and Illustrations. 8vo, Extra Cloth, Bevelled, Gilt Edges, $2 50.

"THE FRIENDLY EDITION" of Shakespeare's Works. Edited by W. J. ROLFE. In 20 vols. Illustrated. 16mo, Gilt Tops and Uncut Edges. Cloth, $25 00; Half Leather, $35 00; Half Calf, $50 00 per Set.

LIFE OF JAMES BUCHANAN, Fifteenth President of the United States. By GEORGE TICKNOR CURTIS. With Two Steel-Plate Portraits. 2 vols., 8vo, Cloth, Uncut Edges and Gilt Tops, $6 00.

CYCLOPÆDIA OF BRITISH AND AMERICAN POETRY. Edited by EPES SARGENT. Royal 8vo, Illuminated Cloth, Colored Edges, $4 50; Half Leather, $5 00.

HISTORY OF CHRISTIAN DOCTRINE. By H. C. SHELDON, Professor of Church History in Boston University. 2 vols., 8vo, Cloth, $3 50.

ADVENTURES IN THE GREAT FOREST of Equatorial
Africa and the Country of the Dwarfs. By PAUL DU CHAILLU.
Abridged and Popular **Edition.** With Map and Illustrations.
Post 8vo, Cloth, $1 75.

LIVINGSTONE'S ZAMBESI. Narrative of an Expedition to
the Zambesi and its Tributaries, and of the Discovery of the
Lakes Shirwa and Nyassa, 1858 to 1864. By DAVID and
CHARLES LIVINGSTONE. Illustrated. 8vo, Cloth, $5 00; Sheep,
$5 50.

THE LAST JOURNALS OF DAVID LIVINGSTONE in Central Africa, from 1865 to his Death. Continued by a Narrative
of his Last Moments, obtained from his Faithful Servants Chu-
ma and Susi. By HORACE WALLER. With Portrait, Maps, and
Illustrations. 8vo, Cloth, $5 00; Sheep, $6 00.

HISTORY OF FRIEDRICH II., called Frederick the Great.
By THOMAS CARLYLE. Portraits, Maps, Plans, etc. 6 vols.,
12mo, Cloth, $7 00; Sheep, $9 90; Half Calf, $18 00.

THE FRENCH REVOLUTION: A History. By THOMAS CAR-
LYLE. 2 vols., 12mo, Cloth, $2 50; Sheep, $3 30; Half Calf,
$6 00.

OLIVER CROMWELL'S LETTERS AND SPEECHES, including the Supplement to the First Edition. With Elucida-
tions. By THOMAS CARLYLE. 2 vols., 12mo, Cloth, $2 50;
Sheep, $3 30; Half Calf, $6 00.

PAST AND PRESENT, CHARTISM, AND SARTOR RESAR-
TUS. By THOMAS CARLYLE. 12mo, Cloth, $1 25.

EARLY KINGS OF NORWAY, AND THE PORTRAITS OF
JOHN KNOX. By THOMAS CARLYLE. 12mo, Cloth, $1 25.

REMINISCENCES BY THOMAS CARLYLE. Edited by J. A.
FROUDE. 12mo, Cloth, with Copious Index, and with Thirteen
Portraits, 50 cents.

BROUGHAM'S AUTOBIOGRAPHY. Life and Times of Henry, Lord Brougham. Written by Himself. 3 vols., 12mo, Cloth,
$6 00.

FROUDE'S LIFE OF **THOMAS CARLYLE.** Part I. **A** History of the First Forty **Years of Carlyle's Life** (1795–1835). By James Anthony Froude, **M.A.** With Portraits and Illustrations. 12mo, **Cloth, $1 00.**

Part II. A History of Carlyle's Life in London (1834–1881). By James Anthony Froude. Illustrated. 12mo, Cloth, $1 00.

AN AUTOBIOGRAPHY. By Anthony Trollope. With a Portrait. 12mo, Cloth, $1 25.

LIFE OF CICERO. By Anthony Trollope. 2 vols., 12mo, Cloth, $3 00.

MARCUS AURELIUS ANTONINUS. By Paul Barron Watson. Crown 8vo, Cloth, $2 50.

A JOURNEY TO ASHANGO LAND, and Further Penetration into Equatorial Africa. By Paul B. du Chaillu. Illustrated. 8vo, Cloth, $5 00; Half Calf, $7 25.

FROM EGYPT TO PALESTINE. Through Sinai, the Wilderness, and the South Country. Observations of a Journey made with Special Reference to the History of the Israelites. By S. C. Bartlett, D.D. Maps and Illustrations. 8vo, Cloth, $3 50.

THE DRAMATIC WORKS OF SHAKSPEARE. With Notes. Engravings. 6 vols., 12mo, Cloth, $9 00.

THE COMMUNISTIC SOCIETIES OF THE UNITED STATES, from Personal Visit and Observation; including Detailed Accounts of the Economists, Zoarites, Shakers, the Amana, Oneida, Bethel, Aurora, Icarian, and other existing Societies. By Charles Nordhoff. Illustrations. 8vo, Cloth, $4 00.

THE ATMOSPHERE. Translated from the French of Camille Flammarion. With 10 Chromo-Lithographs and 86 Woodcuts. 8vo, Cloth, $6 00; Half Calf, $8 25.

A TEXT-BOOK OF CHURCH HISTORY. By Dr. John C. L. Gieseler. Revised and Edited by Rev. Henry B. Smith, D.D. Vols. I., II., III., and IV., 8vo, Cloth, $2 25 each: Vol. V., 8vo, Cloth, $3 00. Complete Sets, 5 vols., Sheep, $14 50; Half Calf, $23 25.

THE LIFE OF JOHN LOCKE. By H. R. Fox Bourne. 2 vols., 8vo, Cloth, $5 00.

THE MILITARY OPERATIONS OF GENERAL BEAURE-
GARD in the War Between the States, 1861 to 1865; including
a brief Personal Sketch, and a Narrative of his Services in the
War with Mexico, 1846 to 1848. By ALFRED ROMAN, formerly
Aide-de-Camp on the Staff of General Beauregard. With Portraits, etc. 2 vols., 8vo, Cloth, $7 00; Sheep, $9 00; Half Morocco, $11 00; Morocco, $15 00. (*Sold only by Subscription.*)

FOLK-LORE OF SHAKESPEARE. By the Rev. T. F. THISEL-
TON DYER, M.A., Oxon.   8vo, Cloth, $2 50.

THE POETS AND POETRY OF SCOTLAND: From the
Earliest to the Present Time. Comprising Characteristic Se-
lections from the Works of the more Noteworthy Scottish
Poets, with Biographical and Critical Notices. By JAMES
GRANT WILSON. With Portraits on Steel. 2 vols., 8vo, Cloth,
$10 00; Gilt Edges, $11 00.

THE HEART OF AFRICA. Three Years' Travels and Adventures in the Unexplored Regions of the Centre of Africa—from
1868 to 1871. By GEORG SCHWEINFURTH. Translated by EL-
LEN E. FREWER. Illustrated. 2 vols., 8vo, Cloth, $8 00.

THE HUGUENOTS: their Settlements, Churches, and Indus-
tries in England and Ireland. By SAMUEL SMILES. With an
Appendix relating to the Huguenots in America. Crown 8vo,
Cloth, $2 00.

THE HUGUENOTS IN FRANCE after the Revocation of the
Edict of Nantes; with a Visit to the Country of the Vaudois.
By SAMUEL SMILES.   Crown 8vo, Cloth, $2 00.

THE LIFE OF GEORGE STEPHENSON, and of his Son, Rob-
ert Stephenson; comprising, also, a History of the Invention
and Introduction of the Railway Locomotive. By SAMUEL
SMILES. Illustrated. 8vo, Cloth, $3 00.

THE VOYAGE OF THE "CHALLENGER." The Atlantic:
an Account of the General Results of the Voyage during 1873
and the Early Part of 1876. By Sir WYVILLE THOMSON,
K.C.B., F.R.S. Illustrated. 2 vols., 8vo, Cloth, $12 00.

DEXTER'S CONGREGATIONALISM. The Congregationalism of the Last Three Hundred Years, as Seen in its Literature: with Special Reference to certain Recondite, Neglected,
or Disputed Passages. With a Bibliographical Appendix. By
H. M. DEXTER. Large 8vo, Cloth, $6 00.